Re-Visioning African Pentecostal-Charismatic
Ecclesiology in the Public Sphere

Re-Visioning African Pentecostal-Charismatic Ecclesiology in the Public Sphere

The James McKeown Memorial Lectures

EDITED BY
Christian Tsekpoe AND
Lord Elorm Donkor

FOREWORDS BY
Eric Nyamekye,
Kwabena Agyapong-Kodua, AND
Cecil M. Robeck Jr.

⌒PICKWICK *Publications* · Eugene, Oregon

RE-VISIONING AFRICAN PENTECOSTAL-CHARISMATIC ECCLESIOLOGY IN THE PUBLIC SPHERE
The James McKeown Memorial Lectures

Copyright © 2024 Wipf and Stock Publishers. All rights reserved. Except for brief quotations in critical publications or reviews, no part of this book may be reproduced in any manner without prior written permission from the publisher. Write: Permissions, Wipf and Stock Publishers, 199 W. 8th Ave., Suite 3, Eugene, OR 97401.

Pickwick Publications
An Imprint of Wipf and Stock Publishers
199 W. 8th Ave., Suite 3
Eugene, OR 97401

www.wipfandstock.com

PAPERBACK ISBN: 979-8-3852-1049-7
HARDCOVER ISBN: 979-8-3852-1050-3
EBOOK ISBN: 979-8-3852-1051-0

Cataloguing-in-Publication data:

Names: Tsekpoe, Christian [editor]. | Elorm-Donkor, Lord Abraham [editor]. | Nyamekye, Eric [foreword]. | Agyapong-Kodua, Kwabena [foreword]. | Robeck, Cecil M. [foreword].

Title: Re-visioning African pentecostal-charismatic ecclesiology in the public sphere : the James McKeown memorial lectures / edited by Christian Tsekpoe and Lord Elorm Donkor ; forewords by Kwabena Agyapong-Kodua, Eric Nyamekye, and Cecil Mel Robeck Jr.

Description: Eugene, OR: Pickwick Publications, 2024 | Includes bibliographical references and index.

Identifiers: ISBN 979-8-3852-1049-7 (paperback) | ISBN 979-8-3852-1050-3 (hardcover) | ISBN 979-8-3852-1051-0 (ebook)

Subjects: LCSH: Pentecostalism—Africa. | Public theology. | Pentecostalism—Doctrines. | Pentecostal churches—Missions.

Classification: BR1644.3 T74 2024 (paperback) | BR1644.3 (ebook)

VERSION NUMBER 09/03/24

Scriptures taken from the Holy Bible, New International Version®, NIV®. Copyright © 1973, 1978, 1984, 2011 by Biblica, Inc.™ Used by permission of Zondervan. All rights reserved worldwide. www.zondervan.com The "NIV" and "New International Version" are trademarks registered in the United States Patent and Trademark Office by Biblica, Inc.™

Scripture quotations marked NKJV are taken from the New King James Version®. Copyright © 1982 by Thomas Nelson. Used by permission. All rights reserved.

Contents

List of Contributors | vii
Foreword—Eric Nyamekye | xiii
Foreword—Kwabena Agyapong-Kodua | xvii
Foreword—Cecil M. Robeck Jr. | xxiii

Introduction: Pentecostal-Charismatic Christianity and the Publish Sphere | 1
—Christian Tsekpoe

1. James McKeown's Concept of Pentecostal Ecclesiology and Its Impact on the Ministry of The Church of Pentecost | 17
   —Opoku Onyinah

2. A Response to Opoku Onyinah's "James McKeown's concept of Pentecostal Ecclesiology and Its Impact on the Ministry of The Church of Pentecost" | 36
   —Lord Elorm Donkor

3. Pentecostal Mission and Social Transformation | 50
   —Emmanuel Kwesi Anim

4. A Response to Emmanuel Kwesi Anim's "Pentecostal Mission and Social Transformation" | 63
   —Allison Norton

5. Ecclesiological Appraisal of Christian Values and Principles in the Public Sphere | 71
   —Peter White

6. A Response to Peter White's "Ecclesiological Appraisal of Christian Values and Principles in the Public Sphere" | 85
   —Christian Tsekpoe

7. Church-State Relations and the Problem of Corruption in Africa | 96
   —Dela Quampah

8. A Response to Dela Quampah's "Church-State Relations and the Problem of Corruption in Africa" | 121
   —Mbanyane Mhango

9. A Pentecostal Response to Home and Urban Mission in Africa | 133
   —Vincent Anane Denteh

10. Pentecostalism and the Lordship of Christ in a Religiously Pluralistic Society | 147
    —Alfred Koduah

11. Re-thinking Church in the Light of COVID-19 | 166
    —Patrick Tetteh Kudadjie

12. Church Governance and National Transformation: A Case of The Church of Pentecost, Ghana | 178
    —Johnny Lartey Peprah

Author Index | 199
Subject Index | 201
Scripture Index | 205

Contributors

Emmanuel Kwesi Anim (PhD, All Nations Christian College) is the Director of the Pentecost School of Theology and Mission and the Acting Pro-Vice-Chancellor of the Pentecost University. Prior to this he was the Principal of the then Pentecost Theological Seminary at Gomoa-Fetteh. Anim is also an Adjunct Lecturer at the Akrofi-Christaller Institute of Theology, Mission and Culture, South African Theological Seminary (SATS) and a Visiting Lecturer at the All Nations Christian College in the UK. Anim is a member of the Translations Committee of the Bible Society of Ghana. His research interest is in Eco-Theology, African Studies, Global Christian Mission as well as Pentecostal and Charismatic Studies. He has a number of publications in these disciplines, including his recent book, *Who Wants to Be a Millionaire? An Analysis of Prosperity Teaching in the Charismatic Ministries (Churches) in Ghana and Its Wider Impact* (Berlin: LIT, 2021).

Vincent Anane Denteh (MTh, South African Theological Seminary) is an ordained minister of The Church of Pentecost and one of the fifteen Executive Council Members of the CoP with the responsibility of governing the over one hundred and fifty-one branches of the CoP worldwide. He is currently the Director of the Pentecost Men's Ministry (PEMEM), which is the men's wing of the CoP worldwide. Prior to these positions, Vincent Anane Denteh has served as a missionary to Ukraine and the Republic of Madagascar, respectively. He was also the Area Head of The Church of Pentecost in Ashanti-Bekwai, Ghana. He holds a BTh in Theology and MTh in Missiology from South African Theological Seminary. Anane Denteh has published eleven books, including the 957-page book,

Revitalising Mission and Missiology: The Way Forward in the Twenty-First Century (Accra: Pentecost, 2019).

Lord Elorm Donkor (PhD, University of Manchester) is the National Head of The Church of Pentecost in the UK. Prior to this position, he was the Principal of the Birmingham Christian College, CoP's theological college for Europe and Middle East region situated in England. Currently, he is a visiting lecturer to the Birmingham Christian College where he teaches Old Testament Survey, Pastoral Studies, Christian Ethics, Pentecostal/Charismatic Studies and Contemporary Christian Leadership. His research interests include Christian ethics, African Christianity, African Pentecostal missions in the West, Pentecostal theology, and the integration of African traditional and Christian moral traditions. He has authored many peer reviewed articles and books, including *Christian Morality in Ghanaian Pentecostalism* (Oxford: Regnum, 2017).

Alfred Koduah (PhD, South African Theological Seminary) served in the full-time ministry of The Church of Pentecost for thirty-seven years (1984–2021). He served in various capacities in this church as district pastor, Area Head and the General Secretary of The Church of Pentecost from 2003 to 2013. Koduah was an Executive Council member of the CoP from 2003–18. He served on many boards including the International Missions Board, Pentecost University Council and was a member of the Board of Trustees of The Church of Pentecost. At the national front, Koduah is the Chairman of the Religious Broadcasts Advisory Council of the Ghana Broadcasting Corporation and a former Vice President of the Bible Society of Ghana. Koduah is an Adjunct lecturer at the Pentecost University, where he teaches Pastoral Studies, Gender Studies and Communicating the Gospel in Contemporary Society. He has authored twenty books to his credit.

Patrick Tetteh Kudadjie (PhD, Akrofi-Christaller Institute of Theology, Mission and Culture) is an ordained minister of The Church of Pentecost. He is a lecturer with Pentecost School of Theology and Mission at Pentecost University (PU) and also serves as the resident minister of Kusi Donkor Worship Centre, a congregation of The Church of Pentecost located in Sowutum, Accra. His research interest include Systematic Theology, Christian Ethics, Contemporary Ethical Issues and African Pentecostalism.

Mbanyane Socrates Mhango (PhD, Regent University) is a member of the National Executive Council of The Church of Pentecost USA Inc., and doubles as the Area head of the Colorado Region, and as the minister in charge of Denver District. He is the Dean of Graduate Studies and the former President of Pentecost Biblical Seminary (PBS) in Wayne, New Jersey, USA. He teaches Systematic Theology, Pentecostal and Charismatic Studies, Practical Theology, Pastoral Studies, Pentecostal Leadership and Spirituality, and Christian Ethics. His research interests are in Systematic Theology, Pentecostal and Charismatic Theology, Intercultural Theology, Ecumenical Theology, and African Immigrant Theology in the West (Europe and North America). He holds a Graduate Certificate in Leadership Studies, a Teaching Certificate in Higher Education, an Advanced Diploma in Pastoral Studies and Church Administration, a Bachelor's Degree in Accounting, a Master of Business Administration (MBA) in Accounting, Finance, and International Business, a Master's Degree (MA), and a PhD in Theological Studies. Mhango is the author of *Manifesting the Spirit: Believers as Sacraments* (Eugene, OR: Resource, 2021), and *Disciples Indeed: Toward True Followers of Christ* (Forthcoming).

Allison Norton (PhD) serves as the Academic Dean at Pentecost Biblical Seminary, USA. She is also the Faculty Associate in Migration Studies and Congregational Life at Hartford International University for Religion and Peace, where she directs the Pastoral Innovation Network of New England. She teaches courses in sociology of religion, immigration, and multicultural and intergenerational ministry. Her research and publications explore the impact of the COVID-19 pandemic on USA congregations, the rise of megachurches in West Africa, the transnational dimension of African Pentecostalism, the role of migration on the worldwide expansion of the Christian faith, and the religious identities of the "new" second generation. Her forthcoming co-authored book is, *Migrant God, Migrant Faith* (with Matthew Krabill, IVP Academic).

Opoku Onyinah (PhD, University of Birmingham) is a lecturer at the Pentecost University. He is the immediate past Chairman of The Church of Pentecost, worldwide. On the National front, he serves as the Chairman for the Board of Trustees of the Ghana National Cathedral; the Chairman of the Governing Council of the National Coalition of Proper Human Sexual Behaviour and Family Values; and the President of the Ghana Bible Society. At the international level, Onyinah is the Co-Chair of the

African Pentecostal Mission of World Pentecostal Fellowship; Co-Chair for Scholars Consultation of Empowered21, Global Council member of the Lausanne Movement, and a Member of the Commission of Christian Unity. He is the author of many scholarly articles and books; his current book is *Apostle and Prophets: The Ministry of Apostles and Prophets throughout the Generations* (Eugene, OR: Wipf & Stock, 2022).

Johnny Lartey Peprah (MTh Trinity Theological Seminary, Legon) is an ordained minister of The Church of Pentecost, Ghana. His twenty-two years' experience of international ministry has taken him to Nigeria, La Cote D'Ivoire, Guinea, Liberia, Togo, Germany, the Netherlands, Mauritius, South Africa, United Kingdom and many parts of Ghana. He is an administrator, theologian, lecturer and assistant registrar at Pentecost School of Theology and Mission (PSTM) of the Pentecost University. He is also the resident minister of Akweteyman Worship Centre—Accra, a CoP congregation of more than one thousand and five hundred (1,500) members. He is currently researching into "Impact Assessment of Indigenous Transformational Leadership Development in The Church of Pentecost on Global Evangelization and Transformation" for his PhD. His research interest include Practical Theology, Pentecostalism, leadership development, global evangelization, church administration, church history, missiology, and development.

Dela Quampah (PhD, University of Ghana) is currently the Area Head of The Church of Pentecost (CoP), Ho, Ghana. He also doubles as an Executive Council Member of the Church with oversight responsibility for all CoP congregations in the Volta and Oti Regions. He also serves as an adjunct lecturer in Christian Ethics at the Pentecost School of Theology and Mission, Pentecost University, Ghana. Prior to these, he was the Dean of Studies and Lecturer at the then Pentecost Theological Seminary, from 2012 to 2015. He worked as a missionary in the Republic of South Africa from 2015 to 2019, where he also helped to train some Ministers of the Church. He has authored some articles and books, including, *Good Pastors, Bad Pastors* (Eugene, OR: Wipf & Stock, 2014).

Christian Tsekpoe (PhD, Oxford Centre for Mission Studies) is a senior lecturer and Head of the Centre for Ministerial Formation and Training at the Pentecost University, Accra-Ghana. Prior to this position, he served as the Director of Postgraduate Studies and Research (2021–2022), the Head of Missions Department (2019–22) and the

Coordinator for the School of Theological Education by Extension (2016–19) all at Pentecost University. He is also a Research Faculty with the Center for Missiological Research at Fuller Theological Seminary, USA, where he has been offered the Global Research Institute post-doctoral fellowship (July–December, 2023). Christian Tsekpoe is an ordained minister of The Church of Pentecost where he also serves as the national chairman for the Home and Urban Missions Committee and the resident minister of A-Lang Worship Centre. His research interests include Pentecostal-Charismatic mission in Africa, intergenerational missiology, witch-demonology as well as African theology and contextualization. He has published many articles and books, including the ground-breaking book, *Intergenerational Missiology: An African Pentecostal-Charismatic Perspective* (Oxford: Regnum, 2022).

Peter White (PhD, University of Pretoria) is an Associate Professor in the Department of Practical Theology and Missiology, at Stellenbosch University, South Africa. His area of specialization is African Pentecostalism and Missiology. White is the immediate past Vice-President of Christian Service University College, Kumasi. He is an examiner for Masters' and PhD theses for University of Pretoria, North-West University, Kwame Nkrumah University of Science and Technology, Kumasi, Ghana, Christian Service University College, Kumasi, Ghana and Trinity Theological Seminary, Legon, Ghana. He is a regular reviewer for a number of peer reviewed Journals both in Ghana and internationally. He has published many peer reviewed journal articles to his credit. White is a bi-vocational minister in the Christ Apostolic Church International with over 20 years pastoral ministry experience. He has worked in several administrative and pastoral positions both in the academia and in the church.

FOREWORD
The Church as an Agent of Transformation

Eric Nyamekye

In this book, Re-Visioning *African Pentecostal-Charismatic Ecclesiology in the Public Sphere,* the editors, Christian Tsekpoe and Lord Elorm Donkor have brought together scholars and ecclesial practitioners to dialogue on a crucial subject, necessary for consideration in contemporary Christianity. Although, the focus is on African Pentecostal-Charismatic ecclesiology, the implications of the explorations in this book transcends African Christianity. The current growth of the Pentecostal movement in Africa and its wider impact, seen in the sending of missionaries by African Pentecostals to all parts of the world as well as the Pentecostalization of History Christianity, makes this book a resource for global Christianity. As the title of suggests, the book examines the public role of the Pentecostal-Charismatic movement in Africa. Taking examples from Africa and the Africa diaspora, the authors assess the current efforts of the Pentecostal-Charismatic movement to influence and transform the public sphere with the principles and values of the kingdom of God. The authors, however, identify serious gaps that the Pentecostal movement must urgently fill to fulfil their divine call as agents of transformation in the nations.

The call of Abraham, and by extension, Israel, was for the salvation of the nations. God's agenda was to work through Israel so that the nations of the world will know that there is only one God (Deut 6:4; Mark 12:29). Through the obedience of Abraham and his offspring, all nations of the earth will be blessed (Gen 22:18). This prophetic responsibility of Abraham and his offspring has been given to the church through faith in Christ Jesus. The Apostle Paul told the Galatian church that,

> So in Christ Jesus you are all children of God through faith, for all of you who were baptized into Christ have clothed yourselves with Christ. There is neither Jew nor Gentile, neither slave nor free, nor is there male and female, for you are all one in Christ Jesus. If you belong to Christ, then you are Abraham's seed, and heirs according to the promise. (Gal 3:26–29)

The implication here is that through Christ, the church has taken on the blessings and responsibilities of Abraham. Through the church, whether Jews or Gentiles, all the nations of the world will come to know and obey the one true God and be blessed. It is therefore, the church's mandate to make this truth known to the nations of the world through the proclamation of the Gospel, the good news of Jesus Christ. This proclamation of the good news must be done through (1) preaching the word, (2) demonstrating good works among the nations and (3) manifesting the wonders of God through signs and wonders. Luke told Theophilus that what he wrote in his former book (the Gospel of Luke), was the record of what Jesus began to do and to teach until the day he was taken to heaven (Acts 1:1–2). It is clear from this Scripture that, Jesus' method of proclamation was both "doing" and "teaching." Secondly, Luke suggest that all that Jesus did and taught in the Gospel narratives was just the beginning of His ministry. The continuation was to be done through the early church as recorded in the book of Acts.

In many cases, the preaching of the word is done with impressive results in the number of converts that are won to faith as seen in the case of African Christianity in contemporary times. Inconsistent with this, however, is the paradox of the increase corruption and evil, incongruent to the transforming power of the Gospel. This suggest that the church is succeeding in the verbal proclamation of the word but seems to be failing in its social action in the public sphere. In Ghana, for example, In spite of our church's impressive numerical grow over the years, the society is still influenced by worldviews, thoughts and arguments which contradict the knowledge of God. According to the 2010 Population and Housing Census, 71.2 percent of Ghanaians claim to be Christians. Beyond population census, the ubiquity of church buildings, bill boards, posters and flyers that portray Christian activities as well as the physical participation of believers in church activities corroborate the numerical growth of Christianity in the country. This notwithstanding, Christianity does not seem to have had the expected transformation on the Ghanaian society. Issues of endemic corruption, bad governance, environmental degradation, and the rampant social mishaps are inconsistent with the huge Christian presence in the country.

This lamentable situation calls for a re-visioning of the church's mandate as agents of societal transformation. This understanding of a re-visioned ecclesiology in the public sphere occupies the *Vision 2023* of The Church of Pentecost (CoP), dubbed "Possessing the Nations: Equipping the Church to Transform Every Sphere of Society with the Values and Principles of the Kingdom of God" (Eph 3:10; Titus 2:13–14). The overall goal of this vision is "a church where members go to possess their nations by transforming every worldview, thought and behaviour with values, principles and lifestyles of the Kingdom of God and thereby turning many people to Christ."[1] This is targeted at equipping members of the church at all levels with the required knowledge, skills and resources to be able to engage their individual sphere meaningfully with the values and principles of the kingdom of God.

Unlike the first James McKeown Memorial Lectures held in 2003 and published in 2004, which focuses on the man James McKeown and the history of The Church of Pentecost, this current volume is concerned with the public role of Pentecostal-Charismatic ecclesiology in contemporary times. This focus is derived from the annual theme of the CoP and the various topics that emerged from such theme. In 2021 the CoP concentrated on building a glorious church revived to possess the nations. It is this goal that informed the choice of theme for the 2021 James McKeown Memorial Lectures. The aim is to bring both scholars and ecclesial practitioners together to dialogue over the current paradox of the parallel increase in both Christian demography and social evil. The leadership of the CoP believes that the problem must be handled from different perspectives, including such conferences and subsequent publications that will emerge from the conference papers. In this current volume, the editors have done well by drawing together scholars and practitioners from multi-disciplinary backgrounds and with divergent experiences to reflect on various topics that are important for the church's mandate in the public sphere.

1. Church of Pentecost, *Vision 2023*, 18 (https://thecophq.org/vision-2023/).

Consequently, the authors of this volume, who are mainly Pentecostal-Charismatics living in Africa and the African diaspora, including the United Kingdom and the United States of America, have contributed to this colossal manual that shed light on the strengths and weaknesses of the movement, whilst providing pointers for the way forward. In this volume, readers will appreciate the perspectives of the authors on subjects such as James McKeown's Pentecostal ecclesiology and its impact on the ministry of the CoP, Pentecostal mission and social transformation, ecclesiological appraisal of Christian values and principles in the public sphere, church-state relations and the problem of corruption in Africa. Others include a Pentecostal response to Home and Urban Missions, Pentecostalism and the Lordship of Christ in a religiously pluralistic society, re-thinking church in the light of COVID-19 and church governance and national transformation: a case of the CoP, Ghana. The book is rich in Pentecostal-Charismatic ecclesiology. The discussions are thorough and challenging. Whilst on the one hand, the authors will keep you comfortable with the achievements of African Pentecostalism, on the other hand, they will make you uncomfortable with obvious weaknesses that leaves room for improvement.

I recommend this book for pastors, lay leaders and all who are interested in understanding role of the Pentecostal-Charismatic movement in the public sphere as well as those who wish to help improve the public image of the church for holistic proclamation of the Gospel in the nations of the world.

Apostle Eric Nyamekye
Chairman, the Church of Pentecost
Chancellor, Pentecost University

Foreword

Apostle Professor Kwabena Agyapong-Kodua

THE CHURCH'S MOST IMPORTANT responsibility on earth is to make disciples of all nations (Matt 28:18–20). This disciple-making mandate is what has been generally referred to as the Great Commission. This assignment was previously misunderstood by many churches and missionaries as they tried to make converts *from* the world and separate these converts from "others." A better understanding of this mandate, however, shows that the church has the responsibility of transforming the systems of the kingdoms of this world and making them align with the principles and values of the kingdom of God. In his farewell prayer, which is generally referred to by theologians as the High Priestly Prayer (John 17:1–26), Jesus prayed for the disciples not to be taken out of the world but to be protected from the evil one. The implication of this prayer is that until the eschatological redemption, which will occur at the Parousia, God is not going to take Christians from the world. Rather, Christians are expected to serve as the salt of the earth and the light of the world (Matt 5:13–16). By this, the church, which represents the kingdom of God, is mandated to bring transformation to the broken and corrupt kingdom of the world.

We clearly see two kingdoms at work in this discourse—the kingdom of the world and the kingdom of God. I carefully use the word "kingdom" in this context to refer to ideologies and philosophies that give a common identity to a people. When the Apostle Paul tells the church in Rome that "Do not conform to the patterns of this world, but be transformed by the renewing of your mind," he was drawing their attention to the patterns of the kingdom of the world which are in opposition to the patterns of the kingdom of God. The believers in Rome may be in the same geographical location, but by becoming Christians, they have changed their status and identity from the kingdom of the world to the kingdom of God. Consequently, their thinking, ideologies or philosophies must be renewed to reflect their new found faith.

It is clear from both in the Old and New Testaments of the Bible that, the issues of kingdoms or nations is core to the heart of God. This is why Jesus spent a lot of time teaching about the kingdom of God throughout His earthly ministry. Gordon Fee, a renowned American-Canadian Pentecostal theologian, argues that to miss or misunderstand the concept of the kingdom of God in reading the Synoptic Gospels is to miss Jesus altogether.[1] Luke tells us in Acts 1:3 that after Jesus' resurrection, he spent forty days on earth, proving to the disciples that He was alive and speaking to them about the kingdom of God. In the book of Revelation 7:9, it is clear that countless multitudes of people from every nation, tribe, people and language will stand before the throne of God. Out of these nations, the kingdom of God is to be formed, hence the purpose of the church's call to facilitate the agenda of reclaiming the kingdoms of this world unto God.

I derive the story of two kingdoms from two cities of the Old Testament Scriptures– the kingdom of Babylon and the kingdom of Jerusalem. These two cities represent the kingdoms of the world and the kingdom of God. In the Bible, the Babylonian kingdom appears in Genesis from the tower of Babel (Gen 11). Babylon was later projected as a powerful kingdom in the book of Daniel but got smashed in the book of Revelation 18:2–3. On the contrary the city or kingdom of God begins in the Garden of Eden (Gen 1). Jerusalem gets projected through aspects of Israel's history and reaches its full glory in the Revelation 21:1–4. It is therefore clear that the Bible gives us an intriguing story of two kingdoms. Each of these kingdoms has a king and operate with ideologies, philosophies, or principles. These ideologies direct the values and behavior of the subjects of these kingdoms. For example, in the story of Babel, we see a people who want to build a tower that reaches the heavens in order to make a name for themselves. Throughout history, the desire and inclination to make a name for oneself has brought about self-centeredness in the world, leading to the level of wickedness, corruption, grid, abuse of all

---

1. Gordon D. Fee, "The Kingdom of God and the Church's Global Mission," in *Called and Empowered: Global Mission in Pentecostal Perspective*, edited by M. W. Dempster et al., 7–21 (Grand Rapids: Baker Academic, 2015), 8.

kinds, lack of integrity, disrespect for others, and perverse immoral behavior the world experiences on daily basis.

To be able to transform such a broken world, there is the need to understand the philosophies that govern the kingdom of the world and replace them with the philosophies and values of the kingdom of God. This understanding of reclaiming and transforming corrupt and crooked systems of the world occupies the core of The Church of Pentecost's Vision 2023—a five-year vision dubbed, "Possessing the Nations." The mantra "I am an agent of transformation" which goes with the vision, clearly shows the focus of The Church of Pentecost (CoP) to help its members see themselves as agents of transformation in the world. In 2021, the CoP's theme seeks to build a glorious church, revived to possess the nations. This focus greatly influenced the choice of the theme for the 2021 James McKeown Memorial Lecture, *Re-Visioning Pentecostal-Charismatic Ecclesiology in the Public Sphere*, and subsequently, the title of this book.

The book emerged mostly from the papers presented at the lecture and contains essays from multi-disciplinary perspectives, responding to how the churches' ecclesiology promotes or impedes their public and social responsibility. Through these papers, authors promote scientific and practical dialogue between academics and ecclesial practitioners on issues that are germane to the growing demography of Christianity in Africa and the African diaspora. The authors offer critical examination, assessment, and reflection on ecclesiology in ways that contributes to global understanding and appreciation of the movement. The authors admit that although African Pentecostal-Charismatics have been quite slow in responding to this public mandate of their ecclesiological responsibilities, there has been a rapid shift in paradigm within recent times. Many Pentecostal-Charismatic churches have responded to the need to influence the wider society positively. These transformational efforts are expected to be evident, not only in church, but also in the homes of the believers, at the offices, the market place, on the streets, in political leadership, traditional chieftaincy institutions, in the schools, hospitals, in the judiciary, architecture, engineering, arts and entertainment, in business and in the media.

The chapters of this book consist of plenary papers and critical responses as well as break-out session presentations. Uniquely, the focus of the book is not only on the failures of Pentecostal-Charismatic Christianity in Africa, the book also identifies some success stories, with practical examples from some Pentecostal-Charismatic churches in Ghana and proposes ways by which Pentecostalism can make much more impact in Africa and beyond. So in this book, the authors have been both sympathetic and critical to the movement. This approach is intended to engender a balanced appraisal of the movement, presenting both the achievements and pointing out areas that need improvement. This book, therefore, encourages Pentecostals to do more, whilst at the same time opposing all forms of complacency and self-preservation in a rapidly changing world.

Pentecostal-Charismatic's dependent on the power of the Holy Spirit to succeed in their mission praxis should be extrapolated to the public sphere. This pneumatological emphasis should permeate the public sphere, where all professions are recognized as God's mission. At Pentecost University, it is our prayer that the kingdoms of the world will be reclaimed and transformed into the kingdom of our God, the Most High and His Son, the Lord Jesus Christ, through the power of the Holy Spirit.

On behalf of the key officers and management of Pentecost University, I would like to thank Apostle Eric Nyamekye, the Chairman of the CoP, Apostle Alexander Nana Yaw Kumi-Larbi, the General Secretary, and Apostle Emmanuel Agyemang Bekoe, the International Missions Director, as well as the entire fifteen-member Executive Council of the CoP for their vision and support which culminated in the revival of the James McKeown Memorial Lectures and subsequently, this volume. I am also grateful to Apostle Dr. Emmanuel Anim, the Director of the Pentecost School of Theology and Mission, (who also doubles as the Ag. Pro Vice Chancellor for Pentecost University) and his team of scholars, for working tirelessly on this project.

I would like to express my profound gratitude to Professor Cecil Mel Robeck Jr., Senior Professor of Church History and Ecumenics at the Fuller Theological Seminary, USA, for writing one of the forewords to the book. I also thank all those who spent time out of their busy schedules to write endorsement for the book. I am grateful to the staff and faculty of Pentecost University as well as colleagues in our sister colleges across the globe, especially, Birmingham Christian College, UK, and Pentecost Biblical Seminary, USA, for their support and contributions in various ways.

I also want to extend our appreciation to Joy Netanya Thompson for reading the text and making valuable editorial suggestions. A very big thanks to Rev. David Amoako Boateng of the Church of Pentecost, Ghana, who also proofread the final text and made valuable suggestions.

Finally, we would like to express our heartfelt appreciation to all the speakers at the James McKeown Memorial Lectures for their insightful presentations and much appreciation to the contributors for working so hard on this project to make it a reality.

Apostle Professor Kwabena Agyapong-Kodua

Vice Chancellor, Pentecost University

FOREWORD
A Global Vision for the Church and Its Ministry

CECIL M. ROBECK JR.

ECCLESIOLOGY IS A TOPIC to which Pentecostals and Charismatics have historically not given much thought. We have been activists, who unfortunately, have taken little time to engage in theological reflection. Until recently, very few Pentecostals gave much thought to ecclesiology, with the exception of Assemblies of God missionary, Melvin L. Hodges, who began writing on the topic in the early 1950s and ultimately authored several small books with ecclesiological reflections tied to missions.[1] While these books contained some theological insights on ecclesiology, they did not explore the topic very deeply.

Over the past decade, ecclesiology has received much more attention in books and articles written or edited by Classical Pentecostal theologians.[2] As you can see from the footnotes below, with the exception of one book originating in Asia, nearly all of the monographs have originated from North America. More recently, the Commission on Faith and Order

---

1. Melvin L. Hodges, *The Indigenous Church: A Theology of the Church and Its Mission* (Springfield, MO: Gospel Publishing House, 1976).

2. Simon Chan, *Pentecostal Ecclesiology: An Essay on the Development of Doctrine* (Blandford Forum: Deo, 2011); Chris E. W. Green, ed., *Pentecostal Ecclesiology: A Reader* (Leiden: Brill, 2016); John Christopher Thomas, ed., *Towards a Pentecostal Ecclesiology* (Cleveland, TN: CPT, 2010); Terry L. Cross, The People of God's Presence: An Introduction to Ecclesiology (Grand Rapids: Baker Academic, 2019); Frank D. Macchia, *The Spirit-Baptized Church: A Dogmatic Inquiry* (London: T. & T. Clark, 2020).

of the World Council of Churches invited Pentecostals to join them in its discussions of what they hoped would be a more robust *global vision* of ecclesiology.[3] In these two edited volumes published by the World Council of Churches, Pentecostal theologians from Latin America, Asia, and Africa received invitations to contribute chapters on ecclesiology in conversation with Faith and Order's earlier volume, *Towards a Common Vision of the Church*. In this way, Pentecostal-Charismatic reflection has also become important in ecumenical discussions. While ecumenical participation has been criticized in much of Pentecostalism for decades, more recently it has received considerable attention, in part because of the growing number of international dialogues in which Pentecostals now participate, and where the topic of ecclesiology is addressed.

The present volume, envisioned as a specific study in Pentecostal-Charismatic ecclesiology by its editors, Christian Tsekpoe and Lord Elorm Donkor, is a welcome addition to Pentecostal-Charismatic ecclesiological thought. By focusing on Pentecostal-Charismatic ecclesiological contributions in the public sphere, they have also made it a topic for ecumenical discussions that extends to the global Church. For decades, Pentecostals have generally tended to avoid addressing the public sphere, with a few obvious exceptions. In South Africa, for instance, Pentecostals struggled over how to address Apartheid for decades, but the work of Frank Chikane and others in the Apostolic Faith Mission of South Africa, enabled that church to turn officially against Apartheid. Typically, Pentecostals and Charismatics have chosen to address public issues only obliquely. Their focus has been on evangelism and mission (love of God), not on social or political, issues shared by Christian and on-Christians alike (love of neighbor).

Often marginalized by secular bodies as well as by other churches, Pentecostals have many times found it difficult to speak up on public issues. With the enormous growth of the Pentecostal-Charismatic Movement, however, a change has begun to take place in the balance of power. For the World Council of Churches to invite theological reflection on the topic of ecclesiology by Pentecostals is what transforms a *common vision* of the Church into a *global vision* of the Church. In the *Common Vision* document, the Pentecostal witness was almost entirely absent. In the *Global Vision* volumes, the Pentecostal-Charismatic witness is quite visible. The recognition of what had been missing from

3. WCC, *Towards a Global Vision of the Church* (https://www.oikoumene.org/sites/default/files/2022-11/TGVC_e_Book_.pdf).

the Common Vision document has caused the entire Commission on Faith and Order to rethink its way of doing theology, and only this year, they increased the number of Pentecostal-Charismatic Commissioners from Classical Pentecostal churches, from one Commissioner, to five, out of a total sixty members. The Pentecostal-Charismatic Movement crosses many denominational likes, but perhaps more importantly its very size now portends the possibility of it becoming a more significant voice on all local as well as global issues facing the Church. The call for further reflection as well as further action on the part of Pentecostal-Charismatics on ecclesiology, together with its implications for what the Pentecostal-Charismatic part of the Church has to offer to the world, could well begin to change the thinking not only of other theologians, but also of local and national politicians and policy makers.

For far too many years, many evangelicals and Pentecostal-Charismatics have argued for the work of evangelism and mission that contribute to the growth of the Church, and meeting the physical and material needs of a world dominated by poverty must be kept separate from one another. Much of that distinction was a reaction against the Social Gospel that gained a footing within more segments of the Church beginning in the late-nineteenth Century. It is a false dichotomy. It is true that Jesus did not send his disciples out to found organizations to overcome the poverty and injustices of His own day, but the physical needs of many of the people that Jesus addressed, touched Him deeply. Jesus urged his followers to give to those in need without calling attention to themselves (Matt 6:1–4). He promised rest, to those who were exhausted from carrying a yoke that was too heavy for them to bear (Matt 11:28–30). When a large crowd followed him around the lake and his disciples tried to convince Jesus to send them away so that they could buy food, Jesus said, "No," and He fed them (Matt 14:13–21). His followers imitated Jesus, when in Acts 6:1–6, they took up the plight of the Hellenistic Jewish widows, against those caring for the Hebraic Jewish widows discriminated in the distribution of food.

One can look at each of these incidents as nothing more than compassionate ministry, something in which most evangelical and Pentecostal-Charismatic churches have long participate, especially among their own. The question, however is, "Is that all the Church should do?" Is there not more that the Church should do? Paul called the Church to submit to the government authorities because God had set them in place (Rom 13:1–5). First Peter 2:13–17 echoes that sentiment, calling for believers to submit to authority at every level, and honoring the king. Importantly, in Jesus' day, and in subsequent years when Paul and Peter wrote to the Christians of their day, none of them lived in societies that were democratic. They were autocratic, governed from the top down, and the Christian community was not well accepted by government leaders. Persecution against Christians soon began, while it was initially local or regional, there were a few times over the next three centuries, when it would grow into a universal purge.

Today, most Christians in North and South America, Europe, Africa, and many parts of Asia have some form of democratic freedom. That often means that Christians are free to live publicly under the Lordship of Jesus Christ, to speak their minds as it reflects their faith, and to influence public policy that impacts the whole population in ways that reflect the kingdom of God. People have a voice. We Pentecostal-Charismatic believers have a voice! The authors in this volume call for a holistic approach to how we should live in the many places that have been desacralized around us. They call us to a holistic approach that takes seriously people of other Christian families as well as people of other faiths, while maintaining our allegiance to the Lordship of Jesus Christ. The whole Church has much to contribute to the larger society. We as members of that Church also have the ability to meet not only the world's spiritual needs through evangelism and mission, but also to contribute something substantial to their many other needs.

During the Second Vatican Council (1962–65), the Bishops of the Catholic Church released a number of extremely important documents that changed that church's focus on the Church from an institutional approach to that of the Church as the People of God. Among the most important documents the Bishops wrote were the Decree on Ecumenism (*Unitatis Redentigratio*), the Dogmatic Constitution on the Church (*Lumen Gentium*), and the Pastoral Constitution on the Church in the Modern World, (*Gaudium et Spes*).

The ecclesiology spelled out in *Lumen Gentium* makes clear that all who have followed Jesus in baptism are Christians.

> The [Roman Catholic] Church knows that she is joined in many ways to the baptized who are honored by the name of Christian. . . . For there are many who hold sacred scripture in honor as a rule of faith and of life, who have a sincere religious zeal, who lovingly believe in God the Father Almighty and in Christ, the Son of God and the Saviour, who are sealed by baptism which unites them to Christ, and who indeed recognize and

> receive other sacraments in their own Churches or ecclesiastical communities.... There is furthermore a sharing in prayer and spiritual benefits; these Christians are indeed in some real way joined to us in the Holy Spirit for, by his gifts and graces, his sanctifying power is also active in them and he has strengthened some of them even to the shedding of their blood. And so the Spirit stirs up desires and actions in all of Christ's disciples in order that all may be peaceably united as Christ ordained, in one flock, under one shepherd.[4]

I would suggest that if Pentecostal-Charismatic believers were to take such a statement seriously, they would soon realize that the 1.3 billion Roman Catholics and arguably the more than half a billion Pentecostal-Charismatic believers have the potential of affecting all of humankind if they could learn to speak with one voice as one Church even in its diversity.

In addition, *Lumen Gentium* is particularly noteworthy in light of what several authors in this volume have contributed. It begins with the following affirmation:

> The joy and hope, the grief and anguish of the men [and women] of our time, especially of those who are poor or afflicted in any way, are the joy and hope, the grief and anguish of the followers of Christ as well. Nothing that is genuinely human fails to find an echo in their hearts. For theirs is a community composed of men [and women] united in Christ and guided by the Holy Spirit, press onwards towards the kingdom of the Father and are bearers of a message of salvation intended for all men [and women]. That is why Christians cherish a feeling of deep solidarity with the human race and its history.[5]

This document moves on to note the major social changes that have touched contemporary society: industrialization, urbanization, mass media, emigration, "socialization," and advancement.[6] It calls upon all Christians to take seriously the nature of humankind, and to work toward that which meets needs, and lifts up and develops the dignity of humankind. In short, *Gaudium et Spes* sets forth the basis for Roman Catholic social teaching. I would note that what the Catholic Bishops wrote here is something to which Pentecostal-Charismatics could all say a hearty, "Amen!" I would only add that this is why Pentecostal-Charismatic believers have much to contribute to the needy of this world.

4. Second Vatican Council, *Lumen Gentium*, no. 15.
5. Second Vatican Council, *Gaudium et Spes*, no. 1.
6. Second Vatican Council, *Gaudium et Spes*, no. 6.

I want to be perfectly clear here. It is not my desire to turn all Pentecostal-Charismatic believers into Roman Catholics. I simply want to point to the facts that in many ways Pentecostal-Charismatics are not that different from those who call the Catholic Church their home. In fact, over 11 percent of all Catholics worldwide identify as Charismatics.[7] Secondly, I want to point out that the world in which we live is a world that we share with other Christians including Catholics, as well as by members of other religions, and those with no faith at all. Finally, I want to suggest that the point of this book, to provide a more holistic approach to the ways that Pentecostal-Charismatics think of themselves as "church" as they face the world. While the number of Christians in the world is still a minority, the number of Christians in the world is now sufficiently substantial, that if we Pentecostal-Charismatic believers were to look at ecclesiology with a global vision, and include others who also name the name of Jesus Christ, we might begin to see some extraordinary changes.

Until quite recently in the West, while scholarship on African Pentecostal and Charismatic studies has been around for decades, much of it has been written by American and European missionaries, historians, theologians, sociologists, and anthropologists. Pentecostal theologians and historians in Africa has received far too little international attention for their own work. This has left those of us in the West with a huge lacuna if we expect to speak with any integrity from a global perspective within any of our academic disciplines. As may be seen in this volume, Ghanaian, South African, and Africans in the diaspora are all producing valuable academic studies that need to be read, digested by those of us in the West. It is my hope that this volume will soon be joined by many other volumes written by African scholars, who are a gift to the whole Church and to the churches in the ecumenical movement.

Cecil M. Robeck Jr.
Senior Professor of Church History and Ecumenics
Special Assistant to the President for Ecumenical Relations
Fuller Theological Seminary, Pasadena, CA, USA 91182

---

7. Alessandra Nucci, "The Charismatic Renewal and the Catholic Church" (https://www.catholicworldreport.com/2013/05/18/the-charismatic-renewal-and-the-catholic-church/). The Charis office has published the number 120,000,000 Charismatic Catholics for over a decade. At least one report I have read, claims that the number may be as high as two hundred million.

INTRODUCTION

Pentecostal-Charismatic Christianity and the Public Sphere

CHRISTIAN TSEKPOE

Background

THIS VOLUME IS THE outcome of the 2021 edition of the James McKeown Memorial Lecture series organized by Pentecost University in honor of the premier superintendent and chairman of The Church of Pentecost, the Reverend James McKeown. The name James McKeown is not only respected in The Church of Pentecost (CoP), he is also revered as a pioneer of Ghanaian Pentecostalism and his contributions have transcended denominations in Ghana and Africa. To hold these lecture series, (which focus on Pentecostal-Charismatic Christianity in Africa and the African diaspora) in his honor is, therefore, apropos. The lecture series and the published materials are intended to promote scientific and practical dialogue between academics and ecclesial practitioners whose works revolve around the global Pentecostal-Charismatic movement. This book aims to offer readers the opportunity to critically examine, assess and reflect on the praxis and theories of their faith, and contribute to the advancements in global understanding and appreciation of the Pentecostal-Charismatic movement in Africa and the African diaspora.

    The title for the book, *Re-Visioning African Pentecostal-Charismatic Ecclesiology in the Public Sphere*, is intended to stimulate conversations around the church's mandate to influence the public sphere as an agent of social transformation. Current demographic statistics on global Christianity reveal that Pentecostal-Charismatic Christianity, in its diverse forms, represents the fastest-growing stream of Christianity, especially in the non-Western worlds of Africa, Latin America, and Asia. Despite its numerical growth in the twenty-first century, there remains a concern about the extent to which the church in Africa is making the desired impact in the public space. As the church grows numerically, the African continent is ironically plagued with many regrettable stories of corruption, bad governance, sexual abuse, gender discrimination and perversion, environmental degradation, robbery, economic crisis (leading to poverty and hunger), wars, and other social vices. The paradoxical increase in these vices in proportion to the demographic growth of the Christian population on the continent has caused many to question the impact of African Christianity on the public sphere. As a response to these observations, the contributors to this volume have engaged the subject from multidisciplinary perspectives and from different backgrounds, covering various thematic areas as will be discussed in the various chapters.

Definition of Pentecostal-Charismatic Christianity

Globally, defining Pentecostalism has continued to be a daunting task because the movement is not monolithic. Its trademarks include multiplicity, dynamism, and spiritual innovation. Nevertheless, there are nexuses that connect the divergent manifestations of the movement, creating its identity as Pentecostalism or, better still, Pentecostalisms. These nexuses provide pointers for some form of definition. In this book, the term "Pentecostalism" is used broadly to describe Christian denominations who believe in the saving power and the Lordship of Jesus Christ whilst emphasizing the practical experience and demonstration of the presence of the Holy Spirit in the lives of people as modeled in the Acts of the Apostles. Such a broad definition of Pentecostalism embraces various shades and waves of Pentecostal innovations in Africa, as the case has been globally. I have argued that such an inclusive definition of the movement is significant due to its variegated nature.[1] In this book, the term "Pentecostal-Charismatic" has been used deliberately and, in many cases, synonymously with Pentecostalism to

---

1. Tsekpoe, "Navigating the Shades and Nexus," 27.

incorporate both those who see themselves as Pentecostals and those who see themselves as neo-Pentecostals or Charismatics.

African Pentecostal-Charismatic Christianity and the Public Space

As has been the character of global Pentecostalism, African Pentecostal-Charismatics have been consistent with intentional evangelism and church planting. According to Julie Ma, "the main *modus operandi* of Pentecostal mission has been straightforward evangelism and church planting from its inception."[2] In terms of social actions, however, the Pentecostals in Africa have been generally slow in their response to the social needs of the communities in which they are located. Until recently, the subject of holistic mission has not been of interest to many Pentecostal-Charismatics in Africa. That is to say that Pentecostal-Charismatics have been concerned with their relationship with God but not their relationship with others and nature. Meanwhile, Tulo Raistrick observes that for the church to fulfil its mission mandate, certain areas must be of a critical concern. These include a transforming relationship with God, transforming relationship with others, transforming relationship with self and transforming relationship with creation.[3] As much as African Pentecostal-Charismatics must not slowdown in their straightforward evangelism, it is equally important for them to see their ecclesiological mandate from a holistic perspective, making way for deliberate social action.

Holistic mission from Pentecostal-Charismatic perspectives should be intentional in striking a responsible balance by combining the proclamation of the gospel, social action, and the demonstration of the power of the Holy Spirit through signs and wonders. This is summarized by Thomas McAlpine and later by Douglas Petersen as "Word, Work and Wonder."[4] Petersen, for example, contends that "the transformational experience of salvation, the ethical actions of social concern, and the empowerment of the Holy Spirit, as seen primarily in the Gospel of Mark, are inextricably

---

2. Ma, "Pentecostal Evangelism," 87.
3. Raistrick, "Local Church," 98–99.
4. Jayakumar, "Work of God," 98–99; see also McAlpine, *By Word, Work, and Wonder*, 2; Peterson, "Word, Work, and Wonder," 255.

linked together in any expression of holistic ministry."[5] The gospel in African Pentecostal-Charismatic Christianity must be good news to the disenfranchised—the poor, the sick, the marginalized, and the disabled. The gospel must also bring economic empowerment, political liberation, environmental awareness, spiritual revival, ethical revolution of people, and total transformation of the public sphere.

The Pentecostal-Charismatic concept of empowerment should not be limited to spiritual empowerment alone. It should be seen as holistic empowerment that brings visible transformation to the public sphere. Asamoah-Gyadu postulates that the Pentecostals' expression of empowerment comes from the word "power" and "relates to the ability to accomplish various tasks. To be empowered, therefore, is to be resourced or made capable of achieving aims and accomplishing feats that would otherwise have remained difficult or impossible to undertake."[6] This understanding must be extrapolated to the public sphere where Pentecostal-Charismatics should depend on the power of the Holy Spirit to grant them the ability to accomplish leadership feats in the fields of marriage and family life, education, politics and governance, sports, arts and entertainment, business, and the media. Veli-Matti Kärkkäinen confirms this possibility when he notes that "Pentecostalism is also characterized by a commitment to social justice, empowerment of the powerless, and a 'preferential option for the marginalized' tracing back to its roots at Azusa Street as a kind of paradigm of marginalization."[7]

In recent times, attention has been drawn to the increasing role and presence of African Pentecostal-Charismatic Christianity in the public sphere, where many of their denominations have started engaging social actions.[8] Francis Benyah argues that although Pentecostals have been generally accused and castigated for concentrating on evangelism and neglecting social concerns, there has been a shift within the last two decades.[9] He points out that "Pentecostal-Charismatic churches are showing sensitivity to local contexts and the biblical mandate to love one's neighbor by responding to the social needs of their constituents."[10] In developing countries, where infrastructural development is highly retarded,

---

5. Peterson, "Word, Work, and Wonder," 255.
6. Asamoah-Gyadu, "You Shall Receive Power," 46–47.
7. Kärkkäinen, "Pentecostal Understanding of Mission," 38.
8. Burgess, "Nigerian Pentecostalism," 29.
9. Benyah, "Pentecostal/Charismatic Churches," 16–30.
10. Benyah, "Pentecostal/Charismatic Churches," 17.

Pentecostal-Charismatic churches are complementing development efforts by drilling boreholes, building clinics, establishing schools, and helping their communities with other social amenities.

In an impressive volume edited by Philip Ohlmann et al., scholars from different backgrounds published a book under the theme, *African Initiated Christianity and the Decolonisation of Development: Sustainable Development in Pentecostal and Independent Churches*. The book explores the ever-increasing contributions of Pentecostal-Charismatic churches in Nigeria, Ghana, Burkina Faso, Zambia, South Africa, and other African counties in general in the public sphere. They argue that these churches are reshaping the notion of sustainable development and are contributing to the decolonization of development.[11] The topics they treated range from environment, gender, social amenities, social transformation, cross-cultural development, decolonization of development, and the whole subject of sustainable development. Coming from the African continent and many of them being Pentecostal-Charismatics, the scholars wrote from an emic point of view, albeit from divergent backgrounds. This volume shows the widespread growth of Pentecostal-Charismatic involvement in the public sphere in Africa. Again, Allan Anderson highlights the contributions of Zambian Pentecostals to their national politics "since the rise of 'born again' President Frederick Chiluba in 1991, who declared Zambia a 'Christian nation' and Nevers Mumba, Vice President from 2003–4 and unsuccessful presidential nominee in 2008 election."[12] In South Africa, Frank Chikane, who is a well-known Pentecostal pastor, has been actively involved in the liberation struggle.[13]

The case in Ghana is not any different from what is happening in many of the other African countries. Many Pentecostal-Charismatic churches are increasingly responding to the social needs of their communities. Francis Benyah lucidly captured the social contributions of four Pentecostal-Charismatic churches in Ghana. These include the International Central Gospel Church, Royal House Chapel International, Action Chapel International, and Manna Mission Church.[14] Their contributions include the provision of education, medical care, rehabilitation, scholarships, and other forms of economic support to the needy and the underprivileged. For example, Central University, owned by Pastor Mensah

11. Ohlmann et al., *African Initiated Christianity*.
12. Anderson, "Pentecostalism," 127.
13. Anderson, "Pentecostalism," 127.
14. Benyah, "Pentecostal/Charismatic Churches," 16–30.

Otabil, founder and leader of the International Central Gospel Church, is among the first private universities to be established in Ghana. Apart from Central University, other Pentecostal-Charismatic churches such as The Church of Pentecost, Action Chapel International, and Perez Chapel International, have their own private universities to augment government efforts in providing tertiary education in Ghana.

In Royal House Chapel International, Benyah identified seven areas of social action that the church is actively engaged in. They include the Prisons Ministry, Community Outreach, Senior Citizens Ministry, School of Restoration, Scholarship Foundation, Feed the Hungry, and Hospital Ministry. These are grouped under what they call "Compassion Ministry."[15] In Action Chapel International, the Archbishop Nicholas Duncan-Williams has founded "Compassion in Action" as an NGO, which supports orphans and provides rehabilitation for drug addicts.[16] Seth Abloh's Manna Mission Church is well known for medical outreach. According to Benyah, Abloh's aim is to "blend Christ-centred compassionate healthcare and effective evangelism, coupled with strategic community development."[17] This model, where evangelism is inextricably linked with social action, has been a major characteristic of Pentecostal-Charismatic understanding of holistic mission. Despite this impressive paradigm shift in recent times, where Pentecostal-Charismatic churches are contributing significantly to social development, the paradox of corruption and other social evil existing parallel to the numerical growth of Christianity is still prevalent in Africa. This needs to be investigated further to identify how the impact of Pentecostals can be felt in the public sphere, not only in evangelism and social actions, but also in moral and behavioral transformation, where the individual church members serve as the salt of the earth and the light of the world.

The Church as Salt and Light in the Public Sphere: The CoP Example

It is important to indicate that the CoP, which is recognized as one of the fastest growing Christian denominations in Africa and the largest

---

15. For details of these ministries, see Benyah, "Pentecostal/Charismatic Churches," 22–26.
16. Benyah, "Pentecostal/Charismatic Churches," 24.
17. Benyah, "Pentecostal/Charismatic Churches," 24–25.

Pentecostal-Charismatic church in Ghana, has identified this paradox of the parallel increase in Christian demography and evil in Ghana and has proposed some approaches as a response. For example, in his inaugural address after his election as the chairman of the CoP, Apostle Eric Nyamekye pointed out that in spite of the impressive numerical growth of Christians in Ghana, where 71.2 percent of the Ghanaian population claim to be Christians, Christianity in the country has yet to positively impact the public sphere. He further noted that the increase in vices such as corruption, environmental pollution, and sexual abuse by employers and university lecturers are worrying observations that the church must respond to.[18] His observation reflects the CoP's position as found in the five-year vision document of the church dubbed, *Vision 2023*. In that vision document, the CoP clearly points out that there is a gap between what the Christian faith professes and the lived experiences of Christians in Ghana and the rest of Africa. It was therefore, explained,

> As a church, it is time for us to focus a lot more attention on the practice of being God's representative on earth. The Church has to focus on being salt and light in this perverse world in order to transform the spiritual, social, economic and political fabric of the nations. We believe that the destiny of our nations is in the hands of the churches.[19]

The reference to being the salt of the earth and light of the world clearly alludes to the biblical foundation from which the CoP derives its public ecclesiology. As salt, the CoP affirms its responsibility to a decaying and corrupt society. As light, the CoP identifies the need to shine in a dark and diabolical world, exposing evil and brightening the destiny or future of the citizens and the generations unborn. According to Brian Woolnough,

> There are two models for the church, that of "an ark" and that of "salt and light." An ark sees the local community as sinful, Godless, and seeks to draw outsiders away from it into the safety of the church, an ark. The "salt and light" model sees the local community as part of God's world, fallen and imperfect, but in which God is working and wishes His people to be involved in it too, being salt and light to flavor and enlighten the whole.[20]

---

18. Nyamekye, "Inaugural Address"; see also The Church of Pentecost, *Vision 2023*.
19. Church of Pentecost, *Vision 2023*, 20.
20. Woolnough, "Implications for the Church," 173.

The *Vision 2023* of the CoP, as stated above, suggests that the church aligns with the salt and light model. The salt and light model derives its source from Jesus' metaphor of salt and light as found in Matthew 5:13–16. In this passage, Jesus describes the centrality of the role his followers play in the transformation of the world. To remain relevant in society, the impact of the disciples must be felt through their ability to stop the world from decay and to make the earth a better place just as the presence of salt provides taste and preserves food from decay. As the light of the world, the disciples are expected to dispel darkness. The inability to do this is described as putting a lamp under a bowl. This is not acceptable practice. Instead, they were expected to let their light shine in the public sphere through their good deeds, and by that bring glory to God's name.

Interpreting this in contemporary terms, the church is expected to "move towards a paradigm shift that will reverse the consequences of the fall, influenced and guided by biblical principles like light to disperse darkness and salt to salvage and preserve from corruption."[21] It is not enough for Christians to profess their faith and participate in all the Christian rituals at church. The church should also not adopt the "ark" model of attempting to redeem people and separate them from the corrupt and perverse society. Rather, the church should play its public role as light and salt by bringing social transformation through their good deeds just as light dispels darkness by shining. The CoP therefore declares,

> *Vision 2023* is an attempt to challenge the church to leave the building. We must move beyond seeing Sunday services as the arena for serving God. If we hope to make a difference in a hopeless world, our people must go and the church must send [its members out] to take the nations for Christ (Rom 10:13–15; 15:20, 21; John 20:21).[22]

By this, the CoP admits the hopelessness of the world without Christian presence. The church then aims at entering the public sphere and demonstrating Christlike character among the nations. The observable increasing social engagement of the CoP based on the *Vision 2023* demonstrates the church's commitment to this paradigm shift. Although the CoP has been slow in boldly engaging the public sphere, the current momentum in the public has been phenomenal. I have argued elsewhere that at its initial stages, the CoP's evangelistic activities did not give much

---

21. Ajulu, "Development as Holistic Mission," 231–32.
22. Church of Pentecost, *Vision 2023*, 22.

attention to social activities. James McKeown, who was the superintendent of the church at that time, seems to have separated social actions from evangelism and concentrated on the latter with the mantra, "Just to Evangelize." This was seen in his statement to Hans Debrunner: "You other missionaries and your African pastors and collaborators labour and sweat with the schools—and then you leave the people on their own, neglecting evangelism—and thus we can harvest where you have sown."[23] This is not surprising because, just like other Pentecostal missionaries who adopted the fundamentalist approach, McKeown was demonstrating the obvious sentiment of his time.[24]

McKeown's statement to Debrunner shows a reaction to the social gospel approach adopted by many of the Historic Mission Churches of the time who, although involved in social activities, failed to proclaim the gospel of Jesus Christ. Onyinah argues that McKeown's strategy was not to reject social action but to concentrate on evangelism and discipleship so that the indigenous disciples themselves can engage in the social actions.[25] It must, however, be acknowledged that the church's mandate should in no way be limited to either the proclamation of the gospel alone or social action alone. In recent times, there has been a radical shift from such limited understanding of the church's mandate to the need for holistic mission. The church's holistic mission has been described as both the vertical and horizontal dimensions of mission, where the vertical dimension represents God's saving action in the life of individuals, and the horizontal dimension represents human relationships in the world.[26] This is what the various authors in this volume have attempted to engage, engendering important conversations for Pentecostal-Charismatics in Africa and the African diaspora, to consider ways by which they can effectively engage the public sphere.

Overview of the Volume

The volume brings together the contributions of different authors in twelve chapters. The first eight chapters emerged from the plenary

23. Debrunner, *History of Christianity*, 325.

24. Tsekpoe, *Intergenerational Missiology*, 99–100; Myers, "Holistic Mission," 120.

25. Personal conversation with Apostle Opoku Onyinah, the immediate past chairman of the CoP. He is one of the few surviving CoP ministers who worked with McKeown as a minister before McKeown's retirement and subsequent departure to the UK.

26. Padilla, "Holistic Mission," 317–18.

presentations of the James McKeown Memorial Lectures, comprising a main speaker and a respondent for each topic. The subsequent four chapters were presentations at breakout sessions. In chapter 1, Opoku Onyinah elucidates James McKeown's concept of Pentecostal ecclesiology and its impact on the ministry of the CoP. He cogently argues that although McKeown's ecclesiology developed from a confluence of existing ecclesiological models as practiced in different church traditions, McKeown developed a unique ecclesiology, namely, Pneumatological Sensitivity, Apostles and Prophets Leadership, Eschatological Consciousness, Existential Encounter, and Light Shining in Darkness. For McKeown, the starting point of the Christian life is the baptism of the Holy Spirit. He therefore sees the church as a Holy Spirit empowered family. McKeown also developed a unique leadership structure by modifying the Presbyterian system to develop a centralized governance and encouraged direct mentoring, accountability, and discipline at all levels. This has ensured continuity for five generations of successful leadership transition in the CoP and still counting. McKeown's eschatological expectations promoted the forcefulness in the churches' evangelistic drive to the admiration of other missionaries. McKeown's wish for every Christian was for them to wait on the Lord and have a personal encounter with him. In the public sphere, McKeown emphasized the need for the Christians to be the salt of the earth and the light of the world. Onyinah concludes that while it is good for the CoP to attempt following McKeown's ecclesiology, there is also the need to remain relevant in the changing world.

Responding to Onyinah's exploration of McKeown's ecclesiology, Lord Elorm Donkor agrees in chapter 2 that although McKeown was not a formal theologian, his reliance on the leading of the Holy Spirit supplied him with relevant understanding of ecclesiology for Pentecostalism, characterized by both continuity and discontinuity. The continuity was identified in the links or affinity with conceptualized ecclesiologies whilst the discontinuity brings out the uniqueness of McKeown's ecclesiology as identified by Onyinah. Donkor argues that Onyinah's position as a former chairman of the CoP as well as his long service in ministry, his scholarship as the first missiologist of the CoP, and his personal association with McKeown, makes him the most qualified to describe McKeown's ecclesiology with such clarity. He indicates that Onyinah's exposition of McKeown's ecclesiology is helpful to clarify misconceptions about what people attribute to McKeown. He concluded that Onyinah's enduring portrait of McKeown's ecclesiology, which has brought the CoP this far, leaves a huge lesson for Pentecostal leaders "to glean new insights that would build tomorrow's church today."

In the next chapter, Emmanuel Anim discusses Pentecostal-Charismatic mission and social transformation in Africa. He uses the CoP and the International Central Gospel Church (ICGC) as case studies and argues that although Pentecostalism in Africa began with the marginalized in society, the movement has contextualized its theology to offer optimism to its patrons in the midst of seemingly disappointing socioeconomic conditions that emerged from bad political leadership. Taking his argument from Acts 6, he postulates that "Pentecostal mission and social transformation is better understood as *diakonia*." As has been the case with evangelicals, *diakonia* was not imperative for Pentecostals since proclamation of the gospel was their priority. In Ghana, this paradigm began to experience significant transformation from the 1980s. In both the CoP and ICGC, education, medical care, hospitality, micro-credit, national peace and security, environmental efforts, and ministry to persons with disabilities have become an integral part of their mission agenda, showing their increasing response to the concerns of the public sphere in Africa.

In chapter 4, Allison Norton responded to Emmanuel Anim by admiring the remarkable evidence of mission as *diakonia* in Ghanaian Pentecostal-Charismatic Christianity. The importance of this, according to her, is the "transformative potential of African Pentecostal theology and praxis as a growing area of study and interest to scholars of community development and political science." She further highlights the public role of Pentecostalism in Ghana using the CoP's response to the COVID-19 pandemic. The setting in Ghana shows clearly how the CoP engaged political structures and partnered with the government to fight COVID from the center of political life and power. In contrast to this, the African migrant churches in the diaspora are still in the margins, re-visioning ways to reach out effectively to the indigenous people of their host nations. Acts of *diakonia* in these transnational contexts may require different approaches. Since there is no one-size-fits-all mission praxis, Norton wonders, how the CoP's mission in the diaspora can meaningfully engage the public sphere from the margins. She concludes that both at home and in the diaspora, African Pentecostalism has the opportunity to re-vision their ecclesiology in the public sphere by being heterogenous in their praxis.

In chapter 5, Peter White deals with ecclesiological appraisal of Christian values and principles in the public sphere. Using the CoP-Ghana as his focus, he contends that "Christian values are embedded in character traits required of every Christian in their places of work and private lives." Since values influence people's behavior and choices about what is good, bad, right, just, lovely, true, or wrong, both the individual Christian and the church as organization should play their specific roles to consciously develop these values. To do this, he points out that the church should be intentional in positioning ethical and God-fearing Christians in strategic places in society, encourage the establishment of Christian professional leaders to mentor younger ones for generational influence, intentionally support Christlike agendas, enforce civic responsibility of the church members, and pray for leaders and those in authority. He carefully concludes that this is not a call for ecclesiasticism, but a call for the church "to equip its members to live godly lives and to be salt and light in their public-square interactions."

The response to this chapter was done in chapter 6 by Christian Tsekpoe, who agrees with Peter White that Pentecostal-Charismatic Christianity must grow beyond the use of Pentecostal jargon and noise-making (though not bad in themselves) and allow the values of the faith they profess to influence the public sphere. He argues that the CoP seems to have developed well thought-out structures with the potential to influence the public sphere positively. These include the model of discipleship as direct mentoring, the periodic royals' conference in Ghana, the Youth Political Chamber, national development conference, building prisons with correctional, moral, and skills training facilities, and many other social interventions. If these structures are used intentionally for the purpose of improving the values and morals of Ghanaians in general, then the public presence of Pentecostal-Charismatic Christianity can be truly felt within the foreseeable future.

Chapter 7 discusses church-state relations and the problem of corruption in Africa. In this chapter, Dela Quampah pointedly alleges that "Africa has become a force to reckon with in contemporary Christianity, but not in contemporary morality." He supports this allegation with what he sees as endemic corruption in many African countries. He argues that although many blame governments for this regrettable state of affairs in Africa, civil societies—including the church—have a crucial role to play in mitigating the menace. Quampah sees the church as an important development partner with the government and argues that since the church in Africa exerts great influence on government through the provision of social amenities, the church should use its presence and influence to fight against corruption. After analyzing some responses of the church to state corruption, he proposes ways by which this relationship can be enhanced. He concludes that although the church may not be equipped to directly fight corruption, it can collaborate with antigraft agencies for a unified effort against the menace.

By way of response to Quampah in chapter 8, Mbanyane Mhango agrees that corruption is antithetical to the image and mission of God. Consequently, the church "partnering with states to fight corruption has theological merit," taking all other factors into consideration. He emphasizes the church's role in behavioral transformation through people's encounter with the gospel since the process of salvation has the potency to change people at the heart or soul level. This, according to him, is essential for curbing what he calls micro-level corruption, which eventually has influence on corruption at the macro level (e.g., large-scale abuse of funds). He debunks the general perception that corruption is as a result of high-level poverty. Such views contradict Christ's teachings on faithfulness. He then puts forward that the church must see corruption through a Christological lens, speak truth to power, and boldly declare corruption as sinful, instead of focusing on a prosperity gospel, which weakens the church's authority to positively confront the sinfulness of corruption. Christians who are privileged to hold high political offices must demonstrate Christlikeness in their duties since their failures discredit the church. After agreeing with Quampah that the church is expected to appropriate theological remedy in fighting corruption, Mhango finally proposes an eschatological view of corruption as a complementing approach to curbing corruption in Africa.

In chapter 9, Vincent Anane Denteh analyzes the CoP's Home and Urban Mission, a special ministry to the marginalized, unengaged, and unreached people groups in Ghana and beyond. He draws attention to the current trend of urbanization, which has taken mission to the marginalized and unreached people groups right in the center of the cities, calling for a paradigm shift in contemporary mission praxis. He points to the model of urban mission in the early church and argues that although urban mission has emerged as a new field today, both the concept and the practice of urban mission has been in existence since the emergence of Christianity. Following the early church, Paul's mission strategy was to evangelize the cities. He identifies the urgency in planting urban churches and the need to develop a theology of mission for the cities as imperative for contemporary Christian mission. Finally, he highlights the concept of megachurches as an emerging strategy for urban mission, which Pentecostal-Charismatics must pay attention to.

Alfred Koduah engages with Pentecostals' response to the lordship of Christ in a religiously pluralistic society, as shown in chapter 10. He opens this chapter by arguing that the affirmation of the lordship of Christ is central to Pentecostal-Charismatic Christianity. He notes that although religious pluralism was given much attention during the modern era, it was given much greater attention during the postmodern era. Again, he points out how globalization aids the widespread influence of religious pluralism and the impact this had on Pentecostalism. He argues that although maintaining the proclamation of the lordship of Christ has become difficult in this pluralistic era, Pentecostal-Charismatics should not shed their firm belief in the lordship of Christ. He concludes by admitting that some church traditions are negotiable and need to be changed, but Pentecostals should be careful not to modify their belief in the lordship of Christ.

In chapter 11, Patrick Kudadjie shows the need to re-think church in the light of the COVID-19 pandemic. The pandemic affected the economic, social, physical and spiritual lives of people across the globe. The pandemic did not spare the church in Ghana just as religious lives were affected in other countries globally. He, however, argues that despite the challenges, the pandemic presented some opportunities such as media innovations in the use of virtual meeting platforms, time consciousness and the importance of small group meetings. He contends that although the direct restrictions of the pandemic have minimized, there is the need for the church to seize the opportunity of the various innovations and encourage the use of the digital space as a sacred space, the judicious use of time for church service, the effective use of small group meetings for discipleship, sustaining social intervention systems, encouraging family and personal devotions, strengthening state-church relations and building health-conscious churches.

Finally, Johnny Lartey Peprah presents a case study of the CoP's church governance and national transformation in chapter 12. He examined the role played by the governance system of the CoP in the national development and transformation of Ghana. He explored the historical trajectory and the administrative structures of the CoP's governance system from James McKeown's era to the contemporary leadership and contends that the CoP has been actively involved in the developmental agenda of Ghana in areas such as moral and spiritual guidance, social welfare and community development, advocacy and social justice, leadership and empowerment, moral accountability and anti-corruption efforts. He presents the CoP's transformational agenda as a model for Ghanaian Christianity.

These excellent contributions provide an overview of the increasing interest of Pentecostal-Charismatic Christianity to engage the public sphere, the gaps that are still left that need our attention, and the way forward for visible social transformation. It is our prayer that this volume will make for valuable reading and stimulate Christians to work hard toward social transformation for a better society.

Bibliography

Ajulu, Deborah. "Development as Holistic Mission." In *Holistic Mission: God's Plan for God's People*, edited by Brian Woolnough and Wonsuk Ma, 229–47. Oxford: Regnum, 2014.
Anderson, Allan. "Pentecostalism and Social, Political, and Economic Development." *Spiritus* 5 (2020) 121–26.
Asamoah-Gyadu, Kwabena. "You Shall Receive Power: Empowerment in Pentecostal/Charismatic Christianity." In *Pentecostal Mission and Global Christianity*, edited by Younghoon Lee et al., 45–66. Oxford: Regnum, 2014.
Barker, Isabelle V. "Charismatic Economies: Pentecostalism, Economic Restructuring, and Social Reproduction." *New Political Science* 29 (2007) 407–27.
Benyah, Francis. "Pentecostal/Charismatic Churches and the Provision of Social Services in Ghana." *Transformation* 38 (2020) 16–30.
Burgess, Richard. "Nigerian Pentecostalism and Civic Engagement: Mission in the Midst of Poverty and Violence." *Amended Paper Theological Education in Africa Conference* (2012) 29–42.
The Church of Pentecost. *Vision 2023: Five-Year Vision Document for The Church of Pentecost Covering the Period 2018–2023*. Accra: Pentecost, 2018.
Debrunner, Hans. *A History of Christianity in Ghana*. Accra: Waterville, 1967.
Goodall, Norman, ed. *The Uppsala Report: 1968*. Geneva: World Council of Churches, 1968.
Jayakumar, Samuel. "The Work of God as Holistic Mission: An Asian Perspective." In *Holistic Mission: God's Plan for God's People*, edited by Brian Woolnough and Wonsuk Ma, 87–101. Oxford: Regnum, 2014.
Kärkkäinen, Veli-Matti. "The Pentecostal Understanding of Mission." In *Pentecostal Mission and Global Christianity*, edited by Younghoon Lee et al., 26–66. Oxford: Regnum, 2014.
Ma, Julie. "Pentecostal Evangelism, Church Planting, and Church Growth." In *Pentecostal Mission and Global Christianity*, edited by Younghoon Lee et al., 87–106. Oxford: Regnum, 2014.

McAlpine, Thomas H. *By Word, Work, and Wonder*. Monrovia: MARC, 1995.

Myers, Bryant. "Holistic Mission: New Frontiers." In *Holistic Mission: God's Plan for God's People*, edited by Brian Woolnough and Wonsuk Ma, 119–27. Oxford: Regnum, 2014.

Nyamekye, Eric. "Inaugural Address." Delivered at his induction service as chairman of The Church of Pentecost. Pentecost International Worship Centre, Atomic, August 25, 2018.

Ohlmann, Philip, et al., eds. *African Initiated Christianity and the Decolonisation of Development: Sustainable Development in Pentecostal and Independent Churches*. London: Routledge, 2020.

Padilla, René. "Holistic Mission." Paper presented at the 2004 Forum for World Evangelization. Pattaya, Thailand, September 29—October 5, 2004.

Peterson, Douglas. "Word, Work, and Wonder as Holistic Ministry." In *Pentecostal Mission and Global Christianity*, edited by Younghoon Lee et al., 255–71. Oxford: Regnum, 2014.

Raistrick, Tulo. "The Local Church, Transforming Community." In *Holistic Mission: God's Plan for God's People*, edited by Brian Woolnough and Wonsuk Ma, 87–101. Oxford: Regnum, 2014.

Tsekpoe, Christian. *Intergenerational Missiology: An African Pentecostal-Charismatic Perspective*. Oxford: Regnum, 2022.

———. "Navigating the Shades and Nexus of Ghanaian Pentecostalism(s): A Search for an Appropriate Metaphor." *Ghana Journal of Religion and Theology* 10 (2020) 27–46.

Woolnough, Brian. "Implications for the Church of Tomorrow." In *Holistic Mission: God's Plan for God's People*, edited by Brian Woolnough and Wonsuk Ma, 160–74. Oxford: Regnum, 2014.

CHAPTER I

James McKeown's Concept of Pentecostal Ecclesiology and Its Impact on the Ministry of The Church of Pentecost

Opoku Onyinah

Introduction

ECCLESIOLOGY SIMPLY MEANS THE study of the church or the doctrine of the church. This necessarily includes the nature of the church, membership of the church, the governance of the church, the images of the church, the ordinances of the church, and church discipline. Attempting to find out Pastor James McKeown's concept of Pentecostal ecclesiology involves exploring his views on how a church should be structured and led. This includes examining his leadership of The Church of Pentecost and assessing how his ideas have influenced its development.

To be able to achieve this, I shall examine a few pieces of literature from evangelical, Catholic, and Pentecostal scholars to dig out their perspectives of ecclesiology. Then, I shall examine McKeown's circular letters, General Council Meeting minutes, and some writings that are already in existence on Pastor McKeown to find out how his concept of the church is reflected in this literature. I shall also examine the existing oral traditions of Pastor McKeown, and some interactions I have had with some of The Church of Pentecost fathers and mothers. I approach this study as someone who had the opportunity to briefly work with him as a pastor.

Concepts of Ecclesiology

I begin by drawing from the Evangelical United Church of Christ's renowned theologian H. Richard Niebuhr's most popular book, *Christ and Culture*, which has been adopted and analyzed by many missiologists. Niebuhr observes five categories of the relationship between the church and society: Christ against Culture, the Christ of Culture, Christ above Culture, Christ and Culture in Paradox, and Christ the Transformer of Culture.

The first type, the Christ against Culture relationship, is "the one that uncompromisingly affirms the sole authority of Christ over the Christian and resolutely rejects culture's claims to loyalty."[1] Here, the church completely opposes the culture. There is a clear line of demarcation between Christianity and culture. Christians are called to holiness and complete separation from the world. In this relationship, the church does not see anything good within the culture and completely rejects the cultural assumptions. It can be said that some of the early Pentecostals held on to this view. Christians were separated from the other people; they were advised not to participate in community gatherings, such as participation in family gatherings, festivals, or chieftaincy affairs. Pastor McKeown's approach, as will be seen, shows that he was not of this type.

The second relationship, which is Christ of Culture, "feels no great tension between church and world, the societal laws and the gospel, the workings of divine grace and human effort, the ethics of salvation and the ethics of social conservation or progress."[2] This is the group which completely assimilates culture into Christianity. This does not mean that the group will completely surrender the church to the recipient culture, but the Christians within emphasize the ideas shared between the culture and Christianity and find no disagreement between them. I will venture to say that some advocates of African theology toe this line.

The third type, Christ above Culture, is a good mediation position between the first two, maintaining that cultural expressions are both good and evil. Therefore, they need to be augmented and perfected by revelation and God's grace through Christ. The Catholic Church can be said to toe this line.

The fourth type, Christ and Culture in Paradox, is the type that attempts to bring a synthesis between the two extremes. They attempt to

---

1. Niebuhr, *Christ and Culture*, 45.
2. Niebuhr, *Christ and Culture*, 83.

"do justice to the need for holding together as well as for distinguishing between loyalty to Christ and responsibility for culture."[3] Basically, this type sees culture as good but corrupted by sin. The outcome of this is often tension between the church and culture. The Christian would like to live within the culture but often realizes it is also necessary to live under the law of God. This becomes the experience of many Christians.

The fifth type, Christ the Transformer of Culture, fits into Pastor McKeown's concept of mission which he used to build The Church of Pentecost. The assumption is that culture is good but corrupted by the fall of humanity. The purpose of the coming of Christ was to redeem humanity from its depraved nature. Since Christ is redeeming all of creation, the church can transform culture to Christlikeness to the glory of God. For with God, all things are possible. The way Pastor McKeown did his work in Ghana, it can be said that his views fall within this type.

Another classic book on ecclesiology is Cardinal Avery Dulles' book, *Models of Church*. In 1974, the Catholic theologian and priest studied the existing writings on ecclesiology and came out with five models, then later added one, bringing it to six. These are Mystical Communion, Sacrament, Servant, Herald, Institution, and Community of Disciples. The first model, Mystical Communion, is the type that stresses community and shows that the mystical community is deeper than an ordinary family. The community is related to one another by the Holy Spirit, which makes the union mystical. The second model, Sacrament, presents the church as the visible manifestation of Christ in the world. The third model, Church as Servant, considers the church as the redeemed people who must commit themselves to social justice. The church must do as Jesus did on earth, helping the needy and vulnerable.

The fourth model considers the church as Herald; in other words, messengers of the good news. This is the faithful people who announce the gospel of the kingdom of God. The church is constantly calling people to hear the good news and calling those within to renew their commitment to the Master. The fifth model, which considers the church as an institution, highlights the structure and administration of the church. It develops the concept, "You are Peter, upon this rock I will build my church" (Matt 16:18). This model places the responsibility of training the laity and administering the church on the clerics, that is, the Pope, bishops, priests, and deacons. It emphasizes the governance of the church.

---

3. Niebuhr, *Christ and Culture*, 157.

For Dulles, however, this should not be the fundamental aim for the church. The Community of Disciples model, the sixth model, emphasizes the church as a community of people who follow Jesus in an unending journey. The devotees follow Jesus in a school that never ends no matter the condition they find themselves in. Pastor McKeown's mission in Ghana shows that most of the principles of this sixth model were also embodied in his concept of ecclesiology.

Another important book on ecclesiology which should be of interest to Pentecostals is the work of the Finnish Pentecostal/Lutheran theologian Veli-Matti Kärkkäinen, *An Introduction to Ecclesiology: Historical, Global, and Interreligious Perspectives*. Kärkkäinen makes a survey of major theological traditions, including Eastern Orthodox, Roman Catholic, Reformed, and Pentecostals. He offers insight into African Americans, women, and contemporary trends in the United States. He touches on major issues, including mission, worship, sacrament, and governance, and the interreligious comparison with Jewish, Islamic, Hindu, and Buddhist communities. He acknowledges the difficulty in defining Pentecostal ecclesiology. However, he considers Pentecostals' concept of the church as charismatic, missionary, and eschatological fellowship. As a Pentecostal, Pastor McKeown operated within the general framework of Pentecostal ecclesiology which was a multiplicity of borrowed concepts.

In a volume edited by John Christopher Thomas, *Towards a Pentecostal Theology*, which comprised contributions from Pentecostal scholars in six continents and of diverse gender, race, and discipline, six areas were identified in Pentecostal ecclesiology. These are the Pentecostal Church as Redeemed Community; the Pentecostal Church as Sanctified Community; the Pentecostal Church as Empowered Community; the Pentecostal Church as Healing Community; and the Pentecostal Church as Eschatological Community. The majority of these are seen in Pastor McKeown's ecclesiology.

Although Pastor McKeown's ecclesiology has certain connections with the various scholarly observations made above, he has a unique ecclesiology which I have placed in five themes: Pneumatological Sensitivity, Apostles and Prophets Leadership, Eschatological Consciousness, Existential Encounter, and Light Shining in Darkness.

Pneumatological Sensitivity

Pastor James McKeown was an Irish missionary who is accredited as the founder of The Church of Pentecost in 1953, although the church's remote origin goes back to 1937 when Pastor McKeown arrived in the Gold Coast. With minimal education, Pastor McKeown relied on what he thought the Bible says and how the Spirit of God led him. This does not mean that McKeown was not interested in reading. He was a man of reading; sometimes he quoted people such as John Bunyan and A. B. Simpson in his pastoral letters.[4] He also encouraged his pastors to read. In a pastoral circular written in the 1950s, McKeown encouraged his ministers:

> Be widely read. If we read good books, we come to learn how little we know. No man is so proud as the man who knows nothing. The man who knows is a humble man. . . . Read, read, read my fellow ministers, get to know. People are looking at us. We may dress like a minister, look like one, but it is when we open our mouth that we reveal what are in us. . . . It is what is within that will determine our true value. . . . Don't even mention your position in the church, you get on with the message of the One Who Loved and gave Himself for you.[5]

Here, we see how McKeown encouraged ministers to read and not pamper themselves with titles. What was important to him was what was in a minister. By "what is within," McKeown was talking about Christ who lives in the Christian in the person of the Holy Spirit.

For Pastor McKeown, the starting point of any Christian is the baptism in the Holy Spirit. This is depicted in the question which he asked Pastor Vanderpuije, the pastor who served as McKeown's chauffeur during his last days. On his last visit to the headquarters of the church in Ghana, seeing the numerous workers, he asked Vanderpuije, "Have these workers been baptized in the Holy Spirit?"[6] For him, to qualify to work at the headquarters of the church one must be baptized in the Holy Spirit. Sometimes the way he placed emphasis on the baptism of the Holy Spirit, like some of the early Pentecostals, showed no clear distinction between the born-again experience and the baptism of the Holy Spirit. For example, in a circular letter to all the assemblies,

---

4. For example, McKeown, "Ghana Apostolic Church, July 27, 1958"; McKeown, "Ghana Apostolic Church, to All Pastors."

5. McKeown, "Ghana Apostolic Church, to All Pastors."

6. Onyinah, "James McKeown," 78.

encouraging them to pray, he wrote, "Begin to pray better, if there is no Holy Spirit in you, you will not pray. If the Holy Spirit is in you, you will pray."[7] In other words, a person cannot pray if the Holy Spirit is not in that person. It is, however, believed that all born-again Christians are baptized by the Spirit into the body of Christ (1 Cor 12:13), and thus have the Holy Spirit in them. By "the Holy Spirit in you," Pastor McKeown might be talking about the baptism in the Holy Spirit as evidenced by speaking in tongues. For him, those who did not speak in tongues were not considered as having the Holy Spirit in them.

Nonetheless, Pastor McKeown's point here can be compared to Dulles' mystical communion that exists among people who have been baptized in the Holy Spirit. McKeown considered all as one family and having one Father. He often called the pastors "my brothers," "my colleagues," or "my friends." It is the Holy Spirit who brings people together. It was Pastor McKeown's concept of the oneness in the family of God that has left people calling him Pastor McKeown instead of Apostle James McKeown. This sort of simplicity and unity within the family is something which The Church of Pentecost must continue to pursue.

Pastor McKeown emphasized that the Christian life is a life of the Holy Spirit. We are filled by the Spirit, walk by the Spirit, and live by the Spirit. Once we live by the Spirit, we shall shine, and not gratify the flesh but give glory to God. He wrote in 1962:

> I am also informed that, in all assemblies where the name was made known and out-doored, great joy filled the hearts of all the members. It is for all now to live up to the standard of this new name. It was on the day of the feast of Pentecost the Church was born: "They were all filled with the Holy Ghost . . ." "Be filled with the Holy Spirit," "Walk in the Holy Spirit." If we so live that the Holy Spirit dwells in us, then our light will shine that all men will see our good works and God our father will be glorified.[8]

Pastor McKeown contended that the most important part of the church's life is the leading of the Spirit, not constitution or rituals. This is what Kärkkäinen observes as Charismatic, and Thomas calls empowered community. McKeown did not believe in rituals. When The Church of Pentecost first drew a constitution, he wrote under the subheading "Constitutions and Rituals":

---

7. McKeown, "Church of Pentecost, January 6, 1964."
8. McKeown, "Church of Pentecost, August 8, 1962."

> We already have our own Constitution. Have we any prescribed form of "ritual" in the Church? I don't know of any. We open our hearts and seek to be led by the Holy Spirit. Has the Bible been taken away from you? Has Jesus been taken away from you? Has the Holy Spirit been taken away from you? Now, if you have Jesus, if you have the Holy Spirit, then you have a fire in you, that is the language of the Bible. "He shall baptize you with the Holy Ghost and fire."[9]

Pastor McKeown was not too stuck to constitutions and rituals. He was opened to the leading of the Spirit. In a pastoral letter to the ministers and general deacons (area finance board chairmen), which was leading to the Thirteenth Session of the General Council meeting, he wrote, "If we commence on the law road, we will end on the low road. We want to commence on the high road." He continued that they needed to meet under the anointing of the Holy Spirit, otherwise, they would sit and "make minutes, rules, and regulations which will turn out to be ropes to strangle the work in future." He emphasized that listening to God would lead them to freedom. He therefore charged them "to bend low before the Lord, come filled with the Holy Spirit." He was not keen to establish committees and boards. Rather, as evidenced in the above discussions, he was keen on listening to the leading of the Holy Spirit rather than creating laws and rules. Here is another approach of his that The Church of Pentecost may need to examine.

It is questionable whether McKeown could have led the church the way he did if he were not the founder. As if he were answering this question, in his analysis "New Wine in Old Wineskins: The Paradox of Preserving the church's Legacies for Succeeding Generations," Christian Tsekpoe contends that by having the Word of God in the background, churches and Christian organizations can, with reasonable freedom, establish principles underlying mission praxis by way of models if only the leaders "are sensitive to the leading of the Holy Spirit to identify what God is doing with a particular context."[10] Thus, it can be stated squarely that the key to steering the affairs of a church in a relaxed way is the use of the Scripture through the revelation of the Spirit—the leading of the Spirit.[11]

---

9. McKeown, "Church of Pentecost, July 24, 1962."
10. Tsekpoe, *Intergenerational Missiology*, 193.
11. McKeown, "Ghana Apostolic Church, March 22, 1960."

Apostles and Prophets' Leadership

Coming from the Apostolic Church, Pastor McKeown believed and practiced apostles and prophets' leadership in church governance. However, reading through some of the circular letters showed that he had his reservations about this type of governance. In 1954, for example, Pastor McKeown issued a pastoral letter to the ministers of the church; he discussed the offices of apostles and prophets and the challenges associated with their operations and functions. He mentioned that some letters he had received entertained doubts about the way some pastors were called to various offices of the church. He concluded:

> "That we all may be one." What a fever rages in group No. 3, cablegrams being sent out, private letters, circulars, in this fever prophecy is active, and I should not be at all surprised if out of this fever there sneaks forth an epidemic of apostles, thus bringing into being that which is not spiritual. Will I continue to write about the confusion? Is this letter intended to bring confusion? Should I hide these things? Shall I sit quiet and let you wanting simplicity into error? I cannot do that, I will speak, I will enlighten you.[12]

From this, we can realize that Pastor McKeown was attempting to find a way to address some of the challenges with the apostles and prophets' governance at the time. Consequently, he adopted the Apostolic Church's practices with some nuance from other church governance.[13] The Church of Pentecost adopted a centralized structure. At the top comes the General Council, which consists of all confirmed ministers of the church, unlike the Apostolic Church, which comprises only apostles and prophets, and elders' representatives. Following the General Council is the seven-member Executive Council that sees to the administration of the church. The regional and national presbyteries, chaired by the apostles and prophets, come after the Executive Council. District presbyteries, headed by pastors, follow the regions and the nations. Last on the administrative structure of The Church of Pentecost are the local presbyteries, headed by presiding elders. Over the years, the Executive Council has been increased to fifteen members. Women's Ministry and Youth Ministry executive committee members have been included in the General Council. The structure has

---

12. McKeown, "Gold Coast Apostolic Church."

13. Apostolic Church, *Apostolic Church*, 22–44; cf. Church of Pentecost, *Final Review Constitution*, 1–27.

some resemblance of Dulles' concept of institution, which sees the clerics with the Pope on top as responsible for training and administration. On the other hand, the structure fits in well with the Ghanaian cultures, especially that of the Akan with its various military organs.[14] It shows Pastor McKeown's willingness to allow Christ to transform a culture for his own glory. Nevertheless, the tension between the centralized type of governance and the decentralized type of governance is evident in this approach. The Church of Pentecost exhibits this tension between granting of autonomy and holding on to the centralized governance in its struggle to grant autonomy to the external branches.

Training was very important to Pastor McKeown. Initially, there was no Bible College. However, one was established in 1954. It appears the patronage was not encouraging; thus, Pastor McKeown wrote circular letters encouraging members to attend the Bible College. In June 1955, he wrote, "The training is good, and our American brothers and sisters are all out to help. I wonder, have the Pastors forgotten that we agreed in Council that at least six of the Pastors and Overseers should, in turn, attend the school each term?"[15] In August that same year, he issued another circular:

> For many years there was a cry for a Bible School. Now, the door has been opened, it is the golden opportunity for everyone to enter this open door.... Let us all together encourage the school and make it a centre from which a stream of workers will flow. If there are in your assemblies those who desire to attend the school, encourage them.[16]

As the patronage continued to be poor and there were some murmurings surrounding the operations of the Bible College, it was closed down. Within The Church of Pentecost, there continues to be mixed feeling on education. While some will go all out for it, others still exercise great caution on too much education.

Consequently, the type of training which he used to provide was the in-service type of training, where the apostles and the prophets had to teach their officers in retreat forms. This was practical ministration that equipped pastors and church officers to discharge their duties. This

---

14. For reading on Akan military organs, see Nukunya, *Tradition and Change in Ghana*, 67–74; Busia, *Position of the Chief in Modern Asante*, 1–22; Rattray, *Ashanti Law and Constitution*, 120–26.

15. McKeown, "Ghana Apostolic Church, June 8, 1955."

16. McKeown, "Ghana Apostolic Church, May 18, 1955."

continued until 1972, when a Bible college was established in Kumasi, only to be closed down after a short period, until it was reopened in 1982, in Accra. This Bible College has now upgraded to a full-fledged university.

One part of Pastor McKeown's leadership style, which has helped to pass on his leadership mantle successfully to five generations, is direct mentorship. He would travel with people, stay in the same house with them, eat with them, and chat with them. He would give them the opportunity to minister while he sat down to enjoy it. This type of mentoring is what Dulles identifies as Community Disciples. The disciples continue until one is completely overwhelmed with the master's principles and values. Tsekpoe has analyzed that Pastor McKeown's simplicity of liturgy, ability to allow vernacularizing, strong indigenous leadership formation, and direct mentoring as aspects of his mission praxis aided the growth of the church in Ghana. Tsekpoe is aware that those factors were already known in the African Pentecostal-Charismatic mission, consequently, he argues that the principles of their practical application in Christian mission can be extrapolated and applied to mission in multigenerational contexts.[17]

Pastor McKeown took discipline in the church as very important. He thought that would bring sanity in the church. Pastors, elders, and church officers who misappropriated church funds, fornicated, or told lies were dismissed. He knew Ghanaians would come and apologize in many such cases, but he would still maintain the decision that had been taken by the Executive Council. He was not interested in dismissal and would have liked to save such people. In 1966, his belief in mentoring and the apostolic type of leadership caused him to believe that the numerous dismissals were the outcome of lack of good apostolic oversight of the ministers; he admonished the ministers to be one another's keepers.[18] He often appealed to the pastors to pray toward such dismissals. In 1962, he wrote, "Meantime I want you to be much in prayer, with the recent dismissal and resignations from the Ministerial Staff, a review of the work as a whole is very important."[19] The Church of Pentecost continues to hold on to the McKeown type of discipline and apostolic leadership as demonstrated in most of the General Council's decisions.[20]

17. Tsekpoe, *Intergenerational Missiology*, 73–101.
18. McKeown, "Church of Pentecost, July 19, 1966."
19. McKeown, "Church of Pentecost, October 12, 1962."
20. These are numerous in various circular letters, e.g., Nyamekye, "To All Assemblies Church of Pentecost."

Eschatological Consciousness

One of the doctrines of the church that was obvious in the mind of Pastor McKeown was the imminent Second Coming of our Lord Jesus Christ. Before closing a session of a church service or convention, Pastor McKeown would often say, "If Jesus tarries," we shall meet tomorrow. This was a visible sign that he strongly believed in the Second Coming of Christ, and that our Lord Jesus could come at any time and, therefore, Christians might live a life of preparedness.

This belief motivated him to embark on aggressive evangelism. Hans W. Debrunner, a missionary and theologian in Ghana in the mid-twentieth century, observed that the success of the Apostolic Church (The Church of Pentecost) in Ghana was its emphasis on evangelism. He remarked that he had met some former Basel missionaries in Germany who had sent reports of the growth of the Apostolic Church in Ghana to their relatives in America. Significantly, one of the missionaries remarked that he wanted to do what the Apostolic Church was doing, "Just to evangelize."[21]

In writing circular letters to members to attend the convention, he would ask them to pray for the Lord to bless them and bring more new converts to Christ. He would write and tell them the number of new converts who had accepted the Lord in rallies that he had attended or reports that he had received. For example, in a circular he wrote to all the assemblies in 1964, he was happy that in Akanter, near Asamankese, seventy-four souls had been won to Christ. He was dreaming of sinners accepting Christ and being added to the church. In the same circular, he continued, "I had a pleasant dream the other night. I dreamed that in Ghana alone 23,000 souls were added to the church. Will our dreams come true?"[22] We dream of things that consume our lives. Pastor McKeown was a man of aggressive evangelism. The desire for aggressive evangelism still consumes the leadership of the church as frequently discussed in various General Council meetings.[23] However, there is always the need to review old practices with new trends in order to be more effective.

---

21. Debrunner, *History of Christianity in Ghana*, 325.
22. McKeown, "Church of Pentecost, May 20, 1964."
23. Church of Pentecost, "45th Session State of Church Address," 19–20.

Existential Encounter

The crux of Pastor McKeown's concept of the church is his emphasis that a believer should have an encounter with Christ. He believed that the Christian should have an existential encounter with the Lord, which should be demonstrated in practical Christian living. Christine Leonard discusses a conversation that went on between Pastor McKeown and a missionary, which shows us some of Pastor McKeown's emphasis on the need to make Christ alive in one's life. When Pastor McKeown was told that he preached very well, he said, "Well my friend, I do not think I preach very well. It would never do back in the UK!" He continued that he had only three messages: the first is Jesus Christ and Him crucified, the second is the baptism of the Holy Spirit, and the third is the power of God to change lives and bring holiness in the church. He continued that he would pray until "the sermon was written on my heart and then my words bring conviction of sin and changed lives."[24] When a young educated person standing there was questioned about how he saw Pastor McKeown, he said, "He directs people always towards Jesus and if you are sharing Christ with him, you cannot lose the way.[25] His focus was to preach Christ until Christ is born in a person's life.

Most of his preaching was based on sanctification, believers setting themselves aside for the use of the master, Christ Jesus. In 1957, in preparation for the members to attend a general convention, he wrote through a circular letter:

> If you are not prepared to give up a besetting sin in your life, DON'T COME. Proverbs 28:13. If you are not sufficiently broken in spirit, and not willing to be reproved, DON'T COME. Proverbs 29:1. We would all like to see the Glory of God manifest at the Convention, right from the very beginning. Malachi 3:1. So please COME in the attitude of surrender to the Lord with a spirit of humility, and a willingness to receive from Him. Psalm 51:17.[26]

Here, his focus was that believers must shun besetting sins so that Christ who lives in them would manifest himself. This is sanctification in the sense that the believer must respond to God in holy Christian

---

24. Leonard, *Giant in Ghana*, 85. From this perspective, McKeown often discouraged pastors to use notes.

25. Leonard, *Giant in Ghana*, 85.

26. McKeown, "Church of Pentecost, March 28, 1957."

living. He thought presenting one's body that way to God was the most important thing. Like Pastor McKeown, Apostle Lord Abraham Elorm Donkor argues that "embodying the character of Christ involves a constant and conscientious practicing (habituation) of the fruit and the gifts of the Holy Spirit."[27] The human being is not left out in the work of the Holy Spirit. The individual must respond. For Pastor McKeown, responding to the call to surrender was more important than church buildings, and it was through surrendering that the Lord could use people as he wants. After reporting about some beautiful buildings that the Lord had given to the church, he requested this:

> Great progress is being made in the church with the erection of church buildings. At Mamprobi, Accra, a miracle has been performed through the faith of the saints there, they have almost completed their beautiful new church building. It is larger than the church building at Kaneshie, with one room at the back, this room is for the Presbytery. Well done, Mamprobi. I have mentioned Kaneshie church building, the last time I visited the Assembly, the Elders were asking permission to extend the building, as it was now no longer able to accommodate the gathering at Sunday morning services. The church building at Akroso became too small to accommodate the saints, they are now nearing the completion of a large block building. Well done, Akroso. Permit me to say, while we are doing a great work in erecting church Buildings to the Glory of God, let us not forget the more important call from God. "Present your bodies as a living sacrifice, HOLY unto the Lord," if we surrender ourselves to the Lord, there is no knowing what God can do in and through us.[28]

Here, he was so careful not to discourage the people for the sacrifice of giving offerings to put up church buildings. However, he did not want them to lose focus by boasting about church buildings. He wanted them to focus on the more important thing—living daily lives that would allow Christ to use them as he wants.

The hidden secret of McKeown's successful life and ministry is what he passed on to the pastors in a pastoral letter sent in 1959—one day of rest each week.[29] In this letter, the apostle (McKeown) requested his

---

27. Elorm-Donkor, *Christian Morality in Ghanaian Pentecostalism*, 197.
28. McKeown, "Church of Pentecost, May 20, 1964."
29. McKeown, "Ghana Apostolic Church, November 10, 1959."

pastors to observe a day of rest where they would wait on God in silence, not praying loudly, singing to work themselves into a happy state, nor engaging in any moving around in "busyness."

> I want you to choose one day each week when you will fast from such luxuries as much talking, going around town, visiting your friends, eating too much, sleeping too much. . . . I want you to choose a quiet spot, it could be the church room, or the room of your dwelling house . . . [or sitting] down under the trees, you will have less noise to contend with. Take your Bibles with all the Bible helps you have, ask God to lead you in reading the Bible. Rededicate your whole life to God. Learn also to wait on God in silence. . . . I am calling you for a day of rest. If you obey me in this, you will find it very hard work, some of you can't wait, you would rather run a mile than wait patiently one minute. It is much easier for some of you to sing than to wait, even it is easier for some of you to keep talking in prayer than to wait on the Lord. Many of you cannot endure the silence, but I am calling on you to wait on the Lord. . . . You will probably feel tired, you may get a little sleepy, then have a little sleep but not all day. After the little sleep, you will then renew your earnest desire in prayer to God. Pray for yourselves, pray for all the people of God, pray for the work of God. When you have pressed with all your power to obey my call to you, you may feel you are getting nowhere, you may feel that you are a useless worthless pastor. This hard day's work, which will be repeated each week will lead you to rest. God is calling you to rest from the works of the flesh, which profiteth little and yield yourselves to the Holy Spirit. You may feel that you are less than you thought you were, but watch your congregation grow, note the change in them. I suggest your wives will be the first to notice the change.[30]

That the issue of rest was very important to Pastor McKeown is evident in what Rev. A. K. Mensah of Zion Church in Ghana told me. He said that at Ho, Pastor McKeown told him this: "Young man, let me tell you something. The most effective medicine in the world is free; you do not have to pay for it. But it takes discipline to take it. That medicine is rest." Pastor McKeown felt every effective pastor (or person) needs a day of rest where the person will do less and allow the Lord to speak to the soul. He did not believe shouting in prayer or singing aloud was to be done. In fact, when it comes to shouting either in prayer, singing, or preaching, he

---

30. McKeown, "Ghana Apostolic Church, November 10, 1959."

often said, "you have more perspiration than inspiration." He believed that observing this day as he suggested, which I consider as the biblical Sabbath, will open the wells of God within a person to gush out for personal refreshment, and positively affect one's ministry. He shared in one of his circulars how God blessed him after such a time of rest.

> It seemed necessary for me to listen to some of them, and to answer some of them, but God said, "Be still and know that I am God." Then came the conflict of thoughts for the morrow, and the duties and cares, but God said, "Be still" and then came the very prayer which my restless heart wanted to press upon Him, but God said, "Be still." And as I listened and slowly learned to obey and shut my ears to every sound, I found after a while that when the other voices ceased, or I ceased to hear them, there was a still, small voice in the depth of my being that began to speak with an inexpressible tenderness, power, and comfort. As I listened, it became the voice of prayer, and the voice of wisdom, and the voice of duty. I did not need to think so hard, or pray so hard, or trust so hard, but that "still small voice" of the Holy Spirit in my heart was God's prayer in my secret soul, was God's answer to all my questions, was God's life and strength for soul and body, and became the substance of all knowledge, and all prayer, and all blessing, for it was the living God Himself as my life and my all.[31]

This is what Cardinal Dulles considers sacrament in ecclesiology, this time, the person becomes a gift. Apostle Mbanyane Mhango of The Church of Pentecost articulates the sacramental role of the believer clearly when he writes, "all believers are sacraments of God's Spirit in Christ. As sacraments, the believers reflect Christ in word and deed. In this way, they fulfil Christ's call as ambassadors and carry out the Great Commission."[32] I believe that this is one of the principles of Pastor McKeown, which the church must reconsider as we embark on "Possessing the Nations'" agenda.[33] In this modern world, where there is work always, even forcing theological institutions to teach on Sundays, the church needs to consider the Sabbatical principle. Encountering Christ is not in numerous programs, singing or praying aloud. Pastors may work all days a week including prayer or business meetings on Sunday. For Pastor McKeown, whether

---

31. McKeown, "To All Pastors."

32. Mhango, *Manifesting the Spirit*, 178–79.

33. The overall theme of The Church of Pentecost for five years, covering 2018–23, "Possessing the Nation."

it is prayer or singing, it could be promoting the works of the flesh. His ecclesiological principles necessarily include a day of rest, which might eventually lead to an encounter with the Lord.[34]

Light Shining in Darkness

Pastor McKeown's belief was that he came to make people the sons and daughters of God who should be able to depend upon God to supply their needs. He believed that if there was a strong church of people who really know Jesus and the Holy Spirit, then everything else would follow.[35] According to Debrunner, McKeown bluntly told him, "You missionaries and your African pastors and collaborators labor and sweat with schools—and then leave the people on their own, neglecting evangelism—and thus we can harvest where you have sown."[36] By this, McKeown was not accusing the missionaries of embarking on such social services. His concern was that they should not do these at the expense of evangelism.

McKeown's stand could be understood that the church had no money to engage in social services. He did not believe the church should beg for money. He often said, "If you beg a white man for money he would tie you to his apron string and pull you along. You can never be independent." He did not allow the church to appeal for funds from the West; neither did he allow the church to solicit funds from the government or borrow money from the bank. His philosophy was to use what you have, for your God can supply you with all your needs. It is a philosophy that, when adopted into a person's life, can help many people who have been encountering financial challenges.

Thus, he did not hold on to the belief that the church should actively engage in social services by establishing schools and hospitals. The people who knew God were going to provide finance, build schools and hospitals, and serve their nations in diverse ways.[37] He stressed in a circular letter in 1962, "If we so live that the Holy Spirit dwells in us, then our light will shine that all men will see our good works and God our father will be glorified."[38] He expected Christians to be lights

---

34. McKeown, "To All Pastors."
35. Leonard, *Giant in Ghana*, 76; Onyinah, "James McKeown," 72.
36. Debrunner, *History of Christianity in Ghana*, 325.
37. Onyinah, "James McKeown," 72.
38. McKeown, "Church of Pentecost, August 8, 1962."

that shine to dispel darkness wherever they are. If Christians play their role of salt and light in the world, wherever Christians are, they will be able to dispel the darkness in society and make tasty the bitterness surrounding it. McKeown's philosophy, therefore, is transforming every sphere of society with the kingdom values. Just as Niebuhr proposed, McKeown believed that the church as the visible representative of Christ must transform culture and make the culture relevant. The church does not function outside the culture.

However, in 1957, when Pastor James McKeown was on furlough, the General Council under the chairmanship of Pastor J. A. C. Anaman decided that an education committee must be formed. The committee was to do all it could to see to it that schools were established for the church.[39] In the following council meeting, Nungua district requested a school, but it was referred to the Educational Unit.[40] Soon after this, the districts that were capable established their own schools. The establishment of schools was placing some financial difficulty on the church. During the 1960 General Council, Elder J. K. Prah was requested to explain the implications of establishing schools since the Ghana government wanted to take over all schools.[41] The church established a secondary school in Kumasi and farms in the era of Pastor McKeown. Unfortunately, both ventures were not successful. Nevertheless, it is the ripples of such ventures that have now metamorphosed into the Social Services Department of The Church of Pentecost. The Church of Pentecost continues to offer various social services; however, the way has never been very smooth. It is yet to take its proper position in the church's general administration.

Conclusion

The ecclesiology of Pastor James McKeown has been identified as comprising multiple ones borrowed from the existing church traditions, and out of which emerged five themes as key in his life and ministry. His emphasis on the leading of the Spirit must always whisper to The Church of Pentecost of whom to follow. His apostolic leadership, where he mentored people who have been able to carry the church for five generations without the church losing its vim, must not be overlooked. A passion

---

39. Church of Pentecost, General Council Meeting, Sekondi, 5.
40. Church of Pentecost, General Council Meeting, Anomabu, 5.
41. Church of Pentecost, General Council Meeting, Akropong-Akuapem, 2.

for evangelism was reflected by his awareness of the imminent return of Christ, which he often proclaimed. This needs to continuously create the passion for lost souls in the church. The hidden secret of his love for the Lord was recognized as his day of rest, which often helped him to encounter his master. The Christian, he believed, must be the salt and light of the world, living in the world without being worldly. The shining light of Christ's representatives on earth must dispel the darkness in the world. Thus, believers themselves must be seen as social services wherever they are. Whereas The Church of Pentecost attempts to follow its founder's concept of the church, there is the call to always review and resist in order to remain relevant in a most changing world.

Bibliography

The Apostolic Church. *The Apostolic Church: Its Principles and Practices.* Bradford: Apostolic, 1937.
Busia, Kofi A. *The Position of the Chief in Modern Asante.* Oxford: Oxford University Press, 1951.
The Church of Pentecost. *The Constitution of The Church of Pentecost.* Accra: General Council of Church of Pentecost, 2018.
———. General Council Meeting, Akropong-Akuapem, April 8–13, 1960.
———. General Council Meeting, Anomabu, March 25—April 1, 1958.
———. General Council Meeting, Sekondi, April 10–22, 1957.
———. "State of Church Address." 45th Session of the General Council Meeting, May 5–8, 2021.
Debrunner, Hans W. *A History of Christianity in Ghana.* Accra: Waterville, 1967.
Dulles, Avery. *Models of the Church.* Dublin: Gill & Macmillan, 1987.
Elorm-Donkor, Lord Abraham. *Christian Morality in Ghanaian Pentecostalism: A Theological Analysis of Virtue Theory as a Framework for Integrating Christian and Akan Moral Schemes.* Oxford: Regnum, 2017.
Hesselgrave, David J. *Communicating Christ Cross-Culturally: An Introduction to Missionary Communication.* Grand Rapids: Zondervan, 1978.
Kärkkäinen, Veli-Matti. *An Introduction to Ecclesiology: Historical, Global, and Interreligious Perspectives.* Downers Grove: InterVarsity, 2021.
Kraft, Charles H. *Christianity in Culture: A Study in Dynamic Biblical Theologizing in Cross-Cultural Perspective.* Maryknoll, NY: Orbis, 1979.
Leonard, Christine. *A Giant in Ghana: 3000 Churches in 50 Years: The Story of James McKeown and the Church of Pentecost.* Chichester: New Wine Ministries, 1989.
McKeown, James. "The Church of Pentecost, to All Assemblies in Ghana, Togo and Dahomey." March 28, 1957.
———. "The Church of Pentecost, to All Assemblies in Ghana, Togo and Dahomey." July 24, 1962.
———. "The Church of Pentecost, to All Assemblies in Ghana, Togo and Dahomey." August 8, 62.

———. "The Church of Pentecost, to All Assemblies in Ghana, Togo and Dahomey." October 12, 1962.
———. "The Church of Pentecost, to All Assemblies in Ghana, Togo and Dahomey." January 6, 1964.
———. "The Church of Pentecost, to All Assemblies in Ghana, Togo and Dahomey." May 20, 1964.
———. "The Church of Pentecost, to All Assemblies in Ghana, Togo and Dahomey." July 19, 1966.
———. "Ghana Apostolic Church, to All Assemblies in Ghana, Togo and Dahomey." June 8, 1955.
———. "Ghana Apostolic Church, to All Assemblies in Ghana, Togo and Dahomey." August 18, 1955.
———. "Ghana Apostolic Church, Circular Letter to All Assemblies." July 27, 1958.
———. "Ghana Apostolic Church, Circular Letter to All Pastors and Overseers." November 10, 1959.
———. "Ghana Apostolic Church, to All Assemblies in Ghana, Togo, and Dahomey." March 22, 1960.
———. "Ghana Apostolic Church, to All Pastors." N.d.
———. "Gold Coast Apostolic Church, Pastor Only. Not to Be Read in the Assemblies." 1954.
———. "To All Pastors." N.d.
Mhango, Mbanyane. *Manifesting the Spirit: Believers as Sacraments*. Eugene, OR: Resource, 2021.
Niebuhr, H. Richard. *Christ and Culture*. New York: Harper & Row, 1956.
Nukunya, G. K. *Tradition and Change in Ghana*. Accra: Ghana Universities Press, 1992.
Nyamekye, Eric. "To All Assemblies Church of Pentecost, Ghana." Circular letter, July 4, 2021.
Onyinah, Opoku. "The Man James McKeown." In *James McKeown Memorial Lectures*, edited by Opoku Onyinah, 55–104. Accra: Church of Pentecost, 2004.
Rattray, Robert S. *Ashanti Law and Constitution*. Oxford: Clarendon, 1929.
Thomas, John C. *Towards a Pentecostal Pentecost*. Cleveland, TN: CPT, 2010.
Tsekpoe, Christian. *Intergenerational Missiology: An African Pentecostal-Charismatic Perspective*. Oxford: Regnum, 2022.

CHAPTER 2

A Response to James McKeown's "Concept of Pentecostal Ecclesiology and Its Impact on the Ministry of The Church of Pentecost"

LORD ELORM DONKOR

Introduction

AN AFRICAN PROVERB STATES that "if the frog comes out of water and tells you the crocodile is dead, do not doubt it." Indeed, being a former chairman who at a point was the longest serving minister of The Church of Pentecost (henceforth CoP), the premier missiologist and ardent scholar, who had the opportunity to work with McKeown as a minister of the CoP, at least from 1976–82, Opoku Onyinah is the most qualified minister to describe Pastor James McKeown's thought and works, particularly his ecclesiology, in such a lucid way. Using reliable materials from oral tradition and archival sources, he masterfully paints a vivid portrait of what McKeown believed, practiced, and taught concerning ecclesiology. Onyinah outlines McKeown's ecclesiology after a general introduction to concepts of ecclesiology in other Christian traditions. Onyinah asserts that although McKeown's ecclesiology has some affinity with Pentecostal and other ecclesiologies, it has some uniqueness as well, which he captures in five thematic areas: "Pneumatological Sensitivity," "Apostles and Prophets' Leadership," "Eschatological Consciousness," "Existential

Encounter," and "Light Shining in Darkness." My response to this paper follows the same thematic order in which it has been presented. It begins with some comments on the connection between McKeown's ecclesiology and other ecclesiological concepts.

Links to Formal Ecclesiological Concepts

Onyinah has shown us that as a Pentecostal, McKeown used "the general framework of Pentecostal ecclesiology which was a multiplicity of borrowed concepts." Obviously, Pentecostalism draws on many traditions. William W. Menzies, a prominent Pentecostal scholar, has demonstrated that Pentecostal theology is a confluence of theological rivers flowing from Wesleyan Holiness teachings, evangelical fundamentalism, Keswick teachings, and the Reformed theology of major voices such as John Calvin and others.[1] Pentecostal ecclesiology conceptualizes the church variously as a community of the redeemed, the sanctified, and the empowered, as well as a community of healing and eschatological expectation. Onyinah shows that the majority of these depictions of the church are seen in the ecclesiology of McKeown in the way he considered the church as a community that is sensitive to the Spirit, a community led by apostles and prophets (Eph 4:11–12), a community with constant expectation of the second coming of Jesus, a community that pursues personal and communal encounter of the Holy Spirit, and a community that is a light shining in the dark world.

Onyinah's view that McKeown's ecclesiology has certain connections with the various scholarly conceptions of ecclesiology discussed in his chapter does not imply that McKeown's ecclesiology was derived from or based on any of those views. In other words, having certain connections with ecclesiological views does not mean McKeown was necessarily aware of any of those, as many of them were conceptualized after McKeown. For instance, even Niebuhr's classic work on *Christ and Culture* was published several years after McKeown had started his ministry in the Gold Coast. Nevertheless, the statement is very important because it could suggest that although McKeown cannot be described as a formal theologian, the Holy Spirit helped him to know the relevant ecclesiology for the CoP and Pentecostalism generally.

---

1. Menzies, "Reformed Roots of Pentecostalism," 78.

Onyinah states that at another level, McKeown's eschatological views are akin to Niebuhr's concept of Christ the Transformer of Culture, but unlike the missionaries whose work Niebuhr referred to as Christ against Culture. Those missionaries advised their followers not to "participate in community gatherings, such as family gatherings, festivals, or chieftaincy affairs." Unfortunately, some people in the CoP had thought that McKeown was of this kind because in his time, members of the CoP were not allowed to participate in traditional family and chieftaincy events or even mingle with other denominations or attend their activities. It was often said that a person who has had a good bath does not need feet washing. This implied that McKeown's CoP was a church that had good teachings and thus her members did not need to go to other churches for anything. A circular issued in 1993 which permitted CoP members to attend events and conferences of other churches suggests that until then it was generally unacceptable for members of the church to participate in the activities of other denominations. It seems that there was a level of exclusivist practices like Niebuhr's Christ against Culture, at least in some segments of the CoP.

Thus, it is comforting to know from the evidence Onyinah provides that such exclusivist practices could not be based on McKeown's views. Sadly, sometimes what leaders believe and espouse is not necessarily what their followers understand and practice. In their book *Talking about God in Practice*, Helen Cameron and her colleagues explain the difficulties and complexities that exists when researchers try to get a group's theological understanding of their practices. To overcome this difficulty, they used a theological action research approach and devised a framework whereby they consider theology as having four voices. The first voice is operant theology, which is the theology embedded in the practices of a group or a church. Espoused theology is the theology drawn from the group's own expression of its beliefs. Normative theology is the theology derived from sources which the group regards as authoritative, and formal theology is the theology of the academy.[2] From the above, it seems clear that although the operant or embedded theology of some practices in the CoP suggests that there were Christ against Culture type of practices, they were not based on the normative theology of McKeown. The implication here is that leaders could hold and teach a theology, but their followers could interpret and practice it differently. Usually, until normative

---

2. Cameron et al., *Talking about God*, 52–56.

theology is formalized through critical academic formulations and kept on record and made widespread, oral traditions can be misconstrued, and different impressions could be created about what a leader believed and practiced. Onyinah's account of McKeown's ecclesiology is helpful in addressing the differences between what McKeown taught and practiced and what is sometimes attributed to him.

Pneumatological Sensitivity

Onyinah reveals that sensitivity to the Holy Spirit was central in McKeown's understanding of the church and Christian life. In agreement with extant classical Pentecostal views, McKeown insisted that only those who spoke in tongues could be considered as having been baptized in the Holy Spirit.[3] He taught that every believer must necessarily desire and earnestly pursue baptism in the Holy Spirit evidenced by speaking in tongues. According to Onyinah, McKeown implied that speaking in tongues offered a sense of guarantee that a person was baptized in the Holy Spirit, and this was crucial for McKeown because it determined how sensitive a believer is to the Holy Spirit. It also determined how a believer communicates with God in prayer and hears from God for their spiritual growth and the church's ministry in the world. In other words, speaking in tongues showed how spiritually sensitive a believer is. Since McKeown saw the church as a community that is sensitive to the Spirit, he wanted to be sure that all members of the community have the capacity to hear, feel, sense, and see from the Spirit of God. A relevant caution, however, with such specific emphasis is that care should be taken that believers who do not speak in tongues are not made to feel as though they were second-class children of God, but instead be encouraged and helped to have the experience the Spirit gives.

Apostles and Prophets' Leadership

Onyinah explains that McKeown adopted some but adapted other aspects of the British Apostolic Church's governance practices and integrated them with other church governance models to produce the CoP governance structure. Whilst holding the belief that the church is a community led by apostle and prophets, McKeown was cautious about the use

---

3. See Menzies, "Spirit Baptism," 175; McGee, "Initial Evidence," 785.

of these gifts because of possible abuses due to human error. Although McKeown had grown up as a British Apostolic and was sent to the Gold Coast by this church, he deviated from some of the Apostolic ways. This is commendable. The courage a leader has to think about their group's practices and search for ways according to God's leading that better capture what is necessary for the group is a theological virtue. Contexts and times change though God and his Word remain unchanged. Therefore, clear leadership is always needed to blaze new trails, focusing on the Holy Spirit, and asking how to understand the nature, purpose, and mission of the church in every time and context.

An aspect of the Apostolic church governance that McKeown kept is the centralized system. Onyinah reveals that the understanding of the church as a community led by apostles and prophets developed into a centralized system of governance that brought tensions. The tension between the centralized type of governance and the decentralized type of governance was evident in McKeown's approach, and this tension has continued in the church and showed up during discussions of whether to grant autonomy to external branches or to hold onto the centralized governance. For instance, in 2017, while Onyinah was the chairman of the CoP, the external branches were given an opportunity to choose whether they wanted to be autonomous of the mother church in Ghana or loosely affiliated to it. It is interesting to note that, at least, the external branches in the Ghanaian Diasporas in the West rejected the offer for autonomy. In the United Kingdom, the National Council (Presbytery) voted against the idea of autonomy and affiliation and chose to remain directly connected to the mother church in Ghana instead of relating to it by a loose affiliation. Maybe sometimes, tensions are anticipated rather than real. This means sometimes such tensions are not only within leadership but also among followers. Probably it is because of the tension between letting go and holding back that McKeown held onto leadership of the church until his retirement, though he could have handed over to the indigenes earlier. Perhaps, like the National Council in the UK, some people did not want him to hand over the reins.

Again, regarding church leadership, Onyinah states that McKeown was not interested in forming committees and boards. Instead, he preferred listening to the leading of the Holy Spirit rather than following constitutions, laws, and rules. Onyinah's observation that the CoP may examine this approach of McKeown does not imply that the use of constitutions, policies, and guidelines is wrong. If those who are involved in the formulation of those policies are filled by the Spirit of God, what they formulate will be God's direction for his church in particular contexts and times. Despite McKeown's emphasis on the infilling of and leading by the Holy Spirit, Onyinah has shown that in the days of McKeown, there were several reports of human weaknesses, some of which may have been addressed heavy-handedly. Arguably, the lack of formal structures and regulations that guide human behavior can be costly. Usually, those who lean too much toward just listening to the Spirit and acting accordingly are shocked when they realize that not all the people they think hear the Spirit, always hear him. "The heart is deceitful above all things and beyond cure. Who can understand it?" (Jer 17:19). In the CoP, ministers have been disciplined or dismissed for flouting policies or sometimes deliberately working against the system. It shows that the core of the human heart is viciously rebellious. Therefore, taming the "tiger" in the human heart cannot be done through just one means of listening to the Spirit, because different people hear the Spirit differently at different times depending on the state of their heart. Some do not hear the Spirit at all when they are bent on serving themselves rather than Jesus Christ who has called and sent them.

To some extent, a discussion on the role of formal regulations and the leading of the Holy Spirit in the church is like the debate on the role of works and grace in the believer's life. Usually, the grace and works debate is used to dichotomize the full truth of the gospel instead of being used to explain the different dimensions of that truth. As grace is the role of God in the human life and works is the responsibility of humans enabled by grace, so is the leading of the Holy Spirit and the use of formal regulations. The Holy Spirit leads and humans write what they perceive the Spirit is directing. Any teaching that pitches the leading of the Holy Spirit against the use of formal regulations or constitutional provisions that are based on Scripture could be divisive. Terry Cross asserts that the work of the Holy Spirit in a believer's life is central to any good understanding of ecclesiology and that "Pentecostal theology desires to wed the intellectual, reflective operation of the mind with the experiential, transformative operation of the Spirit in human life."[4] These two realities should not be separated, but always kept together.

Therefore, it should not be seen as though the Holy Spirit is against constitutions or vice versa. McKeown's reservations with constitutions

---

4. Cross, "Taking the Spirit as Our Guide," 185.

could have resulted from the Apostolic Church's constitutional amendment that he disagreed with, and which led to his dismissal or resignation from the Apostolic Church.[5] Since such a bitter experience may have remained with him, his reluctance for constitutions should be taken as caution rather than dislike. Like grace and works, neither on its own can guide the complex and multidimensional nature of the human heart for constant transformational experiences that translate into practical human behavior which evidences the love of God.

Following the leading of the Holy Spirit in the church must always be interspersed with careful reflective thinking about what is being perceived as coming from the Holy Spirit, then relating it to Scripture and tradition or what has been accepted and done in the past. This is where policies, regulations, and constitutions become useful in holding the human heart from sprinting toward self-centeredness, pride, and division. The danger, though, is when formal regulation replaces the humble search for the leading of the Holy Spirit, or when the search for the leading of the Holy Spirit eliminates any formal regulations. This was McKeown's concern for which he also provided a solution.

Onyinah reveals that whilst McKeown stressed the leading of the Holy Spirit, he also encouraged both theological and leadership training. Since Pentecostals in those days were generally considered averse to theological training, it is very impressive that McKeown encouraged both ministers and non-ministers to go to Bible college.[6] Indeed, this is a leader who was ahead of his time and age. A community led by the Spirit must be a teachable and learning community. Good leadership in the community of God is crucial for the nurturing and mission of the church. McKeown would have been delighted to know that thousands of ministers and lay leaders are now attending theological and leadership training at various colleges of the CoP around the world. Former and current leadership of the denomination have worked hard on the vision to ensure that the church's local ministers receive the right training to remain relevant in the church's mission and to avoid or address false teaching.

Moreover, the ecclesiological view that the church is a community led by the Holy Spirit with gifts embodied as apostles and prophets necessarily requires a constant teachable attitude. Apostle Paul states,

---

5. Worsfold, *Origins of the Apostolic Church in Great Britain*, 263; Turnbull, *What God Hath Wrought*, 13–15.

6. Nel, "Pentecostalism's Tradition of Anti-intellectualism," 27–48; Hollenweger, "Critical Tradition of Pentecostalism," 7–17.

"Christ himself gave the apostles, the prophets, the evangelists, the pastors and teachers, to equip his people for works of service, so that the body of Christ may be built up until we all reach unity in the faith and in the knowledge of the Son of God and become mature, attaining to the whole measure of the fullness of Christ" (Eph 4:11–13). Also, in his last command to the disciples, the Great Commission, Jesus commanded that believers must be taught to do all the things he taught and did (Matt 28:20). Teaching involves learning to understand and is crucial for the mission of the church in the world. McKeown would have endorsed the current CoP vision which encourages all elders to undertake a certificate course in theology and others to be trained in Christian counseling courses.

Considering how Onyinah shows that McKeown was well-read and quoted from prominent authors, it is apt to believe that if he was here today, McKeown would have been open-minded about the possibility of other knowledge fields helping to shed more light on human understanding of God found in Scripture. Possibly, he would have wanted to know what physical scientists have to say about God, what social anthropologists, sociologists, and cultural studies, management, and leadership theorists have to say. Certainly, he would pass all this knowledge through the prism of the Holy Spirit to arrive at what God might be saying now to his church about God's mission in the world.

Such a humble attitude is what the church father St. Augustine referred to as plundering the Egyptians. He explained:

> If those . . . [pagan writers] have said things which are indeed true and are well accommodated to our faith, they should not be feared; rather, what they have said should be taken from them as from unjust possessors and converted to our use. Just as the Egyptians had not only idols and grave burdens which the people of Israel detested and avoided, so also, they had vases and ornaments of gold and silver and clothing which the Israelites took with them secretly when they fled, as if to put them to a better use. . . . In the same way, all the teachings of the pagans contain not only simulated and superstitious imaginings . . . but also liberal disciplines more suited to the uses of truth, and some of the most useful precepts concerning morals. Even some truths concerning the worship of one God are discovered among them.[7]

---

7. Augustine cited in Robertson, *On Christian Doctrine*, Sec. 40.60.

Peter Elliott has shown that apart from a few, many other church fathers held the same view as Augustine. Knowledge in other fields is what helped them to be successful apologetics of their time.[8] Thus, apart from the Scriptures, the community of God led by apostles and prophets needs other forms of knowledge to help interpret its experiences with the hope that it will come to a closer and more intimate knowledge of God. As the church is a community led by apostles and prophets, humility is expected from leaders to study to show themselves approved by God. Onyinah has shown that McKeown was a model in this regard.

Eschatological Consciousness

According to Onyinah, McKeown viewed the church as a community imbued with eschatological consciousness. Since the church is a community that is constantly aware of and expecting the second coming of the Lord Jesus Christ, McKeown focused on evangelism. Once the church is sensitive to the Holy Spirit, it will hopefully be aware of the pain and suffering in the world and be the prophetic voice that God uses to draw all people to himself to bring salvation and healing. It is said that a young salesman, unsuccessful to land a sales deal after all his effort, told his boss that "you can lead a horse to water, but you can't make him drink," to which his boss replied, "Your job is not to make him drink. Your job is to make him thirsty." If through the eschatological consciousness of believers their life and testimony is full of Jesus, they will create a strong thirst in others for the gospel.[9]

Existential Encounter

In the context of McKeown's ecclesiology, Onyinah has shown our readers that the essence of the church on earth is the glory of God realized through encounters with Jesus Christ in the Holy Spirit. He reveals that McKeown's concept of the church stresses that a believer must have an encounter with Christ. For McKeown, every Christian must have an experiential encounter with Jesus Christ, and this encounter should be manifested in practical Christian living. So, like Apostle Paul, McKeown

---

8. Elliott, "Plundering Egyptian Gold."
9. Jeremiah, *Turning Point with God*, 107.

focused on preaching Christ and stressing sanctification until the Lord was formed in his hearers (Gal 4:19).

Onyinah does not leave his readers to wonder what McKeown taught was the method for initiating and sustaining an existential encounter with the Holy Spirit. He reveals McKeown's hidden secret for a successful Christian life, which he taught in a pastoral letter sent in 1959. McKeown taught pastors to have one day of rest each week. "Pastors were to observe a day of rest where they would wait on God in silence, not praying loudly, singing to work themselves into a happy state, nor engaging in any moving around." Apparently, this insight derives from his view of the church as God's people. For the church to remain the people of God, believers must have constant fellowship with God and be transformed into the image and likeness of God. The intimate relationship that God desires from believers is possible only when they dedicate some time to fellowship with God and ponder on him in a way that helps them develop their inner disposition and character to the likeness of God. Gary Millar asserts that the prospect of personal transformation into the image and likeness of God is clearly taught in the Scriptures and that God himself changes people.[10] But an obedient response is expected from humans. In fellowship with him, God transforms believers' relationship with him, their knowledge of him, and their desire for him. "God has designed the local church to be the network of relationships in which we are forced to learn to love, forgive, repent, mourn, build up, rebuke, and encourage."[11] These processes are only possible when individuals set aside time to existentially encounter the living Christ in meditative prayer.

Gregory of Nyssa shared a secret about what happens when a believer encounters God. He said the person devoted to prayer and fellowship with God encounters him through a mystical holiness, a spiritual energy, and an inexpressible disposition.[12] In that encounter, God's holiness, spiritual energy, and life-transforming experience, which changes the believer's desire for and behavior toward God and other people, is imparted. As many believers encounter God in this way, the community of believers is enriched with the ever presence of God. Such a rich fellowship with God is a "real opportunity for finite humans to

---

10. Millar, *Changed into His Likeness*, 238.

11. Millar, *Changed into His Likeness*, 238.

12. Gregory of Nyssa, *On the Christian Mode of Life*, as quoted in Ferguson, *Inheriting Wisdom*, 248.

experience the transcendent God in ways that are almost palpable."[13] Humans' encounter with God is a real event in which human lives continue to be transformed in the life of God forever. McKeown encouraged ministers of the church to long for this type of encounter and to take a day off to rest and to ponder on God. Howard Spring, a noted Welsh writer, is quoted to have said, "The kingdom of God is not going to advance by our churches becoming filled with men [people], but by men [people] in our churches becoming filled with God."[14] Being filled with God happens effectively only when believers have time to read his Word and ponder or meditate on him, especially when they do so without rushing. A day off with sufficient time spent with the Lord as McKeown recommended will change the servants of God and the church they lead. In our fast-paced world, where life moves fast in all directions, McKeown's insistence on a complete rest day in the week for ministers and individuals is highly recommended.

Light Shining in Darkness

McKeown's ecclesiology considers the church as light shining in darkness, albeit, he did not promote social services such as establishing schools and hospitals. His view was that those who will come to know God through the ministry of the church will "provide finance, build schools and hospitals, and serve their nations in diverse ways."[15] McKeown quibbled about the work of other missionaries by saying, "You . . . labor and sweat with schools and then leave the people on their own, neglecting evangelism and thus we can harvest where you have sown."[16] Commenting on this statement, Onyinah suggests that McKeown did not indict the missionaries for carrying out such social services per se. Instead, McKeown's concern was about a lack of holistic mission—mission that involved the salvation of souls. It could be that Onyinah was being gentle with McKeown. On the contrary, it could be that McKeown was ahead of his time because the general evangelical position of

---

13. Cross, *People of God's Presence*, 49.
14. Jeremiah, *Turning Points with God*, 107.
15. Onyinah, "James McKeown," 72.
16. Debrunner, *History of Christianity in Ghana*, 325.

Christian mission at that time was evangelism alone, which was understood narrowly as the verbal proclamation of the gospel.[17]

Thus, even if McKeown was criticizing other missionaries for engaging in social services, he would have been doing so in accordance with the general view of evangelicals at the time. Hence, Onyinah's comment about the holistic view of mission McKeown held is very revealing. On one hand, it shows that being led by the Holy Spirit, McKeown could envision a fuller meaning of Christian mission that many of his contemporaries in the evangelical community could not fathom at that time. Also, McKeown did not allow the church to solicit financial help from Western donors, governments, or banks. This "no borrowing" idea has remained as part of the covenant God made with the church. Today, the fact that world economic processes keep changing and processes for commercial activities are determined by new trends, applying such a covenant must be done with great caution. Like biblical interpretation, contextual factors must always be considered. "McKeown's philosophy, therefore, is transforming every sphere of society with the kingdom values. Just as Niebuhr proposed, McKeown believed that the church as the visible representative of Christ must transform culture and make the culture relevant."

Concluding Remarks

The ecclesiology of a Pentecostal pioneer has been presented by Onyinah who himself has successfully led the CoP and built it into a formidable movement. As Cross has asserted, for the church of Christ to remain relevant in our times and contexts, radical shifts are required, especially in the theological understanding of the nature and mission of the church.[18] Therefore, Onyinah's portrayal of the ecclesiology of the founder of the CoP, one of the largest Pentecostal denominations in Africa, is very timely and relevant. It is important to note that theology requires more than just discursive reasoning and includes an engagement of the whole person within a community where God has given individuals different charisms. Such a community of the Spirit and Word functions as a worshiping, witnessing, forming, reflective whole; "but

---

17. See Noll, *Scandal of the Evangelical Mind*, 109–45; Quebedeaux, *Worldly Evangelicals*; Scherer and Beavan, *New Directions in Mission and Evangelisation*; Stott and Coote, *Down to Earth*.

18. Cross, *People of God's Presence*, 6.

at the heart of all this is the liturgical life of the community."[19] A good understanding of theology leads to a good understanding of ecclesiology, an ecclesiology that does not merely reflect on religious experience but also on lives transformed in the likeness of God.

Such ecclesiology is forged within a community that serves as a hub and a training center where God works through the Holy Spirit to cause personal transformation in obedient believers.[20] Put another way, whereas salvation results from an individual's response to the Holy Spirit, sanctification results from the Holy Spirit's encounter with believers in the community of the church.[21] Hence, a good understanding of the church is necessary for the mission of God in this world. Personal change occurs through individuals' responses to God's Word, yet God has given a context to personal growth. This context is the local church. As a family context, God intends for believers to allow themselves to be forced by the nature of family life to respond in love, in forgiveness, and in repentance, sometimes mourning their weakness, accepting rebuke, encouraging others, and being built up. For that reason, it is important for believers to belong to a church they can call their family and not run from one church to the other in a style that treats churches as religious supermarkets where people could pick and choose based on their preferences. Professor Opoku Onyinah has painted an enduring portrait of the ecclesiology of a Pentecostal pioneer. This ecclesiological view has brought the church this far. It is now left for CoP leaders and other African Pentecostal-Charismatic church leaders to glean new insights that would build tomorrow's church today.

Bibliography

Cameron, Helen, et al. *Talking about God in Practice: Theological Action Research and Practical Theology*. London: SCM, 2010.
Cross, Terry L. *The People of God's Presence: An Introduction to Ecclesiology*. Grand Rapids: Baker Academics, 2019.
———. "Taking the Spirit as Our Guide: A Pneumatic Ecclesiology." *Journal of Pentecostal Theology* 31 (2022) 184–97.
Debrunner, Hans. *History of Christianity in Ghana*. Accra: Waterville, 1967.
Elliott, Peter Thomas. "Plundering Egyptian Gold: Christianity and Culture." Paper presented to the Gonzaga Socratic Club, March 21, 2014.

19. Land, *Pentecostal Spirituality*, 34.
20. Cross, "Taking the Spirit," 187.
21. Cross, "Taking the Spirit," 188.

Ferguson, Everett. *Inheriting Wisdom: Readings for Today from Ancient Christian Writers*. Peabody, MA: Hendrickson, 2004.
Hollenweger, Walter. "The Critical Tradition of Pentecostalism." *Journal of Pentecostal Theology* 1 (1992) 7–17.
Jeremiah, David. *Turning Points with God: 365 Daily Devotions*. Carol Stream, IL: Tyndale, 2014.
Land, Steven J. *Pentecostal Spirituality: A Passion for the Kingdom*. Sheffield: Sheffield Academic Press, 1994.
McGee, Gary. "Initial Evidence." In *New International Dictionary of the Pentecostal Charismatic Movement*, edited by Stanley M. Burgess and Edward M. Van der Mass, 784–91. Grand Rapids: Zondervan, 2002.
Menzies, Glen. "Tongues as 'The Initial Physical Sign' of Spirit Baptism in the Thought of D. W. Kerr." *Pneuma* 20 (1998) 172–89.
Menzies, William. "The Reformed Roots of Pentecostalism." *PentecoStudies* 6 (2007) 78–99.
Millar, Gary. *Changed into His Likeness: A Biblical Theology of Personal Transformation*. London: IVP Academic, 2021.
Nel, Marius. "Rather Spirit-Filled Than Learned! Pentecostalism's Tradition of Anti-intellectualism and Pentecostal Theological Scholarship." *Verbum et Ecclesia* 37 (2016) 27–48.
Noll, Mark A. *The Scandal of the Evangelical Mind*. Grand Rapids: Eerdmans, 1994.
Onyinah, Opoku. "The Man James McKeown." In *James McKeown Memorial Lectures*, edited by Opoku Onyinah, 55–104. Accra: Church of Pentecost, 2004.
Quebedeaux, Richard. *The Worldly Evangelicals*. San Francisco: Harper and Row, 1978.
Robertson, D. W. *On Christian Doctrine*. New York: Bobbs-Merrill, 1958.
Scherer, James A., and Stephen B. Beavan. *New Directions in Mission and Evangelisation*. Vol. 1, *Basic Statements 1974-1991*. Maryknoll, NY: Orbis, 1996.
Stott, John R. W., and Robert Coote, eds. *Down to Earth: Studies in Christianity and Culture*. Grand Rapids: Eerdmans, 1980.
Turnbull, Thomas. *What God Hath Wrought: A Short History of the Apostolic Church*. Bradford: Puritan, 1959.
Worsfold, James E. *The Origins of the Apostolic Church in Great Britain with a Breviate of its Early Missionary Endeavours*. Willington: Julian Literature Trust, 1991.

CHAPTER 3

Pentecostal Mission and Social Transformation

EMMANUEL KWESI ANIM

Introduction

THIS CHAPTER ARGUES THAT Pentecostalism as a modern phenomenon in church history has gained ascendancy and sustained a significant presence in Christianity in Africa. Beginning as a religion of the poor and disenfranchised in society, the movement in its various forms has adapted to their unique contexts and offered hope and optimism in the face of socioeconomic deprivation which characterized most African countries. The case studies of The Church of Pentecost and the International Central Gospel Church, each representing different streams of Pentecostalism, are largely paradigmatic of how Pentecostals are re-visioning their mission praxis by taking integral mission seriously with unique emphasis on social transformation, principally through acts of *diakonia*.[1]

The uniqueness of Pentecostalism lies in primal spirituality and lived experiences. In the West, classical Pentecostalism was born out of the suffering and cry of the marginalized, the oppressed, and the destitute that were disenfranchised and despised in society. The earlier Charismatic movement, in a way, was a mutation of the classical

---

1. A considerable portion of this paper was published in two articles: Anim, "Examples and Concepts of *Diakonia* in West African Christianity"; Anim, "Training for Social Services in Pentecostal Christianity."

Pentecostal movement and its adherents were mostly upwardly mobile youth who had taken solace in the faith or prosperity gospel, which offered hope in the face of seemingly disappointing socioeconomic conditions that had resulted from bad governance by the political elite and successive military regimes.

Who Are the Pentecostals?

Modern Pentecostalism began in the early part of the 20th century as a renewal movement in Christianity. It was founded on the principle of the empowerment and activities of the Holy Spirit in the divine orchestration of human welfare and destiny. Pentecostalism generally emerged as a grassroots movement where many of its early adherents were from the margins and low strata of society. In more recent years, we have seen a great number of Pentecostals in the middle and upper middle class of society. "Thus, at one end of the scale we encounter local Pentecostal congregations that cater primarily to relatively poor farming households or the poorer sections of the urban working classes, while at the other end we encounter upwardly mobile middle-class elements with a relative degree of affluence."[2] The Charismatic churches, also known as "neo-Pentecostal churches," emerged in Africa in the late 1970s as a renewal movement within the larger church bodies, and later began establishing their own congregations.[3] In Ghana, the newer Pentecostal and Charismatic churches are principally urban. Few Charismatic churches are found in the rural communities with notable exception being the Lighthouse Chapel International, which tend to follow The Church of Pentecost model of church planting across all communities.

In his weighty book *The Next Christendom*, Philip Jenkins underscored the significant development and impact of Pentecostalism in the global space. Jenkins observed that the significant growth of the church in Africa was principally in the Pentecostal/Charismatic strand and that these churches were far more traditional, morally conservative, evangelical, and apocalyptic than their northern counterparts.[4] David Barrett and Harvey Cox had previously drawn similar conclusions.[5]

---

2. Long, "Foreword," xi.
3. Anim, "Who Wants to Be a Millionaire?," 85–112.
4. Jenkins, *Next Christendom*, 7–8.
5. Cox, *Fire from Heaven*.

Pentecostal Ecclesiology and Worship

Pentecostal ecclesiology by nature is not liturgical. It is spontaneous and expressive, with singing, dancing, clapping of hands, shouting, rolling on the floor, prostrating, all before the throne of grace. Inspiration is often taken from the celebration of King David, when he "danced before the Lord with all his might" and before the Ark of the Covenant almost naked at the disgust of his wife Michal, the daughter of Saul (2 Sam 6:20). The liberty to dance and celebrate before the Lord is a hallmark of Pentecostal religiosity. Thus, Dena Freeman observes:

> The most readily visible aspect of Pentecostal and Charismatic Christianity in Africa is the ecstatic, Spirit-filled church service, which frequently involves speaking in tongues and outburst of ululations, as well as lively singing and dancing. These church services often last for two–three hours, sometimes all night and in many cases take place several times per week. They are emotionally charged, high-volume gatherings, with pastors "amped up" by sound systems, words to hymns and songs projected karaoke-style, and congregants frequently being moved to stand up, extend their arms upwards and exclaim "hallelujah!"[6]

Diakonia as a Means to Social Transformation

Pentecostal mission and social transformation is better understood as *diakonia* (also written diaconia). In the early years of its development, Pentecostalism, by virtue of its strong eschatological orientation, did not consider *diakonia* or social action a priority. Pentecostals, however, were quick to offer material support to its member congregations as the need arose. The Pentecostal understanding of *diakonia* is often traced to the sixth chapter of the book of Acts, when the early apostles addressed the care for the poor widows in their rapidly growing church. The word *diakonia* may be understood as "the service which the individual Christian as well as the church as a corporate unit is called to render to every needy person in all kinds of suffering and alienation. . . . It may be broad enough to encompass the active concern of God for the relief of the suffering, for meeting the needs of individuals, and for establishing a life of justice and

---

6. Freeman, "Pentecostal Ethic," 12.

dignity for all His creatures."⁷ *Diakonia*, therefore, becomes the conduit for social transformation and socioeconomic uplift.

Mission as Transformation: The Pentecostal Perspective

The subject of whether *diakonia* is a missiological imperative has received considerable attention in recent years. In the past, some saw the primary mandate of the church as evangelism and, therefore, social action or *diakonia* was not considered a priority. Transformation is a process of changing a situation or circumstance for the better. Integral mission therefore provides the framework for transformation. In 1966, the World Congress on Evangelization held in Berlin, Germany, emphasized a traditional evangelical concept of mission, with its primary goal of conversion to Christ through the proclamation of the gospel. Billy Graham maintained that, "if the Church went back to its main task of proclaiming the gospel and people converted to Christ, it would have a far greater impact on the social, moral and psychological needs of men than it could have achieved through anything else it could possibly do."⁸

However, in that same year, evangelical delegates from seventy-one countries met for the Congress on the World Mission of the Church in Wheaton, Illinois, in the United States. The congress ended with the declaration, "We [evangelicals] are guilty of an unscriptural isolation from the world that too often keeps us from honestly facing and coping with its concerns" and the "failure [of the church] to apply scriptural principles to such problems as racism, war, population explosion, poverty, family disintegration, social revolution, and communism."⁹ A defining moment for this holistic mandate was at the International Congress on World Evangelization in Lausanne in 1974, as it affirmed that social action was an integral part of Christian mission:

> God is both the Creator and the Judge of all men. We therefore should share his concern for justice and reconciliation throughout human society and for the liberation of men from every kind of oppression.... We express penitence both for our neglect and

---

7. WCC, *Christians in the Technical and Society Revolutions of Our Time*, 16.
8. Graham, "Why the Berlin Congress," 133.
9. "Wheaton Declaration," 231–44.

for having sometimes regarded evangelism and social concerns as mutually exclusive.[10]

Following the Lausanne Congress, support for broader mission efforts grew among evangelicals, particularly in the Majority World.

Pentecostals and Social Transformation

The quest for independence in Africa was marked by at least two assumptions: first, that the land was filled with natural resources; and second, that African leaders were capable of managing those resources for the benefit of the people. Though the first assumption was true, the second one proved false because of the embedded corruption in the political elite, who left the masses despondent and disillusioned. Against this reality many Charismatic churches emerged with their particular theological orientations of prosperity and well-being, which offered hope in the face of political failure and economic deprivation.[11]

In the past, scholars in development studies did not recognize or pay much attention to the vital role that religion or religious communities played in the process of economic development and social advancement. But equally noteworthy is that Pentecostalism has undergone evolution in its thinking on this subject as well. In Pentecostalism, the debate on the priority and place of social services, vis-á-vis evangelism, has been ongoing for many decades, but it was not until the latter part of the 1980s that Pentecostals began to take the church's role in social outreach more seriously. This is not to say that Pentecostals never gave any attention to this before. Acts of charity or welfare were evident in Pentecostal/Charismatic practices right from the beginning, except that they were not given a precise structure or form.

However, in recent time, we have seen a significant shift of Pentecostal and Charismatic churches towards social outreach and community development in an effort to bring transformation to people and society as a whole. Thus, Freeman rightly observes that the "Pentecostal explosion" has radically altered the religious landscape in much of the developing world, where they are active not only in conducting prayers but also in mobilizing and distributing material resources for human

---

10. Stott, *Making Christ Known*, 24.
11. Anim, "Who Wants to Be a Millionaire?," 333–34.

welfare and development. In this regard, Pentecostals do not "separate religion from development."[12]

In this regard, Freeman observes that "Pentecostal churches are often rather more effective change agents than development NGOs."[13] John Peel has rightly observed, "Christianity has been both a cause and a catalyst of social change in Africa."[14] In Ghana, many Pentecostal and Charismatic churches are broadening their ministries to include a rich variation of *diakonia*. I will focus here on The Church of Pentecost and the International Central Gospel Church (ICGC). This paper looks at two case studies of The Church of Pentecost and the International Central Gospel Church in Ghana, with regards to the churches' sense of mission and transformation.[15]

The Example of The Church of Pentecost and Diakonia

The Church of Pentecost is identified as an indigenous classical Pentecostal church established in Ghana under the leadership of the Irish missionary Pastor James McKeown (1900–1989). From its humble beginnings The Church of Pentecost has grown to become the largest Protestant denomination in Ghana.[16] In 1980, The Church of Pentecost established the Pentecost Social Services (PENSOS) to improve the living conditions of its members and to facilitate the denomination's contribution to the socioeconomic development of the nation. Since its inception, this department has undertaken a wide array of local and national initiatives in *diakonia*.

Education

Presently, The Church of Pentecost has eighty-four basic schools, three vocational schools, and two senior high schools across the country. The vocational schools specialize in fashion design, hairdressing, carpentry,

---

12. Freeman, "Pentecostal Ethic," 2.
13. Freeman, "Pentecostal Ethics," 3.
14. Peel, *Aladura*, 1.
15. See Gifford, *African Christianity*, 80–84; also Anim, "Who Wants to Be a Millionaire?," ch. 6.
16. For a good study on the origins and development of The Church of Pentecost, see Leonard, *Giant in Ghana*; also Tsekpoe, "Local Species in African Soil."

and masonry work. The Pentecost University College was established in 2003 with the vision of offering students academic excellence and empowering them to serve their generation and posterity with integrity and the fear of God. The college has since obtained a Presidential Charter and is now known as the Pentecost University, with a current student population of about three thousand coming from various parts of the country as well as parts of West Africa, particularly Nigeria. The Pentecost Educational Fund, which provides a window of hope and opportunity for brilliant but needy students to further their university education, was expanded the past academic year to benefit more than four hundred students to Pentecost University. The scholarship scheme also covers church members who gain admission to the public universities.

Medical Care

The Church of Pentecost has two hospitals and seven clinics across the country. The Pentecost Hospital in Madina, Accra, is one of the leading facilities for maternal and child health care in Ghana.[17]

Hospitality

In 2014, the church opened the Pentecost Convention Centre (PCC) at Gomoa Fetteh in the Central Region as a facility for conferences and to serve as a Christian hospitality center. The center has nearly three thousand beds, as well as four auditoriums that seat from two hundred to five thousand people. During the COVID-19 pandemic, The Church of Pentecost released the PCC to the Government of Ghana, free of charge, as an isolation center for the treatment of those infected with the coronavirus.

Microcredit

The Church of Pentecost has established nearly forty microcredit schemes across the country. The objective is to financially empower people so that they can develop viable and productive businesses.

17. Pentecost Social Services, "2017 End of Year Report."

Partnerships

The Church of Pentecost (CoP) has collaborated with the Mental Health Authority, the Mental Care Home, the Ghana Heart Foundation, Country-Side Children's Welfare Home, the Ghana Health Foundation, and the Physically Challenged Action Foundation. Ongoing interventions include donations to hospitals, prisons, psychiatric facilities, orphanages, people affected by natural disasters, as well as paying the premiums of the aged and other needy people so that they can benefit from the National Health Insurance Scheme. The church also supports the Ghana Aids Commission, the Bible Society of Ghana, the Scripture Union, and other parachurch organizations, all in an effort to bring about transformation and development in the church and the nation as a whole.

National Peace and Security

Since 2018, The Church of Pentecost has seconded five of its full-time ministers to serve in the Ghana Armed Forces and the Prisons Service of Ghana. In terms of advocacy, the church plays a significant role in the National Peace Council (NPC), in which the Immediate-Past Chairman, Apostle Professor Opoku Onyinah, has served as a member since 2016. The NPC is an independent statutory body established in 2011 by an act of Parliament of the Republic of Ghana to prevent, manage, and resolve conflict, and to build sustainable peace.[18]

Environment

On September 8, 2019, The Church of Pentecost launched a nationwide campaign on sanitation and environmental care, and the church is working with the government and other private businesses to address the country's enormous sanitation problem.

People with Disabilities

The church is working to ensure that all its facilities will be easily accessible to those with disabilities.

---

18. See Ministry of the Interior, "National Peace Council."

The Example of the International Central Gospel Church

The ICGC is a Charismatic church established in 1984 in Accra. From its humble beginning of about twenty members who met in a classroom, the church has expanded into hundreds of branches across the country, as well as overseas into Europe and North America. The main branch, the Christ Temple in Accra, has some five thousand worshipers each Sunday. Drawing on his own humble experience, Mensa Otabil, the founder and general overseer of the ICGC, motivates his congregation by saying, "If you believe God, no matter the colour of your skin, the country you come from, or the economy of the world, you can still believe for a big God to give you a big ability to achieve big things for His glory."[19] Otabil continues, "God has put much into us, so do not underestimate, undervalue, underuse what you have. Do not cry, pity, or fear using what you have."[20] He goes on to explain how it works: "In order to excel and expand, you need an inquiring mind. Ask why, how, when and where. Practice analyzing things. When you do, you have a learning process going on that will expand you and sharpen your seed-gift."[21] By the 1990s,

> It was becoming obvious that Otabil's teachings had struck a chord with the upwardly mobile youth who saw every opportunity to a better their lot for the future. However, there were some obvious limitations to Otabil's messages in particular and the Faith Gospel in general. First, it did not address the glaring issue of high illiteracy, especially amongst the rural population, and what sense they could make of the rhetoric. Second, the faith message did not address the level of dependency on limited government resources and how exactly people were to harness their potential or obtain capital to invest in profitable businesses. The less economically endowed inadvertently turned to deliverance and prophetic ministries for supernatural succor to cope with life's vicissitudes.[22]

Despite those limitations, ICGC has become one of the leading churches in terms of support for health services in Ghana. In the past ten years, Christ Temple has given regular monthly financial support to the

---

19. Otabil, *Four Laws of Productivity*, 134.
20. Otabil, *Four Laws of Productivity*, 62.
21. Otabil, *Four Laws of Productivity*, 61. For further analysis of Otabil's teachings, see Gifford, *Ghana's New Christianity*, 113–39.
22. Anim, "Who Wants to Be a Millionaire?," 248.

Children's Cancer Unit at the Korle-Bu Teaching Hospital in Accra.[23] It is believed that the ICGC's regular support led to a significant reduction in the percentage of children forced to abandon treatment due to lack of financial support from 48 percent in 2010 to less than 9 percent in 2017.[24] As part of its thirty-fifth anniversary celebration in 2019, ICGC donated electroconvulsive therapy (ECT) machines to the Accra, Ankaful, and Pantang Mental Health Hospitals, worth many thousands of dollars. A donation of 3,500 pints of blood to the National Blood Service was part of the same anniversary celebration.[25]

The church also established Central Aid in 1988 as a human-oriented development agency. Its social interventions are many, varied, and impressive. For example, it offers regular support to the cardio-thoracic unit of the Korle-Bu Teaching Hospital and supports the physically disabled, the blind, and those suffering from breast cancer. It has also provided very generous scholarships to brilliant but needy students to pursue education in secondary, technical, and vocational institutions. This gesture is without prejudice to gender, religion, ethnicity, disability, or denomination.

Pentecostals and the COVID-19 Pandemic

In Ghana, we see this link between religion and development in the response to the current COVID-19 pandemic. This crisis has made things extremely hard for some individuals and families. The lockdown experienced in the country for about six months or more had adverse economic implications as many people lost their jobs or had their incomes slashed because they couldn't leave their homes to seek their daily bread. In April 2020, in response to the effects of the pandemic, The Church of Pentecost released its multipurpose, three-thousand-bed Pentecost Convention Centre to the Government of Ghana to serve as an isolation center for individuals undergoing treatment for the coronavirus. This facility in Ghana's Central Region was offered free of charge to augment the government's efforts to address the problem.[26] This action by the church has

---

23. Modern Ghana, "ICGC Christ Temple."
24. Tannor, "ICGC Donates Electro-Convulsive Therapy (ECT) Machines."
25. Benghan, "ICGC Donates Therapeutic Machines to MHA."
26. Pentecost News, "Pentecost Convention Centre to Serve as Isolation Centre."

been applauded by many in the country as a testimony to the goodness of God and the necessity of the church in times of crisis.

Along with The Church of Pentecost, other Pentecostal and Charismatic churches have arisen to address the effects of the pandemic. The International Central Gospel Church, under the leadership of Otabil, responded by providing substantial amounts of money to needy members in the church and to health institutions in the form of personal protective equipment (PPE). Churches have also donated to a government fund that was established to help people cope with the crisis and have, in addition, collaborated with the government to help distribute food to deprived communities.

Conclusion

Pentecostal churches have embraced a pragmatic approach to addressing human needs through the provision of social services. This involvement has yielded commendable results, drawing attention to the fact that "the faith dimension should be added to development work."[27] This underscores the significance of Pentecostal churches in the provision of social services as part of the development process and human flourishing.

Bibliography

Adeyemo, Tokunboh. "Africa's Enigma." In *Faith in Development: Partnership between the World Bank and the Churches of Africa*, edited by Deryke Belshaw et al., 31–38. Oxford: Regnum, 2001.

Anim, Emmanuel Kwesi. "Examples and Concepts of Diakonia in West African Christianity" In *International Handbook of Ecumenical Diakonia: Contextual Theologies and Practices of Diakonia and Christian Social Services: Resources for Study and Intercultural Learning*, edited by Godwin Ampony et al., 203–12. Oxford: Regnum, 2021.

———. "Training for Social Services in Pentecostal Christianity—Discoveries in Ghana." In *International Handbook of Ecumenical Diakonia: Contextual Theologies and Practices of Diakonia and Christian Social Services: Resources for Study and Intercultural Learning*, edited by Godwin Ampony et al., 620–27. Oxford: Regnum, 2021.

———. *Who Wants to Be a Millionaire? An Analysis of Prosperity Teaching in the Charismatic Ministries (Churches) in Ghana and Its Wider Impact*. Berlin: LIT, 2020.

---

27. Tsele, "Christian Faith in Development," 210.

———. "Who Wants to Be a Millionaire? An Analysis of Prosperity Teaching in the Charismatic Ministries (Churches) in Ghana and Its Wider Impact." PhD diss., All Nations Christian College, 2003.
Benghan, Bernard. "ICGC Donates Therapeutic Machines to MHA." *Ghanaian Times*, June 19, 2019. http://www.ghanaiantimes.com.gh/icgc-donates-therapeutic-machines-to-mha/.
Bosch, David. *Transforming Mission: Paradigm Shifts in Theology of Mission*. Maryknoll, NY: Orbis, 1991.
Cox, Harvey. *Fire from Heaven: The Rise of Pentecostal Spirituality and the Reshaping of Religion in the 21st Century*. Reading: Addison-Wesley, 1995.
Freeman, Dena. "The Pentecostal Ethic and the Spirit of Development." In *Pentecostalism and Development; Churches, NGOs and Social Change in Africa*, edited by Dena Freeman, 1–38. London: Palgrave Macmillan, 2012.
Gifford, Paul. *African Christianity: Its Public Role*. London: Hurst & Company, 1998.
———. *Ghana's New Christianity: Pentecostalism in a Globalizing African Economy*. Bloomington: Indiana University Press, 2004.
Graham, Billy. "Why the Berlin Congress." *Christianity Today*, November 11, 1966.
Jenkins, Philip. *The Next Christendom: The Coming of Global Christianity*. Oxford: Oxford University Press, 2007.
Jordheim, Kari. "Bridge-Building and Go-Between: The Role of the Deacon in Church and Society." In *Diakonia as Christian Social Practice: An Introduction*, edited by Stephanie Dietrich et al., 187–202. Oxford: Regnum, 2014.
Leonard, Christine. *A Giant in Ghana: 3000 Churches in 50 Years: The Story of James McKeown and the Church of Pentecost*. Chichester: New Wine Ministries, 1989.
Long, Norman. "Foreword." In *Pentecostalism and Development: Churches, NGOs, and Social Change in Africa*, edited by Dena Freeman, vii–x. London: Palgrave Macmillan, 2012.
Ministry of the Interior, Republic of Ghana. "National Peace Council." https://www.mint.gov.gh/national-peace-council/.
Modern Ghana. "ICGC Christ Temple Donates ¢200,000 to Korle-Bu Children's Cancer Unit." January 26, 2020. https://www.modernghana.com/news/981360/icgc-christ-temple-donates-200000-to-korle-bu.html.
Myers, Bryant. *Walking with the Poor: Principles and Practices of Transformational Development*. Maryknoll, NY: Orbis, 1999.
Ohlmann, Philipp, et al., eds. *African Initiated Christianity and the Decolonization of Development: Sustainable Development in Pentecostal and Independent Churches*. London: Routledge, 2020.
Otabil, Mensa. *Four Laws of Productivity: God's Foundation for Living*. Tulsa, OK: Vincom, 1991.
Peel, John D. Y. *Aladura: A Religious Movement among the Yoruba*. Oxford: Oxford University Press, 1968.
Pentecost News. "Pentecost Convention Centre to Serve as Isolation Centre for COVID-19 Patients." April 23, 2020. https://thecophq.org/pentecost-convention-centre-to-serve-as-isolation-centre-for-covid-19-patients/.
Pentecost Social Services. "2017 End of Year Report." The Church of Pentecost General Headquarters, 2017 Executive Summary Reports Compiled for the 43rd Session of the General Council Meetings, May 2–5, 2018.

Phiri, Isabel Apawo. "An Overview on the Imperative of *Diakonia* for the Church." https://www.oikoumene.org/resources/documents/an-overview-on-the-imperative-of-diakonia-for-the-church.

Sider, Ronald J., et al. *Lifestyle in the Eighties: An Evangelical Commitment to Simple Lifestyle*. Westminster Press, Philadelphia, 1982.

Stott, John. *Making Christ Known: Historic Mission Documents from the Lausanne Movement, 1974–1989*. Carlisle: Paternoster, 1996.

Tannor, Mabel Faith. "ICGC Donates Electro-Convulsive Therapy (ECT) Machines to Accra, Pantang, and Ankaful Hospitals." *Graphic Online*, June 19, 2019. https://www.graphic.com.gh/news/general-news/ghana-news-icgc-donates-electro-convulsive-therapy-ect-machines-to-pantang-and-ankaful-hospitals.html.

Tsekpoe, Christian. "Local Species in African Soil: The Development of James McKeown's Mission Models and Their Implications for the Church of Pentecost, Ghana." PhD diss., Oxford Centre for Mission Studies, 2020.

Tsele, Molefe. "The Role of the Christian Faith in Development" In *Faith in Development Partnership between the World Bank and the Churches of Africa*, edited by Deryke Belshaw et al., 203–18. Oxford: Regnum, 2001.

Turner, Harold W. *Religious Innovations in Africa: Collected Essays on New Religious Movements*. Boston: Hall, 1979.

"The Wheaton Declaration." *Evangelical Mission Quarterly* 2 (1966) 231–44.

White, Theresa J. "Diakonia." https://www.oikoumene.org/resources/documents/diakonia.

World Council of Churches. *Christians in the Technical and Society Revolutions of Our Time: The Role of the Diakonia of the Church in Contemporary Society: A Report to the World Conference on Church and Society*. Geneva: World Council of Churches, 1966.

———. "Kairos for Creation: Confessing Hope for the Earth—The Wuppertal Call." https://www.oikoumene.org/resources/documents/kairos-for-creation-confessing-hope-for-the-earth-the-wuppertal-call.

CHAPTER 4

A Response to Emmanuel Anim's "Pentecostalism as a Public Religion in Ghana and Beyond: Responses in Pandemic Times"

ALLISON L. NORTON

IN THIS TIMELY AND relevant chapter, Emmanuel Anim has reminded us that indeed the transformation of Pentecostalism toward increased intentionality in seeking the social transformation of communities via development initiatives and nation-building efforts cannot be overstated. Pentecostals across the world, and especially in the Global South, have increasingly become involved in various projects aimed at the betterment of the lives of both their own members and the wider community. There is power in naming and outlining in concrete terms the evidence of this transformation, as has been done in the two case studies of The Church of Pentecost and the International Central Gospel Church. We catch a glimpse of the remarkable range of Ghanaian Pentecostal experiments in *diakonia* evidencing a re-visioning of mission praxis that continues to adapt to the context and the times. This is especially important because the transformative potential of African Pentecostal theology and praxis is a growing area of study and interest to scholars of community development and political science, but also because it is highly relevant to church leaders and members, who are deeply concerned with what it means to live out a faithful, spirit-filled life in this time and place.

In this chapter I will highlight two implications related to the role of Pentecostalism as a public religion both in Ghana and beyond—first, recognizing the impact of the current COVID-19 pandemic on the church's response in Ghana; and secondly, focusing on the transnational nature of the church with implications for the mission of the church in the West. Continuing in the spirit of discussions on the missional model of Rev. James McKeown, I will highlight the "flexibility" model, or what others deem the inherent pragmatism of Pentecostalism in its adaptability to its various contexts and cultures. The lived experiences of Pentecostalism entail circular movement between theory and practice, as Pentecostal spirituality is a social practice. As such, it brings theology into conversation with daily experience, resulting in creations of lived theology arising from experiences of its adherents. It is in this dialogue with the mundane—the political, economic, and social worlds inhabited by Pentecostals—that the pragmatic orientation that is characteristic of global Pentecostalism becomes apparent.[1]

First, as outlined in the case study of The Church of Pentecost, COVID-19 has accelerated the church's work toward social transformation in the public sphere—beyond caring only for the needs of individual church members, The Church of Pentecost has partnered with the government through public health education efforts, supporting lockdown enforcements, the giving of funds, donations of personal protective equipment (PPE), the use of the Convention Centre as an isolation center, and more. The church has complemented the governments' efforts in providing essential services during an essential season. This early-COVID response of the church in the form of social services is Pentecostal flexibility and pragmatism on full display. Due to the pandemic response of the church, Pentecostalism has reinforced its relevance not only to adherents, but to the nation of Ghana at large, bringing religion into the public sphere in new ways.

Many scholars have argued that Pentecostals, in most cases at least, focus primarily on personal, spiritual, moral, and ethical transformation rather than directly engaging in political and structural solutions to social challenges. The Pentecostal movement has been perceived as focused on personal salvation to the neglect of the transformation of society more holistically. Scholars such as Allan Anderson have suggested that one weakness within Pentecostalism is its exclusion of the social

---

1. Wariboko and Oliverio Jr., "Pentecostal Spirituality as Theory and Praxis of Theology."

implications of Pentecostal spirituality and theology.[2] Likewise, Douglas Petersen has criticized Pentecostalism for its "self-serving purposes" and "neglect [of] the social responsibilities that should accompany this phenomenon."[3] Indeed, the social implications of Pentecostalism are often a consequence of the personal renewal of its adherents, rather than its prime aim. However, Pentecostal communities are more frequently aligned with political and social causes than is often thought to be the case. Over the last two decades, Pentecostal and Charismatic churches have risen to the forefront of public-facing Christianity, as they have addressed social needs that are not met by traditional political and governmental responses.[4] But what continues to be evident, however, is that Pentecostals are less inclined to seek political solutions for social challenges such as poverty, violence, and climate change.

In The Church of Pentecost's *Vision 2023*, we see a definition of "possessing the nations" that evidences Pentecostal concern with individuals, but also a political theology in which nations themselves need to be transformed and brought into alignment with the kingdom of God. This raises questions for the church and the broader Pentecostal community about the relationship between the church and the state. It further drives the church to consider the appropriate realm for such transformation of the nation state to occur—does it require structural change, new policy and law, and increased partnership with government entities toward such change? The church has mobilized and empowered the laity for engagement in different spheres of public life. In this way, Pentecostalism does not just manifest itself as a public religion in Ghana through the use of modern media or community development work—it also reshapes the public sphere itself into a spiritual domain, as Christians take their faith out of their private and ecclesial lives into the political domain, broadly considered.

Drawing on Anim's description, I argue that we are seeing a further re-envisioning of mission praxis in Ghanaian Pentecostalism—a re-envisioning of the role of Pentecostalism in social work that combines the empowerment of the individual as an agent of transformation with an emphasis on approaches that engage in political and structural solutions

---

2. Anderson, *Introduction to Pentecostalism*, 208.

3. Petersen, *Not by Might, Nor by Power*, 229.

4. Benyah, "Pentecostal/Charismatic Churches and the Provision of Social Services in Ghana"; Burgess, "African Pentecostal spirituality and Civic Engagement"; Kalu, *African Pentecostalism*.

to the challenges unearthed by the pandemic. The COVID-19 pandemic has exposed the limitations of social engagement that is exclusively oriented toward individual agency or that avoids engagement in political and structural solutions to social concerns. COVID-19 has revealed challenges besetting health structures and infrastructures that call the Pentecostal community to rethink what social action is necessary.

Here, I draw on Musa Gaiya's distinction between centripetal churches and centrifugal churches. Centripetal churches are those that "tend to be inward-looking, channeling human and financial resources into the church and not routinely using them for social and human development."[5] In contrast, centrifugal churches shift toward an outward-looking orientation, employing resources toward social and political improvement beyond the church or the congregation itself. The pandemic has transformed religious activities in religious communities across the nation toward a more centrifugal orientation, forcing some religious groups to extend their frontiers to meet not just the spiritual but also the mundane needs of their members (through the sharing of food, resources, etc.). What we see in the mission praxis of The Church of Pentecost in response to the pandemic is the embrace of a strongly centrifugal model, as the church has worked in collaboration with political elites to bridge binaries between religion and politics to work toward the welfare of the people of the nation during a time of crisis. This has not been without controversy.

During the first several months of the pandemic, from March to June 2020, The Church of Pentecost (CoP) used Facebook to disseminate several posts focused on combatting the pandemic via both spiritual and pragmatic means, bridging the spiritual and the mundane and doing so in partnership with Ghana's government. These posts highlighted the CoP's support of and joint effort with the government of Ghana in combating the virus, highlighting the role of the church in providing support for public health education and donations of money, PPE, and its own convention center for government use as a COVID-19 isolation center. In analysis of the public's comments made in response to these posts, I found that while many comments expressed support and pride in the church's role in partnering with the government to provide social and medical services in response to the pandemic, there was also an ambivalence or resistance to this "centrifugal" orientation of the church's

---

5. Gaiya, "Charismatic and Pentecostal Social Orientations in Nigeria," 63–64.

sociopolitical engagement over fears of scarcity and the perceived lack of prioritization of the church's own members.[6]

Stemming from this reality, my question for Pentecostal church leaders is this: What aspects of Pentecostal theology might provide a necessary framework for the kind of social engagement we are seeing in response to the pandemic—social engagement that is broader in its emphasis and with a stronger orientation toward social transformation than traditionally espoused in the past? In other words, how are lived Pentecostal theologies being constructed that shift beyond seeing transformation as exclusively in the realm of personal empowerment? What does it mean to stress that "I am an agent of transformation" in such a manner that also addresses structural realities and is able to both build on the strengths inherent in the movement, while correcting some of the weaknesses that have been unearthed by the pandemic crisis?

Secondly, I focus in this chapter on the implications of the church's mission re-envisioning from the diaspora setting. As a supranational institution, The Church of Pentecost anchors diaspora Ghanaians in the United States and many other countries to the religious and social values, cultures, and beliefs of their land of origin even as they seek to adapt to new contexts by mapping out new trajectories and identities. In Ghana, as in many other African nations, a key feature of centrifugal or progressive Pentecostalism is its focus on nation-building and national transformation through diverse forms of social, economic, and political engagement. With a view from the church in the United States, my questions now are: How might mission praxis and social transformation look different in the view from the diaspora? How might we continue to expand our understanding of social transformation and re-envision our missiological praxis acknowledging that there is no one-size-fits-all approach?

Pentecostalism is often argued to be a public religion *par excellence*. As Adrian Van Klinken has argued, this is due to the reality that the movement refuses "to accept the marginal and privatised role which theories of modernity as well as of secularisation use to reserve for religion. Pentecostal Christianity manifests itself publicly, engages with social and political issues, and in the meantime reshapes the public and political sphere by its dualist religious epistemology in which the world

---

6. Apaah and Norton, "Combating COVID-19 and 'Possessing the Nations.'"

is the scene of a spiritual battle between God and the Devil."[7] Pentecostalism, the "all-encompassing Spirit" directs and guides each aspect of life; everything—from the individual to the community, from the field to the city, from the nation to the world—is imbued with spiritual significance and has spiritual meaning. In other words, Pentecostalism is capable of integrating programs of evangelism and social concern into a unified effort because Pentecostals do not separate the spiritual from the physical, but instead integrate the two holistically. This provides a foundation for involvement in issues of social transformation that is truly derived from the Pentecostal way.

In the view from the diaspora in the United States and North America, much of the work toward social transformation that has been initiated by African immigrant congregations has been characterized as reverse mission, a concept that has gained traction in the literature on transnational Pentecostal churches. This is a vision of restoration, as Western nations are conceptualized as the former missionary-sending nations that are now the prime fields of missionary endeavor. However, as Richard Burgess argues, studies of reverse mission tend to measure success in terms of soul-wining of indigenous converts—which is based on a narrow concept of mission as evangelism and church-planting.[8]

What happens if we view the work of "possessing the nations" in diaspora not only through the lens of evangelism and church planting, but also through the work of these congregations in various kinds of civic and social activity in the communities in which the congregations are located and in which members reside? We know that despite many African transnational churches' efforts toward developing flourishing multicultural communities in the West—winning the "indigenous" population—the social composition of Pentecostal churches in the US and Europe has remained predominantly African. In response, some congregations have adapted their worship style and ritual practices in their host societies. However, social action and adapting the concept of "possessing the nations" to Western settings can also help overcome this barrier by enabling churches to make meaningful connections in their local communities in societies that are increasingly unreceptive to traditional evangelistic techniques and who are reluctant to attend church or identify with institutionalized religion. When surveying non-Ghanaian members of The Church

---

7. Klinken, "Pentecostalization of Public Spheres."
8. Burgess, "Megachurches and 'Reverse Mission.'"

of Pentecost in the US and Europe, one of the main findings is that these attendees strongly desire that the church place greater emphasis and priority in its social outreach in the community.[9] For many non-Ghanaian attendees, the church is not doing the business of the church if it is not emphasizing social transformation. Engaging in social initiatives in the wider society, however, will necessarily look different in the West compared to the activities of the church in Ghana.

This calls for heterogeneity in how the church re-envisions its mission. A small Pentecost International Worship Center located in a diverse neighborhood in Chicago will have a very different approach to development and acts of *diakonia* from that of The Church of Pentecost headquartered in Ghana. The US Government is not likely to contact them personally to seek their direct partnership in combating COVID-19 in the United States. What does it look like to "possess the nation" from the margins, rather than the center, of political life and power? This requires the deployment of multiple visions toward "possessing the nations," transforming society, and acting as agents of transformation in the public sphere. It requires building local partnerships with other entities currently engaged in social transformation, building trusting relationships with nonprofit organizations, local governments, and other churches from a posture of humility and openness to learn from these long-standing entities and work collaboratively toward the transformation of the local community in which the church is located. Ultimately, in both of these spheres—the church's response to COVID-19 in Ghana and the work of possessing the nations from the view of the diaspora—Pentecostal communities have the opportunity to recognize the inherent pragmatism of Pentecostalism in its adaptability to its various contexts and cultures and to continue to re-envision our social engagement and mission, following in the footsteps of Pastor McKeown's flexibility.

Bibliography

Anderson, Allan. *An Introduction to Pentecostalism: Global Charismatic Christianity.* Cambridge: Cambridge University Press, 2004.
Apaah, Felicity, and Allison L. Norton. "Combating COVID-19 and 'Possessing the Nations': Insights from Ghana's Megachurches." Paper presented at American Academy of Religion, San Antonio, TX, November 20–23, 2021.

---

9. Donkor et al., *Winning and Retaining Members.*

Barker, Isabelle V. "Charismatic Economies: Pentecostalism, Economic Restructuring, and Social Reproduction." *New Policital Science* 29 (2007) 407–27.

Benyah, Francis. "Pentecostal/Charismatic Churches and the Provision of Social Services in Ghana." *Transformation: An International Journal of Holistic Mission Studies* 38 (2021) 16–30.

Burgess, Richard. "African Pentecostal Spirituality and Civic Engagement: The Case of the Redeemed Christian Church of God in Britain." *Journal of Beliefs & Values* 30 (2009) 255–73.

———. "Megachurches and 'Reverse Mission.'" In *Handbook of Megachurches*, edited by Stephen Hunt, 243–68. Leiden: Brill, 2020.

Donkor, Lord Elorm, et al. *Winning and Retaining Members from Non-Ghanaian Backgrounds in North America and Europe: The Experience at The Church of Pentecost (Cop) Missions Fields*. Unpublished report.

Gaiya, Musa A. B. "Charismatic and Pentecostal Social Orientations in Nigeria." *Nova Religio* 18 (2015) 63–79.

Kalu, Ogbu. *African Pentecostalism: An Introduction*. Oxford: Oxford University Press, 2008.

Klinken, Adriaan van. "The Pentecostalization of Public Spheres." March 17, 2014. https://adriaanvanklinken.wordpress.com/2014/03/17/the-pentecostalisation-of-public-spheres/.

Petersen, Douglas. *Not by Might, Nor by Power: A Pentecostal Theology of Social Concern in Latin America*. Eugene, OR: Wipf & Stock, 2011.

Wariboko, Nimi, and L. William Oliverio Jr. "Pentecostal Spirituality as Theory and Praxis of Theology." *Pneuma* 44 (2022) 1–4.

CHAPTER 5

Ecclesiological Appraisal of Christian Values and Principles in the Public Sphere: Ghanaian Pentecostal Approach

PETER WHITE

Introduction

GOD LOVES THE WORLD and never ceases to engage with it. This deep faith conviction motivates the churches to engage in the public space.[1] The church and state have been in existence since the Old Testament. Although in the Old Testament, the word "church" was not used, God used Israel as his instrument and the concept of the church. Within this covenant relationship, Israel became the *light* to reveal God to the nations. Similarly, God also appointed prophets and judges to point out the direction of his will for other nations.[2] In the Old Testament, we read of Moses, who was raised in Egypt but was later called and used by God to deliver the Israelites from Egyptian bondage and authority. We also read of Nehemiah and Daniel serving in public spaces, and prophets such as Isaiah, Jeremiah, and Ezekiel serving as prophetic voices, speaking boldly against social injustices and inequalities, and bringing order.

In the New Testament, Jesus assigned the church to go to all the world to preach the gospel and make disciples that would observe

---

1. Lutheran World Federation, "Church in the Public Space," 8.
2. Bosch, *Transforming Mission*, 16–20, 62.

(practice) the word of God (Matt 28:20). The challenge we have in contemporary society is the fact that the majority of Christians have not realized that the world of work is a mission field in which to project good Christian principles and values. Therefore, Christianity and Christian values have been limited to selected days for church activities. In addition to the biblical references, Ciuraru notes that "democracy is a political system that allows its actors participation in shaping the public sphere. In view of this understanding of democracy, the Christian religion can play a bigger role in the public sphere, if it is recognized as a partner in the implementation of public policies and governance."[3]

In Höschele's definition of ecumenism, he explains the functions and relations of the church both with the wider ecumenical body and with related organizations and communities. He noted that the functions of the church include but are not limited to worshiping, prophetic voice, redemptive declarations, and the unitive functions. He argues that within the core functions of the church, it creates missional relations with non-Christian religions, society, culture, and the state. This missional relation of the church is also extended to include how the church functions and relates to the whole inhabited world.[4] Consequentially, Höschele's concept of the functions and relations of the church outlines a simplified perspective of the role of the church in the public sphere.[5] In other words, "God's engagement with the world moves the church's theology and praxis into the world—into public spaces."[6]

As a matter of fact, Christ does not want his church to be meaningless in society or to be pushed to the periphery, but to be right at the center of things, right where the action is.[7] The church in this regard is called to participate in the mission of God (*missio Dei*) and transform society.[8] Kudadjie and Aboagye-Mensah submit that "the church has a valid case to be involved in the affairs of the state in all aspects including national politics."[9]

---

3. Ciuraru, "Christian Values and Public Sphere," 93.
4. Höschele, "Defining Ecumenics," 107.
5. Höschele, "Defining Ecumenics," 107.
6. Lutheran World Federation, "Church in the Public Space," 9.
7. Hendriks, "Change of Heart," 275; also see Sarpong, "What Church?," 9.
8. World Council of Churches, "The Church," 53, 60; Balia & Kim 4, 31; Bosch, *Transforming Mission*, 389–92.
9. Kudadjie and Aboagye-Mensah, *Christian and National Politics*, 33.

In light of the above, if we claim that Ghana is a Christian country, it intrinsically means that majority of the people in public and private service are Christians. If this is the case, why then do we still have open platforms for corruption, shoddy contract deals, lazy workers, and people willing and ready to compromise and bend rules for their personal and relational gains? This, therefore, calls for a reflection on the missional call of the church to disciple and serve as the prophetic voice for society. Since the focus of this chapter is on Ghanaian Pentecostal churches, and The Church of Pentecost (CoP) is noted to be one of the leading Classical Pentecostal Churches in Ghana, I wish to quote relevant information of the church that resonates with the focus of this chapter.

One of the popular banner headlines of the CoP website is the statement of Apostle Eric Nyamekye which states, "In the coming years, The Church of Pentecost will strive to become a Church whose members go to possess or take their nations by influencing every worldview, thought and behavior with Kingdom principles, values, and lifestyles, thereby, turning many people to Christ." Furthermore, the *Vision 2023* of the CoP reports:

> The church seeks to contribute to a God-fearing society with hardworking and committed citizens; a society where there is the display of Christ-like behavior and the demonstration of a high level of integrity; a society with a considerable reduction in social injustice, corruption, crime rate, and other social vices; a society whose members are law-abiding citizens and where there is a reasonable reduction in wayward or deviant characters.[10]

These statements resonate well with the focus of my argument, and even more, they are in line with the third approach of the CoP's *Vision 2023*—Transforming Society:[11]

- Deploying Members as Agents of Transformation
- Community Transformation
- Church/Government Partnership

In view of the above discussions, this chapter will focus on the ecclesiological appraisal of Christian values and principles in the public sphere from a Pentecostal perspective.

---

10. Church of Pentecost, *Vision 2023*, 9.
11. Church of Pentecost, *Vision 2023*, 24, 46.

Christian Values and Principles in the Public Sphere

Values are important and lasting beliefs or ideals shared by members of a culture about what is good or bad, desirable or undesirable. Values have major influence on a person's behavior and attitude and serve as broad guidelines in all situations. Values influence choices one will make under certain circumstances.[12] Religious values and morals deal with ideas that safeguard or uphold the lives of religious adherents in their relationship with one another and the world around them. Such values deal with issues such as truth, love, justice, right and wrong, and respect for people and property.[13]

Christian values and principles are character traits that provide inner sanctions on our particular motives, intentions, and outward conduct. It is often referred to as moral excellence, goodness, and conformity of life and conduct with the principles of morality. It is a well-known fact that Christian teaching and theological virtue do not originate from humans. They are imparted by God through Christ and then practiced by the believer through the help of the Holy Spirit.[14] Christian values can be described as having godly excellence, godly goodness, or godly righteousness. They are the application of a conscious will to do what is right from God's revealed Word and from personal responsibility. They encompass integrity, honesty, modesty, and purity. Values are not only there to serve as a guide for our daily lives or decisions but also to help us give the best of ourselves.[15]

The challenge we are facing in various communities and places of work is that many Christians are unable to stand firm on their Christian convictions, values, and principles. The end result is that such people become conformists to non-Christian standards rather than transformists. Apostle Paul admonished the Roman Christians in his letter urging them not to conform to the world's standards but to be transformed by the renewal of their minds (Rom 12:2). This statement could possibly serve as one of the antidotes to the commonly accepted statement, "If you can't beat them, join them." It should be noted that Christian

---

12. Mbiti, *Introduction to African Religion*, 195.

13. Mbiti, *Introduction to African Religion*, 11.

14. Encyclopedia Britannica Online, s.v. "Virtue in Christianity," https://www.britannica.com/topic/virtue-in-Christianity.

15. Collins English Dictionary, s.v. "Christian Virtues," https://www.thefreedictionary.com/Christianvirtues.

values and principles are embedded character traits required of every Christian in their places of work and private lives. They are developed through personal and organizational conscious efforts and through the help of the Holy Spirit.

The Role of the Church in Developing Christian Values and Principles of Their Members in Public Service

It is not enough to talk of Christian values and principles without bringing in the role of the church. "Churches have a public dimension, as they are called and sent to be transformative agents in the world. With their vision of the common good, churches contribute to public life. This does not only happen through their speaking and acting inside, but also through the way in which they create space outside the church."[16]

The report of the Faith and Order Commission of the World Council of Churches on the church states that "the Church is not merely the sum of individual believers among themselves." The report acknowledges that the church is fundamentally a communion in the Triune God and a communion whose members participate in the life and mission of God.[17] The report further noted that "the Church, as the body of Christ, acts by the power of the Holy Spirit to continue his life-giving mission in prophetic and compassionate ministry and so participates in God's work of healing a broken world."[18]

As the body of Christ, it is our call to disciple our members to develop Christlike character. Though this is not an event, it requires a conscious commitment. Although the church has a general call for maturing believers, everyone also has a personal responsibility to aspire for Christian maturity. This is what Apostle Paul refers to as "working out your own salvation with fear and trembling" (Phil 2:12–13). This approach to Christian maturity is known as discipleship.

According to Asamoah-Gyadu, discipleship is human experience and decision leading to change and transformation with respect to absolute allegiance to God.[19] It is one of the core components of mission and it is one of the ways through which the believer is transformed into

---

16. Lutheran World Federation, "Church in the Public Space," 16.
17. World Council of Churches, *Resource Book*, 18.
18. World Council of Churches, *Resource Book*, 8.
19. Asamoah-Gyadu, "Conversion," 176.

the image and character of Jesus Christ.[20] Transformation in this regard is a process of profound and radical change that orients people, organizations, and society in a new direction and takes them to an entirely different level of effectiveness. It implies a basic change of character and little or no resemblance to the past configuration or structure. It is a complete change in the appearance or character of something or someone, especially so that the thing or person is improved.[21] As churches and Christians, we are shaped by the gospel message, the liberating power that transforms us to live a life that reflects the gospel.[22] The church, therefore, has a huge responsibility in nurturing its members to be responsible and relevant with respect to Christian values and principles at their various places of work.

The Intentional Positioning of Ethical and God-Fearing Christians in Strategic Places in Society

One of the areas the church has not done well is in the intentional grooming of people for strategic social positions. This approach was used by God when people like Nehemiah and Daniel had the opportunity to serve in public service (Neh 2; Dan 6:1–3). Many of the Pentecostal churches are so focused on the spiritual perspective of their call but do very little as far as their social impact is concerned. They are good with church planting and training pastors but fail to intentionally and strategically orient their members and leaders to aspire for strategic social positions.

Further to the above, it is very important for churches to create room to engage their members who are in public service to see their work as a call rather than a profession to make money through crooked means. The problem of society is not only solved by prayer but also by intentionally grooming people to serve God's divine purposes in public and private sectors of society.

Ghana is known to be about 71.2 percent Christian and the Pentecostals are in the majority. Pentecostals constitute about 28.3 percent, Protestant 18.4 percent, Catholic 13.1 percent, and others 11.4 percent of

---

20. Bosch, *Transforming Mission*, 56; Walls and Ross, *Mission in the 21st Century*, 25–35; Wright, *Mission of God*, 391; Kretzschmar, "Indispensability of Spiritual Formation," 344–45.

21. Cambridge Dictionaries, s.v. "Transformation," http://dictionary.cambridge.org/dictionary/english/improve.

22. Lutheran World Federation, "Church in the Public Space," 9.

the Christian population.[23] Based on the fact that Pentecostal churches have the lion's share in Ghanaian Christianity, it is possible for them to lobby for certain positions in government and the public sector. The same applies to other church traditions. Agbiji and Swart note that despite some Christians being involved in politics and governance, it is hardly evident how Christians are impacting the situation. In such a situation, it is justifiable to argue that churches as part of community structures are required to contribute to the goal of good governance.[24]

The reason we are finding it difficult to deal with some minority groups that are seeking attention in Ghanaian society in the name of human rights and religious rights is that they have deliberately positioned some of their members to influence decisions and policies at various places. We are finding it difficult to deal with the Chinese influence in African communities because the Chinese government seems to have made intentional efforts to strategically position Chinese business people in various communities in Africa. They come in to establish their presence through businesses and partnerships. They have gone further to send their best brains to high-class institutions and countries to learn their technologies and skills that would in the end be used to the benefit of China. They have dedicated schools and institutions for African languages and culture. It is time, therefore, for the church to learn from some of these strategies for influence and impact.

In *Vision 2023* of the CoP, it was noted that the church "shall be committed to rolling out programmes to strategically engage/disciple the nation's existing governance structures (the Executive, Judiciary and Legislature) within the framework of fulfilling our prophetic responsibility to the nation. Ministry to politicians as well as raising leaders for the nation's governance structures will therefore be given special attention."[25] Although it is good to see it written, I am hopeful that the church would make it a point to see it materialized for strategic reasons.

---

23. World Atlas, *Religious Beliefs in Ghana*.
24. Agbiji and Swart, "Christian Religious Leadership," 10.
25. Church of Pentecost, *Vision 2023*, 13, 52.

Encouraging Established Christian Professionals and Leaders to Mentor Younger Ones for Generational Influence

One of the easiest ways that would enable the church and Christians to positively influence the public sphere is through mentorship. Mentorship is very important in every sphere of life. It is the process by which a more experienced person imparts advice, support, insight, and knowledge to a less experienced person.[26] It is a system of support and encouragement given to less experienced people to enable them to maximize their potential, develop their skills, improve their performance, and be groomed for higher professional and social responsibilities.[27] The ultimate purpose of mentorship is to change the behavior of mentees in such a way that they function more fully and effectively academically, professionally, spiritually, and socially.[28]

One of the areas the church has also not done much is in the conscious effort to groom talented and skillful young Christians for the world of work. Although some churches have chosen to do so through their schools, this agenda is still in the mushroom stage without intentional and conscious efforts toward it. As a matter of fact, the kind of church, country, or community we want to see in the future depends on the conscious effort being made by the current leadership to groom younger ones. Specific biblical examples of such efforts can be seen from the grooming of biblical characters such as Esther (Esth 2:8–18), Daniel and his three friends (Dan 1:3–21), Jesus Christ and his disciples, and Paul's mentorship of Timothy and Silas. One of the greatest factors affecting mentorship in contemporary times is the desire for fame and the "get-money-quickly" syndrome among the youth. Despite this challenge, there are still genuine young men and women who are willing for such opportunities.

Intentional Support for Christlike Agenda, Doctrines, and Policies

As a country, we have allowed foreign ideologies and principles to be imposed on us by donors and some of our European counterparts who

---

26. Alred et al., *Mentoring Pocketbook*, 46.
27. Parsloe, *Coaching, Mentoring, and Assessing*, 67.
28. Masango, "Mentorship," 1.

come in with their selfish interests and parochial agenda. In light of this, the church has the power to make clear its positions on policies and subtle ideas that would undermine our cultural values and principles. Ghanaian Christians are good with prayers, but this approach is not enough if we are not ready to be the prophetic voice to ensure that the right things are done without political bias. As part of the proclamation (evangelism) mandate of the church, the church was also assigned a prophetic role of advocacy. The church must continue to echo her prophetic role and be the voice of the voiceless. The church must denounce and combat all that degrades and destroys people and society.[29]

Ghanaian Christianity is challenged with the proliferation of "prophets" who claim to be called by God, but their praxis appears not to conform to the biblical text. They are taking advantage of innocent and vulnerable people. It is the task of the Christian community to make clear the practices that are unbiblical yet are being accepted into the Christian communities. The challenge some of us face as Pentecostal scholars is that non-Pentecostal theologians and scholars bracket all unorthodox praxis as Pentecostal traditions. This has therefore affected the image of the Pentecostal communities and churches in a negative way.

In view of this, it is important for the Pentecostal churches, especially the classical Pentecostal churches, to properly document their doctrines and praxis, as well as educate their pastors and members on them. I can say for a fact that the CoP has done very well as far as documentation and availability of their policies and doctrinal positions are concerned, but the same cannot be said of some other classical Pentecostal churches in Ghana.

Enforcing Civic Responsibility of the Church and Members

Civic responsibility is the responsibility of citizens in a society to exhibit certain attitudes and actions related to participation in society and democratic governance. Civic responsibility is associated with involvement in church, government, and memberships with voluntary associations. Actions and attitudes relating to civic responsibility are displayed through political, civil, environmental, and economic advocacy.

The goal of civic responsibility is to create social participants and develop responsible citizens within the community and government. It

---

29. WCC, *Resource Book*, 2–3.

includes but is not limited to supporting the community, civic action, setting a positive example, and adopting beneficial values. Adopting beneficial values requires accepting and utilizing values that benefit society instead of the individual. Setting a good example involves acting in an ethical manner regarding society's guidelines, laws, and rules.[30] Examples of our civic responsibilities are: civility, hard work, fulfilling tax obligations, maintaining peace and order, and promoting justice and fairness.

Biblical examples have taught us to pay our taxes (Matt 22:16–22; Rom 13:1–7), submit to government, and obey societal regulations (Rom 13:1–7).[31] One of the reasons many churches have lost the moral right to be the prophetic voice to boldly speak against certain government policies and corrupt practices in our communities is the fact that some of the churches have also contributed to many of our social challenges through unethical behaviors and compromise. Some churches, Christian organizations, and Christian businesspeople have compromised on their responsibility of paying required taxes to the government for the running of the country. Some underreport their tax values, while others connive with public service officials to bypass approved regulations and processes. The mind-boggling questions are:

- Can those involved in such practices be bold to question government when certain obligations and promises are not met?
- Can we be bold to question the corrupt practices in society if we are part of those nurturing them?

To be the salt and light of the world, as said by the Lord Jesus Christ in Matthew 5:13–16, we must work on ourselves as the body of Christ and encourage members of our churches to live responsible Christian

---

30. Reference, s.v. "What Is Civic Responsibility?," https://www.reference.com/world-view/civic-responsibility-66a4800099c91789.

31. Let every soul be subject to the governing authorities. For there is no authority except from God, and the authorities that exist are appointed by God. Therefore whoever resists the authority resists the ordinance of God, and those who resist will bring judgment on themselves. For rulers are not a terror to good works, but to evil. Do you want to be unafraid of the authority? Do what is good, and you will have praise from the same. For he is God's minister to you for good. But if you do evil, be afraid; for he does not bear the sword in vain; for he is God's minister, an avenger to *execute* wrath on him who practices evil. Therefore *you* must be subject, not only because of wrath but also for conscience' sake. For because of this you also pay taxes, for they are God's ministers attending continually to this very thing. Render therefore to all their due: taxes to whom taxes are due, customs to whom customs, fear to whom fear, honour to whom honour (Rom 13:1–7 NKJV).

lives. In a nutshell, we should be publicly righteous and our churches should be formation centers for public righteousness.[32]

The Call of the Church to Pray for Leaders and Those in Authority

The issue raised above cannot have the required impact when our ethical praxis is not backed by prayer for our community, nation, and all those in authority. Precedence in Scripture has given us ideas on the importance of prayer for a successful public life and the relevance of the church in society. In Jeremiah 29:7, God, through the prophet Jeremiah, admonished the Israelites to seek the peace and prosperity of their host city (Babylon). They were encouraged to pray to the Lord for the city because if the city prospers, they will also prosper. Although someone may say this message was specifically for the Israelites in exile, I believe the call for prayer for the nations is still relevant for our time Further to the above, in Apostle Paul's epistle to Timothy he wrote:

> I urge, then, first of all, that petitions, prayers, intercession, and thanksgiving be made for all people, for kings and all those in authority, that we may live peaceful and quiet lives in all godliness and holiness. This is good, and pleases God our Saviour, who wants all people to be saved and to come to a knowledge of the truth. (1 Tim 2:1–4 NKJV)

Additionally, Christians who are in public or private service can also learn from the spirituality and praxis of Bible characters that served in public spaces. Nehemiah and Daniel were noted to be people of prayer in their public services. Nehemiah was not a preacher or pastor. In fact, he was not even in church. Nehemiah was a Jewish cupbearer to King Artaxerxes, who reigned from the city of Susa in what is today's Iran. We would naturally assume that because he held a high position as the king's own cupbearer, he would be comfortable where he was. However, when he heard of the condition of Jerusalem, he went to his closet and prayed. His prayer later gave him favor before the king and he was subsequently allowed to go to Jerusalem with resources on the authority of Artaxerxes (Neh 2:4–10). In Nehemiah 8:9 we read that he became a governor but still did not allow that position to influence his prayer life and the promotion of a godly agenda.

32. Mouw, *Uncommmon Decency*, 33–38.

Daniel was also noted for his prayer life in spite of his position in public service (Dan 2:16–19; 6:5–10; 9:1–23; 10:1–12). Daniel's strength lay in his devotion to prayer and is a lesson for us all. It is not just in the bad times but on a daily basis that we must come to God in prayer. The lesson one could learn from Daniel and Nehemiah's approach to public service is that it is not enough to encourage people to live their lives according to Christian values and principles. We have to be conscious of the fact that not all men are of a good conscience, therefore, we have to back our Christian principles with prayer and intercession. Furthermore, the prayer and intercession of Nehemiah and Daniel helped them to have favor before the people in authority despite their non affiliation to Jewish principles, and later led to the fulfillment of God's divine purpose. In Apostle Paul's admonishing, he outlined the end result of praying for leaders and people in authority. He also noted that it is the will of God for believers to do so.

Conclusion

I wish to submit that the aim of this chapter is not to promote ecclesiasticism. That is a situation in which the church seeks to control the state. Instead, the church is called to equip its members to live godly lives and to be salt and light in their public-square interactions. Philippians 4:8 admonishes us to think on "whatsoever things are true, whatsoever things are honest, whatsoever things are just, whatsoever things are pure, whatsoever things are lovely, whatsoever things are of good report." This suggests that by meditating on Christian virtues we will start practicing them through the help of the Holy Spirit.

This chapter discusses the role of the church in promoting Christian principles and virtues in the public sphere. In order to achieve the objective of the chapter, the author used ecumenical, relevant church documents and literature study to support various arguments. The focus of the chapter led to discussions under the following subheadings: Christian values and principles in the public sphere; the role of the church in developing Christian values and principles of their members in public service; the intentional positioning of ethical and God-fearing Christians in strategic places in society; encouraging established Christian professionals and leaders to mentor younger ones for generational influence; intentional support for Christlike agenda, doctrines, and policies; and enforcing civic responsibility of the church and members; as well as the call of the church to pray for leaders and those in authority.

In the light of the various discussions in the chapter, I want to state that the gospel we preach is political, and therefore the church is a political community. We are political in the sense that we are a "contrast community" whose life is ordered under Christ and should be markedly different from other communities. Our power does not come from wealth, social position, or military power. Instead, it comes from Christian love, prophetic witness, generosity, and sacrificial service. By implication, the church is called to participate in God's mission that brings life in abundance to all—not only to church members.

Bibliography

Agbij, Obami M., and Ignatius Swart. "Christian Religious Leadership and the Challenge of Sustainable Transformational Development in Postmilitary Nigeria: Towards a Reappraisal." *KOERS—Bulletin for Christian Scholarship* 80 (2015) 1–13.

Alred, Geof, et al. *The Mentoring Pocket Book*. London: Management Pocket, 1998.

Asamoah-Gyadu, Johnson Kwabena. "Conversion, Converts, and National Identity." In *Wiley-Blackwell Companion to World Christianity*, edited by Lanin Sanneh and Michael J. McClymond, 176–89. Oxford: Blackwell, 2016.

Balia, Daryl, and Kirsteen Kim, eds. *Witnessing to Christ Today*. Vol. 2, *Edinburgh 2010*. Oxford: Regnum, 2010.

Bosch, David Jacobus. *Transforming Mission: Paradigm Shifts in Theology of Mission*. 20th anniversary ed. Maryknoll, NY: Orbis, 2014.

The Church of Pentecost. *Vision 2023: Five-Year Vision Document or The Church of Pentecost Covering the Period 2018–2023*. Accra: Pentecost, 2019.

Ciuraru, Marius Liviu. "Christian Values and Public Sphere: Giuseppe Lazzati's Paradigm." *Agathos* 6 (2015) 90–97.

Hendriks, Jurgens. "A Change of Heart: Missional Theology and Social Development." In *Religion and Social Development in Post-Apartheid South Africa: Perspectives for Critical Engagement*, edited by Ignatius Swart et al., 275–88. Stellenbosch: Sun, 2010.

Höschele, F. Stefan. "Defining Ecumenics Fifty Years after Mackay." *Communio Viatorum* 55 (2013) 105–36.

Kretzschmar, Louise. "The Indispensability of Spiritual Formation for Christian Leaders." *Missionalia* 34 (2006) 338–61.

Kudadjie, Joshua N., and Robert Kwesi Aboagye-Mensah. *The Christian and National Politics*. Accra: Asempa, 1991.

The Lutheran World Federation. "The Church in the Public Space." https://www.lutheranworld.org/sites/default/files/dtpwchurches_in_public_space.pdf.

Masango, Maake. "Mentorship: A Process of Nurturing Others." *HTS Teologiese Studies/Theological Studies* 67 (2011) 1–5.

Mbiti, John S. *Introduction to African Religion*. New York: Praeger, 1975.

Mouw, Richard J. *Uncommon Decency: Christian Civility in an Uncivil World*. Rev. and expanded ed. Downers Grove, IL: InterVarsity, 2010.

Parsloe, Eric. *Coaching, Mentoring, and Assessing: A Practical Guide to Developing Competence*. London: Page, 2001.

Sarpong, Peter Kwesi. "What Church, What Priesthood for Africa?" In *Theological Education in Africa: Quo Vadimus?*, edited by J. S. Pobee and J. N. Kudadjie, 6–17. Geneva: World Council of Churches 1990.

Walls, Andrew, and Cathy Ross, eds. *Mission in the 21st Century: Exploring the Five Marks of Global Mission*. Maryknoll, NY: Orbis, 2008.

World Atlas. "Religious Beliefs in Ghana." https://www.worldatlas.com/articles/religious-beliefs-in-ghana.html.

World Council of Churches. "The Church: Towards a Common Vision." In *Ecumenical Vision for 21st Century*, edited by M. Lorke and D. Werner, 61–62. Geneva: World Council of Churches, 2013.

———. *Resource Book WCC 10th Assembly, Busan 2013*. Geneva: World Council of Churches, 2013.

Wright, Christopher J. H. *The Mission of God: Unlocking the Bible's Grand Narrative*. Downers Grove, IL: InterVarsity, 2006.

CHAPTER 6

A Response to Peter White's "Ecclesiological Appraisal of Christian Values and Principles in the Public Sphere: Ghanaian Pentecostal Approach"

CHRISTIAN TSEKPOE

IN THIS PRESENTATION, PETER White rightly points out that the church's mandate to the public sphere is found in both the Old and New Testaments of the Bible. He agrees with Hendriks, Jurgens, and Peter Kwesi Sarpong that "Christ does not want his church to be meaningless in society or to be pushed to the periphery . . . but . . . to be right at the centre of things, right where the action is"[1] because "the church in this regard is called to participate in the mission of God (*missio Dei*) and transform society." Indeed, the church's mandate of being the salt of the earth and the light of the world is clear in Jesus' teachings as found in Matthew 5:13–16. This is again corroborated in what has come to be known as the Great Commission, which mandates the followers of Jesus Christ to "go and make disciples of all nations, baptizing them in the name of the Father and of the Son and of the Holy Spirit" (Matt 28:19). This understanding of mission has broadened the church's perspective to see mission beyond "the proclamation of the historical,

---

1. Hendriks, "Change of Heart," 275; also see Sarpong, "What Church?," 9.

biblical Christ as Saviour and Lord, with a view to persuading people to come to him personally and so be reconciled to God."[2] Mission should also be "equated with social transformation resulting from God's action in history through human agency."[3] This carries the notion that mission should be vertical as well as horizontal. Vertical in the sense that the gospel must be preached to reconcile humans to God the Father through Christ the Son. Horizontal in the sense that mission must engage the public sphere by responding to issues of humans' relationships in the world. Consequently, Norman Goodall argues:

> A Christianity which has lost its vertical dimension has lost its salt and is not only insipid in itself, but useless for the world. But a Christianity which would use the vertical preoccupation as a means to escape from its responsibility for and in the common life of man is a denial of the incarnation, of God's love for the world manifested in Christ.[4]

This understanding of the church's mandate gives no room for Christians (and in this context, Pentecostal-Charismatics) to just give verbal ascent to Pentecostal-related mantras or slogans. It also gives no room for just labeling churches as Salt and Light Ministries or Worship Centers. Again, this ecclesiological mandate gives no room for just using stickers or raising giant billboards and making flyers with beautiful and catchy religious phraseologies. As much as these labels or mantras or slogans are great and apropos for announcing the presence of the church and aiding what Michael Green calls presence evangelism,[5] it is critical for the church to understand, see, and approach its mandate in practical terms, consciously working toward visible and identifiable social transformation. This, therefore, calls for a reflection on the missional call of the church to disciple and to serve as the prophetic voice for society.

This is to say that the presence of the church in the communities must not only be seen in symbols and inscriptions. Instead, the church's presence must be felt in speech, in conduct, in love for God and neighbor, in purity and in the demonstration of faith in everyday life. Just as the saltiness of salt is not felt in its bag and the brightness of light is not experienced until it moves out of its manufacturing box, so also will the

2. Padilla, "Holistic Mission," 11.
3. Padilla, "Holistic Mission," 11
4. Goodall, *Uppsala Report 1968*, 317–18.
5. Green, *Evangelism through the Local Church*.

impact of the church be hidden under the cover of church buildings until the church begins to positively influence the public sphere (Luke 10:27; 1 Tim 4:12). Again, the presence of the church must not only be heard in shouts and loud noise. Pentecostal-Charismatics in Ghana have been accused of making loud noise at church to create a nuisance for residents living close to church buildings. This gives the church a bad image in the public space and should not be encouraged. I am by no means saying Pentecostals should mute their microphones and be hushed in their services. Responsible shouting and vibrancy are some of the birthmarks of Pentecostalism. Even on the Day of Pentecost, "a sound like the blowing of a violent wind came from heaven" (Acts 2:2).

The subject matter here is not just about noise making, the emphasis of my argument is that Pentecostal-Charismatic ecclesiology should go beyond just "making joyful noise unto the Lord" in the church room. It should also go beyond dancing and vibrancy. Pentecostal-Charismatic Christianity in Ghana should begin showing signs of maturity by responding to what Bill Bright, founder of Campus Crusade, and Loren Cunningham, founder of Youth with a Mission (YWAM), call "The 7 Mountains of Societal Influence." They listed these seven mountains as religion, family, education, governance, media, arts and entertainment, and business. They proposed that for the church to effectively and truly transform society positively, its members must strategically reach these facets of society and demonstrate the values and principles of their faith.[6] In Ghana, if the huge number of Pentecostal-Charismatics who go to church on Sundays and on weekdays begin to demonstrate true Christian values and principles in these facets of society as outlined, the church's saltiness and brightness would not be hidden or undermined.

Pentecostal-Charismatics in Africa seem to be doing quite well in terms of evangelism and church planting, leading to the exponential numerical growth of Christianity in Africa within the past one hundred years. Based on current demographic statistics on global Christianity, including Todd Johnson's "Counting Pentecostals Worldwide," it has been argued that at the moment, Pentecostal-Charismatic Christianity, in its diverse forms, represents the fastest growing stream of Christianity, especially in the non-Western world.[7] Additionally, it has been generally observed that Christianity is growing in Africa and the rest of

6. Bright and Cunningham, "7 Mountains of Societal Influence."
7. Asamoah-Gyadu, *Contemporary Pentecostal Christianity*.

the Global South more rapidly than in other parts of the world. African Christianity has grown by 2.8 percent per year, followed by Asia (2.13 percent) and Latin America (1.20 percent). Comparably, the growth rate in the Global North is quite low—Oceania (0.98 percent), North America (0.58 percent) and Europe (0.04 percent).[8]

Although the church in Ghana has contributed significantly to the development of the wider society, there remains much concern about whether Christianity on the continent in general, and Pentecostal-Charismatic Christianity in particular, is making the desired impact in the public sphere commensurate to the current numerical growth rate. This is the major concern of Dr. White. He pointed out that Ghana is known to be about 71.2 percent Christian and the Pentecostals are in the majority, constituting about 28.3 percent, whilst Protestants are 18.4 percent, Catholics, 13.1 percent, and others 11.4 percent. Although, Ghana's constitution indicates that Ghana is a secular nation, these statistics seems to tell us otherwise, and as a result, many people argue that Ghana is actually a Christian nation.

Dr. White, therefore, draws out this logic, "If we claim that Ghana is a Christian country, it intrinsically means that the majority of people in public and private services are Christians." He further asked, "If this is the case, why then do we still have open platforms for corruption, shoddy contract deals, lazy workers, and people willing and ready to compromise and bend rules for their personal and relational gains?" He then offered some challenging proposals that Pentecostal-Charismatics in Ghana and Africa can consider critically and reflectively as a response to the gap in their public ecclesiology. These include:

1. The role of the church in developing Christian values and principles of their members in the public service,
2. The intentional positioning of ethical and God-fearing Christians in strategic places in society,
3. Encouraging established professionals and leaders to mentor younger ones for generational influence,
4. Creating the platform for constant interaction with Christians in public services,
5. Intentional support for Christlike agenda, doctrines, and policies, and

---

8. Johnson, "Christianity 2018," 20–28.

6. Enforcing civic responsibility of the church and members.

The rest of this chapter will critically reflect on these issues and propose additional suggestions for Pentecostal-Charismatic ecclesiology in the public sphere.

The Church of Pentecost Model of the Church's Influence in the Public Space

White begins this discussion by indicating, "It is not enough to talk of Christian values and principles without bringing in the role of the church. . . . The church therefore has a huge responsibility in nurturing its members to be responsible and relevant with respect to Christian values and their various places of work." In The Church of Pentecost's (CoP) *Vision 2023*, the church intends to equip it members and unleash them to go and transform society. Under the subtopic "Equipping the Church," the CoP's *Vision 2023* indicates,

> We need to be intentional about the purpose of every believer—being like yeast and influencing the contexts in which they find themselves until they have transformed it to reflect the glory of God (Matt 13:33). Understanding the priority and purpose of the Church is necessary for equipping Christians and sending them to affect the spiritual and moral darkness in our societies. If our members are well-equipped and intentionally released into the nations, the spiritual and social capital we have inherited and the material resources we have at our disposal are likely to touch the communities of the world, bringing a great multitude under the rule of the Kingdom of God.[9]

This agrees with White's proposal for the church to be responsible for developing Christian values and principles of their members in the public service. In The Church of Pentecost, for example, discipleship has been one of the ways by which the church attempts to help its members develop such values. Discipleship in the CoP developed from its informal stage of direct mentorship, usually in the form of apprenticeship until intentional and formal structures began to develop. Some of the formal structures of discipleship in the CoP include new converts classes, Sunday morning Bible study groups, home cell groups, officers' retreats, lay

---

9. Church of Pentecost, *Vision 2023*, 8.

leaders school, and formal theological education for full-time ministers, ministers' wives, and some lay leaders.[10]

Additionally, in recent times The Church of Pentecost has organized a number of conferences for royals in Ghana. These conferences attract chiefs, queens, and other royals across the country to the Pentecost Convention Centre in Gomoah-Fetteh in Ghana. The aim of this conference is to help Christian chiefs appreciate the need to allow Christian principles and values to permeate their leadership and governance. The conferences respond to very difficult issues that bother the relationship between the practices of the traditional chieftaincy institution and the Christian faith. Many topics have been treated over the years, including pouring of libation, animal sacrifice, fortification of the body, forced polygamy, feeding of ancestors, the use of alcoholic beverages, chewing of spices and spitting on an individual's face to make the person strong, divination, rituals of the black stool, and traditional oath swearing.[11] Through these efforts, the CoP now has ministry to the palace, where some of the pastors of the church offer voluntary chaplaincy services to many of the palaces in Ghana.

Furthermore, the CoP has created what is known as the Youth Political Chamber. The vision of the political chamber is "to raise politicians, statesmen and diplomats for Ghana and the world who shall be real 'salts and lights' in this morally challenging post-modern world."[12] This vision is inspired by the Vision 2018 of the CoP and derived from Proverbs 29, which states, "When the righteous are in authority, the people rejoice; but when a wicked man rules, the people groan. The king establishes the land by justice, but he who receives bribes overthrows it" (vv. 2, 4 NKJV). The chamber is intended to train selected young people into political leadership by intentionally exposing them to the constitution of Ghana, public speaking, and parliamentary proceedings. The chamber also aims at encouraging the young people to run for leadership positions in their respective Student Representative Councils and the National Union of Ghana Students at the university campuses. In their various communities they shall be encouraged to vie for leadership positions as assembly members and unit committee members.[13] The mission of the Youth

---

10. For detailed explanation of these formal discipleship structures in the CoP, see Tsekpoe, "Discipleship and Ordained Ministry," 206–15.

11. Tsekpoe, "African Traditional Oath-Swearing," 131–38.

12. Church of Pentecost Youth Ministry, "Political Chamber."

13. Church of Pentecost Youth Ministry, "Political Chamber."

Political Chamber indicates that "undergirded by principles drawn from God's word, the chamber seeks to instill into emerging leaders virtues such as hard work, patriotism, honesty, integrity, sacrificial service, social justice and diligence." Its core values include (a) Leading with integrity and selflessness, (b) Being real examples of faith in Christ, and (c) Using one's political career to bless the entire world.

Beyond the Youth Political Chamber, the CoP also set out to hold the first ever National Development Conference from July 26–27, 2023, at the Pentecost Convention Centre at Gomoah-Fetteh in the Central Region of Ghana. This conference is under the theme, *Moral Vision and National Development*. The conference is expected to bring together all the arms of government in Ghana—the executive, the legislative and the judiciary. As the name and the theme for the conference suggest, it is expected that issues of moral uprightness and social development will be discussed extensively. Whilst the Youth Political Chamber is limited to only members of the CoP, the National Development Conferences targets particular groups of people, irrespective of their religious affiliations. To ensure maximum participation, the leadership of the church extended invitations to the leadership of the two major political parties in Ghana to encourage their members to attend the conference.[14] As Dr. White indicated, many of the politicians in Ghana claim to be Christians. Conferences of this nature are a good way to remind them of their roles as salt and light of the world and to encourage them to reflect their Christian values and principles in their political career.

Other public spaces where the CoP has been very instrumental include building prison facilities to decongest some prisons in Ghana, building police stations to enhance security in the nation, constructing boreholes for deprived communities, and building clinics and CHIPS compounds to provide health facilities for some communities that need it. The CoP has also been at the forefront of environmental care campaigns and tree planting projects in Ghana. All these attempts of the CoP have attracted divergent public opinions from the Ghanaian observers. One of the critics of the CoP's social actions is the Ghanaian comedian Kwaku Sintim Misa, popularly known as KSM, who ridicules the church's prisons project by stating that it is only in Ghana that churches build prisons whilst the government builds a cathedral.[15] This statement can also be understood

---

14. Pentecost News, "NPP to Participate in National Politicians' Conference"; also see Pentecost News, "Church of Pentecost Delegation."

15. GhanaWeb "It's Only in Ghana Churches Build Prisons."

from the background that some Ghanaians have not been happy with the government's decision to build a national cathedral.

These sentiments notwithstanding, many have applauded the various social interventions of the CoP in recent years. These activities are directed at entering the public space and influencing these spaces with the principles and values of the kingdom of God. In the two prisons that have been built by the CoP in Ghana so far, one is situated at Ejura in the Ashanti Region of Ghana and the other one is situated at Nsawam in the Eastern Region of Ghana. I have personally paid visits to these two prisons to observe the facilities within provided by the church. It is heartwarming to see that there are skills training facilities such as workshops for carpentry, tailoring, shoe making, and *kente*[16] weaving. Other facilities include a fully furnished church building and a baptistery. To make good use of these facilities, the CoP employs a few full-time pastors in some of the prisons to help in the training and discipleship of the inmates to rehabilitate and transform them into responsible citizens before they complete their prison terms.[17]

With these and many other social interventions, it can be concluded that the CoP is providing an important model for the Pentecostal-Charismatic church's influence in the public space. However, there has not yet been an empirical assessment on the extent to which these social interventions and the discipleship structures discussed earlier are being successful. Further, it is not very clear how other Pentecostal-Charismatic denominations in Ghana respond to the public sphere. There is the need for further research in the country to identify the extent to which these efforts are being fruitful and to propose modifications and recommendations for further public ecclesiological engagements by Pentecostal-Charismatic churches in Ghana.

Again, Peter White cogently argues that "As a matter of fact, the kind of church, country, or communities we want to see in the future depends on the conscious effort being made by current leadership to groom younger ones. Specific biblical examples for such efforts can be seen from the grooming of biblical characters such as Esther (Esth 2:8–18), Daniel and his three friends (Dan 1:3–21), Jesus Christ and his disciples, and Paul's mentorship of Timothy and Silas." By pointing to these biblical characters, Peter White is proposing what I call direct mentoring in The

16. *Kente* is a Ghanaian traditional textile that is woven with strips of silk and cotton threads.

17. Personal observations at both the Ejura Prisons and Nsawam prisons of Ghana.

Church of Pentecost.[18] Hilborn and Bird defined Christian mentoring as "A relational experience in which one person empowers another by sharing God-given resources and a lifelong relationship, in which a mentor helps a protégé reach his or her God-given potential."[19] In my personal research about James McKeown, who is recognized as the founder of The Church of Pentecost, I discovered that McKeown was firmly convinced that leaders who understand and work with God's mission can only be raised if converts are effectively and genuinely discipled.[20]

It is appropriate to argue that it will not do well for us in this generation to apply McKeown's discipleship or mentorship and praxis on a one-on-one basis. It is, however, important for us to know it is also apropos to apply the principles McKeown worked with to our contemporary contexts with responsible freedom if those principles have produced the desired results and continue to show signs of relevance. As Peter White proposed, this mentoring should not be limited to the church room, it must be targeted to the government, business, arts and entertainment, media and technology, education, and family spheres. We seem to be doing well in terms of the religious, and we must keep it up without slowing down. The CoP's Political Chamber and Politicians Conference should consider using this direct mentoring approach in its training, where responsible leaders intentionally mentor younger ones with Godly values and encourage them into political leadership. If McKeown was able to mentor people long after he left Ghana and even after his death—his impact is still being felt not only in the CoP but within Ghanaian Pentecostalism today—then the principles behind his direct mentoring approach can be extrapolated into the church's efforts to mentor the next generation in business, traditional and political leadership, arts and entertainment, media and technology, and education. Again, Dr. White argues,

> As a country [Ghana], we have allowed foreign ideologies and principles to be imposed on us by donors and some of our European counterparts who come in with their selfish interests and parochial agenda. In light of this, the church has the power to make clear their positions on policies and subtle ideas that would undermine our cultural values and principles.

18. Tsekpoe, "Direct Mentoring," 21–33.
19. Hilborn and Bird, *God and the Generations*, 170.
20. Personal interviews with Apostle Rigwell Ato Addison, a former General Secretary of The Church of Pentecost who was also an interpreter to Rev. James McKeown, February 20, 2018.

> Ghanaian Christians are good with prayers, but this approach is not enough if we are not ready to be the prophetic voice to ensure that the right things are done without political bias. Footnote number not included.

What Peter White is calling for in this regard is the fact that beyond praying and fasting and social interventions, Pentecostal-Charismatic churches in Ghana must be bold to reject what is evil and intentionally support Christlike agendas, doctrines, and policies in the nation. This we must not take lightly at all. I recount two cases in point within the Ghanaian community, which gives me the signal that if the church takes its prophetic mandate to the nations seriously, it will be able to fulfil its mandate of being the salt of the earth and the light of the world (Matt 5:13–16). First was the attempt to introduce comprehensive sexuality education into the Basic School Curriculum in Ghana. The leaders of the Christian community in Ghana spoke boldly and publicly about this and the action was reversed. Second was the attempt to push for the bill on the floor of parliament on the subject of "the promotion of proper human sexual rights and Ghanaian family values bill, 2021." The overwhelming support given to this bill by the Christian community in Ghana made its rejection by parliament very difficult.

It is, therefore, important to emphasize here that the issues raised by Dr. Peter White in these James McKeown Memorial Lectures are not just issues of theory to be discussed and left till the next James McKeown Memorial Lectures. They are real issues that confront society and require the church's reflection and critical response in contemporary times. As we do this, our appraisal of Christian values and principles in the public sphere will be pragmatic and effective. The role of Pentecostal-Charismatic churches as the salt of the earth and the light of the world will be realized and the Ghanaian society will become a better place to the glory of God.

Bibliography

Bright, Bill, and Loren Cunningham. "The 7 Mountains of Societal Influence." https://www.generals.org/the-seven-mountains.

The Church of Pentecost. *Vision 2023: Five-Year Vision Document for the Church of Pentecost Covering the Period 2018–2023*. Accra: Pentecost, 2018.

The Church of Pentecost Youth Ministry. "Political Chamber." https://www.penteagle.org/youth-ministry-homepage/political-chamber/.

GhanaWeb. "It's Only in Ghana Churches Build Prisons—KSM Mocks." July 29, 2019. https://www.ghanaweb.com/GhanaHomePage/NewsArchive/It-s-only-in-Ghana-Churches-build-prisons-KSM-mocks-767555.

Goodall, Norman, ed. *The Uppsala Report 1968*. Geneva: World Council of Churches, 1968.

Green, Michael. *Evangelism through the Local Church*. London: Hodder & Stoughton, 1990.

Hendriks, Jurgens. "A Change of Heart: Missional Theology and Social Development." In *Religion and Social Development in Post-Apartheid South Africa: Perspectives for Critical Engagement*, edited by Ignatius Swart et al., 275–88. Stellenbosch: Sun, 2010.

Hilborn, David, and Matt Bird. *God and the Generations: Youth, Age, and the Church Today*. Carlisle: Paternoster, 2002.

Johnson, Todd M. "Christianity 2018: More African Christians and Counting Martyrs." *International Bulletin of Mission Research* 42 (2017) 20–28.

———. "Counting Pentecostals Worldwide." *Pneuma* 36 (2014) 265–88.

Padilla, C. René. "Holistic Mission." *Occasional Paper No. 33*. https://lausanne.org/wp-content/uploads/2007/06/LOP33_IG4.pdf.

Pentecost News. "NPP to Participate in National Politicians' Conference." March 14, 2023. https://thecophq.org/npp-to-participate-in-national-politicians-conference.

———. "The Church of Pentecost Delegation Meets NDC Leadership Over Upcoming Politicians' Conference." March 9, 2023. https://thecophq.org/general-secretary-meets-ndc-leadership-over-upcoming-politicians-conference.

Sarpong, Peter Kwesi. "What Church, What Priesthood for Africa?" In *Theological Education in Africa: Quo Vadimus?*, edited by J. S. Pobee and J. N. Kudadjie, 6–17. Geneva: World Council of Churches, 1990.

Tsekpoe, Christian. "African Traditional Oath-Swearing: An Evaluation from a Ghanaian Pentecostal Perspective." *E-Journal of Humanities, Arts, and Social Sciences* 1 (2020) 131–38.

———. "Direct Mentoring as a Model of Discipleship in Multigenerational Contexts: Experiences from an African Pentecostal Church." *Pentecostal Education: A Journal of the World Alliance for Pentecostal Theological Education (WAPTE)* 6 (2021) 21–33.

———. "Discipleship and Ordained Ministry in The Church of Pentecost, Ghana." In *Towards a Global Vision of the Church*. Vol. 1, *Explorations on Global Christianity and Ecclesiology*, edited by Cecil M. Robeck Jr., et al., 215–26. Geneva: World Council of Churches, 2022.

CHAPTER 7

Church-State Relations and the Problem of Corruption in Africa

DELA QUAMPAH

Introduction

AFRICA HAS BECOME A force to reckon with in contemporary Christianity, but not in contemporary morality. The rising figures in Christian conversion appear to have made little impact on the endemic nature of corruption on the continent. Though governments are often upbraided for the situation, as they control an enormous portion of national resources and their allocation, it is contested that civil society, including the church, is partly blamable. Although the concept of the separation of powers was introduced in Africa by colonialists, the holistic worldview of the African could not uphold the practice. The church exerts influence in the corridors of political power in Africa because it provides a significant fraction of the socioeconomic infrastructure such as educational and health care institutions.

Society perceives the church as the bastion of morality that should influence state institutions for good governance, transparency, probity, and accountability, but the antigraft impact of the church remains questionable. On occasion, the church itself is accused of simony, misappropriation of resources, and the manipulation of the vulnerable. Although the church in Africa has contributed to reforms by challenging autocratic and abusive regimes to consolidate democracy, allegations of hegemony, power abuse, and corruption continue to dog the church in Africa. The isolated cases of anticorruption initiatives by the church in some African countries is appreciated; nevertheless, a more intentional and rigorous approach would serve society better. The church could therefore engage indirectly in supporting government in the antigraft drive by setting up relevant sponsoring advocacy and public education, and resourcing anticorruption agencies.

Corruption, which is often defined as using public office for personal gain, is a universal human problem. However, its manifestation and intensity vary with the context. Kunhiyop is convinced that "although Africans know that corruption in all its forms is illegal and undesirable, it seems to have a hold on them everywhere they go."[1] The World Economic Forum report of 2018 estimates the global cost of corruption at $2.6 trillion, or 5 percent of the global gross domestic product (GDP), observing that businesses and individuals pay above $1 trillion in bribes annually. A Transparency International report indicates that African countries pay a whopping sum of at least US $50 billion each year in illegal financial transactions. Various reasons are advanced for the prevalence of corruption in Africa, and as the government is the main controller of the nation's resources, it is normally upbraided for either actively or passively promoting graft. Attempts are often made by civil society organizations, such as the church, to hold the government accountable for the judicious use of the nation's wealth. This has serious implications on church-state relations, as the church on the one hand supports the government as a partner in national development, while on the other hand sometimes functions as a critic or an opponent of government policy.

Relations between the church and state in Africa records a checkered narrative, as they fluctuate between the strict observance of the church-state divide and the occasional active intervention of the church in governance. Using the reflective approach, I have examined the interaction of church and state as it relates to responsible and transparent governance in Africa to identify areas of cooperation and conflict. Additionally, I have isolated some of the causal factors of corruption and examined its impact on society. Finally, I have assessed the response of the church to state corruption and suggested ways to enhance the church-state partnership in controlling the canker of corruption and promoting economic development in Africa.

---

1. Kunhiyop, *African Christian Ethics*, 165.

Relationship between the Church and State

Traditionally African societies maintain a holistic approach to life, which brooks no distinction between the sacred and the secular spheres of community life. Kings in Africa, in Mbiti's estimation, are not just political leaders, but they are "mystical and religious heads, the divine symbols of their people's health and welfare."[2] The pervasiveness of African religiosity, therefore, extends spiritual influence to every sphere of communal and personal life.[3] This is evidenced by the numerous taboos attached to chieftaincy, setting high ethical standards for the chief as the moral model of the community.[4] It is therefore asserted that "in both the traditional setting and some contemporary institutions, the challenge of moral excellence is regarded as a benchmark for those in leadership."[5] In the African worldview the religious, political, and socioeconomic spheres of life are in a symbiotic relationship, as they closely interact and have an impact on each other.[6] In such traditional societies, religion was part of the public life and institution. It gave the moral and divine justifications to social and political order of the community; the separation of powers between the state and the church is therefore foreign to African sociocultural norms.

The separation of powers between the religious establishment and the state, and for that matter church and state, was introduced into Africa by European colonial powers that arrived on the continent in the fifteenth century. This led to the separation of the public domain from the private sphere, thus limiting religion and religious practices to the private space.[7] The potential challenge in relegating religion to the private sphere is the undermining of the social roots of morality,[8] as it cannot be denied that divorcing private morality from public morality significantly erodes the virtues of communal responsibility and accountability, which consequently promotes graft. Furthermore, Nsereko suggests that "the modern State does not enjoy the absolute loyalty of the citizen's allegiance compared to the kings of yesterday." And he concludes that the state shares

---

2. Mbiti, *African Religions and Philosophy*, 177.
3. Assimeng, *Social Structure of Ghana*, 130.
4. Akrong, "Religion and Traditional Leadership in Ghana," 200.
5. Quampah, *Good Pastors, Bad Pastors*, 42.
6. Agbiji and Swart, "Religion and Social Transformation in Africa," 2.
7. Ennin, "Religious Institutions in Governance in Africa," 1.
8. Coetzer and Snell, "Practical-Theological Perspective on Corruption," 33.

this loyalty with organized religion or the church.[9] Coetzer and Snell are convinced that the only reason people insist on the separation of religion from governance is for them to indulge in graft:

> When religion is regarded within the public sphere as disruptive, archaic and the suggestion is made that it belongs within the realm of private life, history teaches that it leads to the re-evaluation of the practicality of the separation between state and religion. The primary motivation appears to be corruption in the expenditure of state funds and self-enrichment.[10]

The relationship between the church and state in Africa since postcolonial times has been complex and intricate. And it is debatable to assert that the influence of religion, and for that matter the church, was ever totally separated from the state. To Asamoah-Gyadu, "All over Africa, for example, religion and politics encroach upon each other," and he is convinced that in postcolonial Ghana, "religion and politics have interacted in even more profound ways."[11]

The Church as Partner in Development

The socioeconomic influence of the church in many African states is significant. From the colonial era to post-independence days, churches have sacrificed to complement the government's efforts in providing socioeconomic infrastructure such as schools, hospitals, and orphanages. In 1964, when Zambia became independent from Britain, two-thirds of their secondary schools were run by the Catholic Church, as well as a higher proportion of primary schools.[12] In Ghana, statistics reveal that:

- The Catholic Church has established 1,825 primary schools, 948 junior high schools, 52 senior high schools, 8 teacher training colleges, 1 university, and 45 health institutions.[13]
- The Presbyterian Church of Ghana has 490 nurseries, 973 primary schools, 388 junior high schools, 5 vocational institutions, 25 senior high schools, 5 colleges of education, 1 university, 4 nurses training

---

9. Nsereko, "Religion, the State, and the Law in Africa," 28, 269–87.
10. Coetzer and Snell, "Practical-Theological Perspective on Corruption," 35.
11. Asamoah-Gyadu, "God Bless Our Homeland Ghana," 165.
12. Lungu, "Church, Labour, and the Press in Zambia," 395.
13. Ayaga, "Planning for Church and State," 39.

institutions, 11 primary health care centers, 8 health centers, 4 hospitals, and 13 clinics.[14]

- The Methodist Church has founded 719 kindergartens, 1,017 primary schools, 483 junior high schools, 20 second cycle schools, 22 tertiary schools, 1 university, 2 hospitals, and 20 clinics.[15]
- The Church of Pentecost owns 96 basic schools, 2 senior high schools, 2 skills development centers, 1 vocational training center; 1 university, 3 hospitals, and 5 clinics.[16]

The significant contribution of religious institutions to the socio-economic progress of the nation makes them a formidable force to be reckoned with by governments in many African countries; this position is reinforced by the fact that many of the government officials are products of mission schools. Obviously, good governance and efficient management of national resources would impact the progress of the mission schools and the health facilities, which is one reason the churches express concern about good governance and oppose state corruption. For instance, when in Zambia the government wanted to reform education by excluding religious education from the curriculum and introducing scientific socialism or Marxism, the churches protested, and the then government of President Kenneth Kaunda reviewed the proposal to accommodate the views of the church leaders.[17]

Sociocultural Influence of the Church

The role of moral advocacy by the churches in many African countries is also informed by the sociocultural impact of Christianity. In Lungu's view, "In addition to playing a leading role in the country's education history, the churches had also become the main moulders of socio-cultural values among various tribes in Zambia."[18] Indigenous customs and values have been effectively influenced by a Christian mindset toward institutions such as marriage and family, and in many areas of personal and communal life, Christian principles now overwhelm indigenous

---

14. Presbyterian University–Ghana, "Historical Background."
15. Ghanian Chronicle, "Contribution of the Methodist Church."
16. Church of Pentecost, "Membership Hits Over 4.2 Million."
17. Lungu, "Church, Labour, and the Press in Zambia," 396–97.
18. Lungu, "Church, Labour, and the Press in Zambia," 395.

traditional values. Obviously, the church is supposed to function as the conscience and moral bastion of the nation. And Bansah suggests that the "drive for holistic, accelerated, and sustainable development lies in the use of sound religious teachings and values as a moral force in public life and political discourse."[19]

Besides, Christian institutions on occasion broker peace between feuding state institutions. For instance, the Ghana Catholic Bishops' Conference (GCBC) and the Christian Council of Ghana (CCG) collaborate with the state to address some social and political problems in the country. These Christian bodies have intervened on some occasions to convince striking workers in essential services such as health and education to rescind their decision. For instance, the GCBC and the CCG mediated to restore dialogue between the Ghana Registered Nurses Association and the government when relations between the two bodies came to a head.[20] And the two organizations again spent many hours to broker a truce between the government and striking university teachers.[21]

Governance

It is asserted that governance in most African countries is characterized by neopatrimonialism and clientelism.[22] Neopatrimonialism is a governance approach, where leadership is personalized and executed through a network of clients who are patronized and coerced for blind loyalty.[23] Clientelism is similar to neopatrimonialism and entails a reciprocal relationship wherein a superior's generosity sustains a subordinate, who then mobilizes political support for their patron.[24] In Saah-Dade's opinion, "Clientelism is designed to protect the interest of the ruling elite and prevent clash or uprisings as a political factor."[25] This approach to governance clearly becomes a recipe for corruption and manipulation.

Thus, even established democratic institutions like Parliament are not immune to neopatrimonialism, which erodes accountability and

---

19. Bansah, "Religious and Moral Education," 108.
20. Cited in Gifford, *African Christianity*, 70.
21. Cited in Gifford, *African Christianity*, 70.
22. Ennin, "Religious Institutions in Governance in Africa," 39.
23. Lindberg, "What Accountability Pressures Do MPs in Africa Face?," 117–42.
24. Ennin, "Religious Institutions in Governance in Africa," 39–40.
25. Ennin, "Religious Institutions in Governance in Africa," 39–40.

sound democratization.[26] For instance, Agyeman-Fisher, reports that the Director of Research of the National Development Party (NDP) Dr. Samuel Mensah expressed concern about "the manner chiefs, the clergy and opinion leaders demanded money from political parties during electioneering."[27]

Church Involvement in Public Life

In many African countries, post-independence history has seen much church activity in public life as the clergy, who are relatively well-informed, engage with issues of politics and governance.[28] Scholarly opinions on the trajectory of church and state relations in postcolonial Africa comprise two divergent views. One opinion, which is pessimistic, views the churches as institutions that are patronized by governments to legitimize their leadership, whether covertly or overtly.[29] And Konings further observes that approaches to leadership in the church and state in Africa appear to be similar and symbiotic:

> It has been claimed that church and state leaders in Africa show common interests and sentiments, and form, with other well-positioned social groups such as businessmen, an informal coalition of elites who seek to exercise hegemonic control over society.[30]

Additionally, due to similarities in leadership style, the church can easily liaise with the state to protect and preserve their privileged position in society.[31] It is therefore suggested that since the ideological sources of political and religious leaders are similar, as a result, political leaders have used their power to influence the church and perpetuated poverty and corruption on the continent.[32]

Kudadjie and Aboagye-Mensah are advocates for church participation in politics as they assert, "We ourselves are clear in our mind,

---

26. Ennin, "Religious Institutions in Governance in Africa," 39–40.
27. Agyeman-Fisher, "James Bond of Ghanaian Journalism."
28. Quayesi-Amakye, "Pentecostals and Contemporary Church-State Relations in Ghana," 2–18.
29. Konings, "Church-State Relations in Cameroon's Postcolony," 45–46.
30. Konings, "Church-State Relations in Cameroon's Postcolony," 45–46.
31. Konings, "Church-State Relations in Cameroon's Postcolony," 45–46.
32. Agbiji and Swart, "Religion and Social Transformation in Africa," 1–20.

that the church has a valid case to be involved in the affairs of the state in all aspects including national politics."[33] It is asserted that religious groups, and for that matter the church, constitute the most formidable form of associational life in Africa, with the capacity to speak truth to power.[34] Similarly, Yirenkyi's survey on church-state relations advances two major reasons for church involvement in political process; the first is that the public considers the clergy as a category of people with the capacity to confront the state without the fear of intimidation. Second, the laity think it is an ethical obligation for the church to engage in politics to fulfill its role as the conscience of society and become, as it were, the "voice of the voiceless."[35]

On the other hand, segments of the church fraternity think the church should not participate in politics because, the idea of active church involvement in politics has no biblical support, and they further advise that active partisan politics would only result in the fragmentation of the church. The church therefore encounters a paradoxical situation with its involvement in the affairs of the state. On the one hand, if the clergy expressed concern about governance, they are advised to stick to preaching and stop meddling in politics; on the other hand, if the clergy stayed aloof from politics, they were criticized for being indifferent to the important task of nation-building.[36]

Benefits of the Church in Politics

The more optimistic view of the relations of Christian churches in Africa postcolony appreciates the church as a leading voice in civil society groups that demand accountability of the state. Indeed the churches have demonstrated "capacity to challenge authoritarian regimes, urging for reform, advocating political change and even presiding over change itself."[37] The political struggles in Africa in the 1990s, which Mazrui terms "Africa's second liberation struggle,"[38] offered the Catholic Church and other religious organizations the opportunity to contribute

---

33. Kudadjie and Aboagye-Mensah, *Christian Social Ethics*, 3.
34. Gifford, *African Christianity*.
35. Yirenkyi, "Christian Churches in National Politics," 329.
36. Yirenkyi, "Christian Churches in National Politics," 330.
37. Konings, "Church-State Relations in Cameroon's Postcolony," 46.
38. Mazrui, "Africa since 1935," 725–43.

positively to the struggle for democratic governance.[39] It is suggested for instance that in Ghana, because the church supports good governance, it played a key role in returning the country to the constitutional rule of the Fourth Republic in 1992.[40] To Gifford, the Christian Council of Ghana (CCG) did such a remarkable job in this 1992 democratization process by serving the government with memos, producing and distributing literature, and holding workshops that he concludes "the CCG is among the most impressive Christian Councils in sub-Saharan Africa."[41] Similarly, the Catholic Bishops of Cameroon responded to persistent election malpractices at their 2003 conference by demanding a transformation of the electoral process. They wrote to Parliament to request the composition of an independent electoral commission that will allow the unhindered participation of all political parties.[42]

The Peace Council of Ghana (PCG), which has mediated to resolve conflicts relevant to vote rigging, is appreciated for its significant contribution to the smooth transitions in Ghana's democratization process. This particular Peace Council evolved from the initiative of the Catholic Church in 1995 to restore peace in an intertribal conflict, when it established the Northern Ghana Peace Project which later developed into the Centre for Conflict Transformation and Peace Studies (CECOTAPS). Currently, the following Christian bodies are represented on the PCG: the Catholic Bishops Conference, the Christian Council of Ghana, Ghana Pentecostal and Charismatic Council, and the National Council for Christians and Charismatic Churches.[43]

Defining and Analyzing Corruption

To reiterate, corruption is simply defined as using public office for personal gain; however, the phenomenon is more complex than any single definition can encapsulate. Graft always involves two parties, where one party either entices a potential benefactor with a gift, or someone extorts valuables from a victim for offering them public service. In either case both parties could be branded as corrupt, depending on their response.

---

39. Ennin, "Religious Institutions in Governance in Africa," 3.
40. Norman, "Separation of Church and State."
41. Gifford, *African Christianity*, 71–72.
42. Konings, "Church-State Relations in Cameroon's Postcolony," 58.
43. Awinador-Kanyirige, "Ghana's National Peace Council."

Ndiyo provides a more comprehensive definition of corruption as "the offering, giving, receiving or soliciting, directly or indirectly anything of value to influence improperly the actions of another party."[44]

Oftentimes "corruption" is paired up with "bribery" in the phrase "bribery and corruption," but bribery is just one aspect of the umbrella term "corruption." Corruption, or graft, comprises bribery, fraud, conflict of interest, etc. Myint presents a list of items which constitute corrupt behaviors: "bribery, extortion, fraud, embezzlement, nepotism, cronyism, appropriation of public assets and property for private use, and influence peddling."[45] Kunhiyop thinks, "Corruption also manifests in outright theft, match-fixing, examination fraud, kickbacks, illegal awarding of contracts and the like. In the political sphere it manifests itself in vote rigging, the purchase and sale of votes, and the falsification of election results."[46]

One of the reasons corruption seems to be endemic in Africa is the low level of patriotism and loyalty of the citizens to the state. It is suggested that since colonial state administration—which the Africans inherited—comprised Europeans who were perceived as foreigners plundering our resources, loyalty and allegiance to the imperial governor was at best superficial and at worst hypocritical. Coetzer and Snell opine that "it is fair to conclude that neither loyalty to the state nor any shared sense of identity and belonging had been cultivated by colonizing powers across generations of imperial rule, having experienced government as distant and impersonal."[47]

According to Makumbe[48] and Cochrane,[49] the contemporary upsurge of global consumerism practices, coupled with the destabilization of value systems and moral authority, are promoting corruption in both developed and developing countries. The African cultural practice of giving gifts to influential people is often cited as a sociological factor that perpetuates corruption on the continent. Giving such gifts to traditional rulers who settle litigation in the community often blurs the line

---

44. Ndiyo, *Poverty to Sustainable Development*, 175.
45. Myint, "Corruption," 33–58.
46. Kunhiyop, *African Christian Ethics*, 165.
47. Coetzer and Snell, "Practical-Theological Perspective on Corruption," 34.
48. Makumbe, "Fighting Corruption in the SADC and Sub-Saharan Africa," 1.
49. Cochrane, "Corruption and the Role of Religion in Public Life," 3.

between objective administration of justice and partiality. Thus, conflict of interest becomes indistinct.[50]

To Leite and Weidmann corruption is also attributed to rent-seeking behavior of state and non-state actors, especially in resource rich countries.[51] Auty describes rent-seeking as the practice whereby social groups like unions and businesspeople spend their resources urging governments for special favors instead of working hard to improve their performance.[52] The result is that government officials discriminate in favor of their political cronies. In such cases, state resources are directed to projects that will benefit their cronies or to businesses that serve their personal interest to the neglect of what will benefit the populace. Auty concludes that such a situation makes corruption an illegal obligation, limiting resources available for investment and undermining efficiency.[53] It has been observed that since the public sector is the key player in the economy of many African countries, the effects of political corruption and the misapplication of resources are correspondingly severe.[54]

Effects of Corruption

Undoubtedly, corruption seriously undermines democratization and governance in Africa. Lindberg has insightfully deduced from the Transparency International Corruption Perceptions Index that in some African countries the level of political rights of the citizens corresponds with the level of corruption in those nations.[55] To Zalot, corruption exerts pressure on state coffers because the cost of the bribes and kickbacks would be factored into the pricing and quoting of projects of national interest.[56] Proper planning and quality output in public project execution are compromised, as public and civil servants may be more concerned about their personal benefits from contracts rather than serving the best interest of the public. In the view of His Excellency John Dramani Mahama, an ex-president of Ghana, "Corruption involving state funds amounted

50. Ennin, "Religious Institutions in Governance in Africa," 46.
51. Leite and Weidmann, "Does Mother Nature Corrupt?"
52. Auty, "Resource Curse in Developing Countries," 226.
53. Auty, "Resource Curse in Developing Countries," 207.
54. Werlin, "Consequences of Corruption" 77.
55. Lindberg, "What Accountability Pressures Do MPs in Africa Face," 117–42.
56. Zalot, *Roman Catholic Church and Economic Development in Sub-Saharan Africa*.

to mass murder, as it deprived government of the resources to address the needs of the people, and must not be countenanced."[57]

According to Transparency International,

> Corruption in African countries is hindering economic, political and social development. It is a major barrier to economic growth, good governance, and basic freedom, such as, freedom of speech or citizens' right to hold government to account. More than this, corruption affects the wellbeing of individuals, families and communities.[58]

Combating Corruption

The magnitude of the effect of corruption on developing economies has challenged civil society groups to set up organizations to combat the canker, and although some African governments claim they are fighting corruption, their efforts appear to be superficial. The Political Science Department of the University of Ghana conducted a survey in 2018 which revealed that the most corrupt institutions in Ghana are the Police Service, the Ministries, the Parliament of Ghana, the Presidency of the Republic of Ghana, and Ghana Education Service.[59]

According to Keulder, the *Afrobarometer* surveys in eighteen African countries in late 2019 and early 2020 reveal that a sizeable number of citizens are convinced corruption is on the rise in their countries, but control initiatives by their governments were insignificant. He concludes, "Africans think their governments aren't fighting corruption hard enough."[60] Biggs reports that Ghana, for instance, has lost seven points on the Corruption Perceptions Index (CPI) since 2014, moving from forty-eight in 2014 to forty-one in 2019.[61] Biggs suggests this decline was ascribable to the suspension of twelve high court judges in the wake of allegations of bribery captured in a documentary by an investigative journalist,[62] and the murder of Ahmed Hussein-Suale in early 2019 for his work in investigative journalism.

57. Ghanaian Chronicle, "Corruption as Mass Murder . . ."
58. Transparency International, "Citizens Speak Out about Corruption."
59. MyNewsGH, "Police, Presidency, Parliament."
60. Keulder, "Africans Think Their Governments Aren't Fighting Corruption."
61. Biggs, "Ghana Suspends Seven High Court Judges."
62. Biggs, "Ghana Suspends Seven High Court Judges."

The most prominent antigraft agencies are therefore nongovernment setups, such as Transparency International, whose Corruption Perceptions Index has proved to be one of the most reliable data sources on corruption globally. Additionally, the World Bank Group works with the public and private sectors and civil society to prevent corruption and provide solutions to the impact of graft, and also works toward improving attitudes and values required to curb corruption.[63]

Some positive developments in the battle against corruption in Ghana have been identified by Transparency International (TI) "In 2017, the Office of Special Prosecutors was established, which has the power to investigate and prosecute cases of corruption. In 2019, a right to information bill was also passed." And in the estimation of TI, "These efforts, combined with the enhanced performance of the Auditor General's Office, offer hope for improvement."[64]

Some of the most effective anticorruption endeavors in Africa were executed by the daring Ghanaian investigative journalist Anas Aremeyaw, whose Tiger Eye PI project exposed corruption in the Ghana Football Association, resulting in the life suspension of its president, Mr. Kwesi Nyantakyi.[65] The second project undertaken by Aremeyaw, titled "Ghana in the Eyes of God," revealed judicial corruption in Ghana in September 2015 and led to the suspension of twelve high court judges for taking bribes.[66]

The Church and Corruption

It is often contested that the much touted expansion of Christianity in Africa has not necessarily translated into improved morality, as there appears to be a mismatch between the Christian percentage of the population of African nations and their Corruption Perceptions Index (CPI) score. This is revealed in the table below, where the positions of selected African countries in the 2020 CPI of Transparency International are indicated. The total number of countries compared for the ranking was 180.

---

63. Yirenkyi, "Combating Corruption."
64. Transparency International, "Where Are Africa's Billions?"
65. Patterson, "Betraying the Game."
66. Agyeman-Fisher, "James Bond of Ghanaian Journalism."

Ghana, Zambia, Nigeria, Gabon, and Zimbabwe

COUNTRY	SCORE	RANK/ POSITION	CHRISTIAN POPULATION	NATIONAL POPULATION
GHANA	43	75	71.2%	24,658,823
ZAMBIA	33	117	95.5%	18,383,955
NIGERIA	25	149	46.3%	158,503,197
GABON	30	129	80%	1,800,000
ZIMBABWE	24	157	86%	12,700,000

The Old Testament prophets were vociferous in their condemnation of graft, economic manipulation, and oppression of the poor, as for instance the following passage from Amos 8:3–5 reveals:

> "In that day," declares the Sovereign Lord, "the songs in the temple will turn to wailing. Many, many bodies—flung everywhere! Silence!" Hear this, you who trample the needy and do away with the poor of the land, saying, "When will the New Moon be over that we may sell grain, and the Sabbath be ended that we may market wheat?" skimping the measure, boosting the price and cheating with dishonest scales, buying the poor with silver and the needy for a pair of sandals, selling even the sweepings with the wheat.

The New Testament records in Acts 8:18 Simon's attempt to induce Peter with money for the ability of Holy Spirit impartation, and since then, the practice of paying bribes for church offices has been labeled "Simony." In an interview with Mbanyane Mhango, he contends that "church-state relations and the problem of corruption is a theological issue," and the church should examine it from God's perspective by classifying it as grossly immoral (2 Pet 1:4).[67] Mhango is convinced that the church "can play a huge role in rooting out the loathsome problem of corruption in Africa."[68]

Drawing inspiration from Jesus' salt and light metaphor (Matt 5:13–16), Mhango proposes the "salt and light model" as a theological response to the canker of corruption in Africa. In his view, salt and light

---

67. Mhango, personal interview, November 5, 2021. Mbanyane Mhango is the president of Pentecost Biblical Seminary in Wayne, New Jersey.

68. Mhango, personal interview.

have self-evident characteristics that are difficult to manipulate or misapply. He therefore contends, "salt is used to preserve food or materials from decay whereas light is used to illumine. Salt and light remind the church's telos is to fight against corruption or moral decay in society in as much as it shines in darkness."[69]

The Christian church has since the time of Martin Luther been often accused of maleficence. To Dummet, some of the corrupt practices that characterize the Catholic Church include "simony in the papal court, or pluralist bishops, or priests with concubines and children"[70] and today we can add "pedophile priests" to the list; practices which undermine the moral authority of the church. To Dario's mind, "The socio-economic and political system itself appears to be built on corruption and thrives in it. Even the Church and other religious organizations are themselves not completely free from corruption."[71]

Scholarly opinions on the response of the church to corruption are diverse and varied. One segment of observers thinks the church itself is corrupt and has no moral right to criticize state corruption. And in certain instances, it is observed that Christians are themselves actively participating in corruption, hence they are regarded as a part of the problem, with no solution to offer. For example, to Dairo's mind the neo-Pentecostal churches practice "sacred corruption" by the privatization and commercialization of Christianity.[72] Anderson and Tayviah have observed that religion—which is supposed to have a positive impact on the morality of Ghanaians—appears to be failing in that respect.[73] To them, "the Christianity expressed by majority of the Pentecostal/Charismatic and Neo-prophetic churches in Ghana today focuses primarily on business, the search for niche, hegemony, materialism and wealth creation."[74]

It appears politics and Christianity make strange bedfellows, as efforts by some African leaders to, as it were, "Christianize" their nations only resulted in a travesty. The Zambian example, where President Frederick Chiluba declared Zambia a Christian nation only for the nation to experience an escalation of corruption and mismanagement, is a case in point. According to Kunda,

69. Mhango, personal interview.
70. Dummet, "How Corrupt Is the Church?," 619.
71. Dairo, "Privatization and Commercialization," 243.
72. Dairo, "Privatization and Commercialization," 139.
73. Anderson and Tayviah, "Corruption in the Wake of High Religiosity," 113.
74. Anderson and Tayviah, "Corruption in the Wake of High Religiosity," 117.

Eight years after President Frederick Chiluba officially declared Zambia to be a "Christian nation," the declaration is largely meaningless, according to church leaders and officials. On December 30, 1991, Zambia's newly installed president declared this small, southern African nation a Christian state, despite opposition from some Christian and Muslim leaders. Prominent church officials interviewed by Ecumenical News International (ENI) this week said that the declaration had become increasingly "hollow," as Zambia faces mounting social, political and economic problems, including widespread corruption.[75]

In July 2007 the media in Zimbabwe exposed the adulterous acts of Pius Ncube, the Catholic archbishop of Bulawayo, who was a fierce critic of President Robert Mugabe. According to McGreal, "Archbishop Ncube has denounced Zimbabwe's president as a murderer, mobilized the country's Catholic bishops to issue a pastoral letter likening the struggle against the present regime to the liberation war against white rule."[76] All of which offers a good illustration of the idiom, "those who live in glass houses do not throw stones."

A case from Sierra Leone involving a top government official who claims to be a Christian is reported by the news outlet *This Is Africa*: "Fatmata Edna Kargbo, the State Chief of Protocol Officer [sic] to Sierra Leone's President Julius Maada Bio, has been placed on leave after giving testimony of how God favored her at the church of Prophet T. B. Joshua's Synagogue Church of All Nations. Kargbo, a career diplomat and civil servant is being investigated by Sierra Leone's Anticorruption Commission. Questions continue to be raised on the source of her wealth. There has been outrage in the country after her testimony on how she was living in a single room apartment and now resides in a luxurious house."[77] Another example occurred in Ghana in May 2011, when Bishop Vaglas Kanco, General Overseer of the Vineyard Chapel International of Ghana, was jailed for eighteen months for duping a British woman out of £120,000 under the pretext of praying to "sanctify the check" she had issued to someone.[78]

In other instances, political leaders manipulate division in the Christian community to their own advantage. For instance, Agbiji and

75. Kunda, "Eight Years after Zambia Became a Christian Nation," para. 1.
76. McGreal, "Secret Camera in Archbishop's 'Love Nest,'" para. 3.
77. Mbamalu, "Sierra Leone," para. 2.
78. Bokpe, "Clergy under Fire," 1, 3.

Swart point out that whilst "ZANU-PF and its president then, Robert Mugabe, were routinely intimidating and attacking religious leaders such as Archbishop Pius Ncube for criticizing the bad policies of the government, Mugabe sought to woo other Christians. For his part, the leader of this sect [African Apostolic Faith] Madzibaba Nzira announced a prophecy that Mugabe was the divinely anointed king of Zimbabwe and that no person could dare to challenge him."[79]

A more appreciative view of the role of the church in social transformation insists that the church has the moral right, and it has indeed proven to be one of the few institutions in Africa that could boldly challenge and criticize the secular state effectively. Konings opines, "The other view of the socio-political role of mainline Christian churches in the African postcolony tends to be more optimistic. It regards churches as the masthead of civil society, pointing to their proven capacity to challenge authoritarian regimes, urging reform, advocating socio-political change and even presiding over change itself."[80] Konings supports his position by indicating that the National Episcopal Conference of Cameroon (NECC) responded to electoral malpractices in 2003 by submitting a draft proposal to amend electoral laws to Parliament in 2006.[81]

A lot of Christian leaders and Christian organizations have shown concern about corruption in Africa and have made some efforts to help bring the menace under control. For instance, a communiqué issued by the Catholic Bishops' Conference of Nigeria is reported by *The Premium Times*:

> The Catholic Bishops' Conference of Nigeria (CBCN) on Friday in Abuja expressed worry over the lack of accountability and transparency at all levels of government in Nigeria, saying the situation is responsible for the massive poverty and insecurity in the country. The bishops said by failing to uphold probity in the deployment of public resources, President Goodluck Jonathan, state governors and other public office holders should be regarded as human rights abusers.[82]

According to Jere, the Church of Central Africa Presbyterian (CCAP) in Malawi took the following measures to address corruption in the country:

---

79. Agbiji and Swart, *Religion and Social Transformation in Africa*, 7.
80. Konings, "Church-State Relations in Cameroon's Postcolony," 46.
81. Konings, "Church-State Relations in Cameroon's Postcolony," 58.
82. Abdulmalik, "Catholic Bishops Blast Jonathan, Governors," paras. 1–2.

i. The CCAP Synod has issued anticorruption communiqués condemning and rebuking the state for rampant corruption.

ii. The CCAP Synod has carried out inclusive advocacy and anticorruption sensitization campaigns with the goal of promoting awareness on the evils of corruption and how the church and congregants could refrain from the malpractice.

iii. The CCAP Synod, through the church and society, has participated in various national anticorruption forums, workshops, and conferences, and structured short courses in promoting good governance.

iv. The CCAP Synod has collaborated and partnered with both local and international agencies in anticorruption activism, including Dan-Church Aid, Malawi Economic Justice Network (MEJN), and Human Rights Consultative Committee (HRCC).[83]

In another instance, the Secretary General of The Christian Council of Zambia (CCZ) condemned the high incidence of corruption, which has been perpetrated even by Christians, and requested effective measures to control this vice.[84] The CCZ Secretary General Suzanne Matale is convinced the focus of Christianity is predominantly ethical, therefore there is contradiction between the percentage of Christians and the high levels of corruption in Zambia, saying, "The levels of corruption in Zambia are very saddening. If more than 75 percent of the Zambian population is Christian and we are forced to hold more than one Church service in our churches, it means that we have more people going to churches and that even the congregants are involved in these corrupt practices."[85]

Besides issuing communiqués, tangible efforts have been made by some churches and Christian groups to address the problem of corruption in Africa. A model strategy occurred in Cameroon, where the diocese of Bafoussam launched an anticorruption campaign which took place July 3–5, 2019, when the Africa Faith and Justice Network (AFJN) and the Justice and Peace Commission of the diocese of Bafoussam (JPCDB) organized a study of the problem of corruption in two primary schools, two high schools, and two health centers. The focus was to determine the facts about the existence of corruption and assess its impact on individuals, institutions, and society. Furthermore, the study was to help

83. Jere, "Public Role of the Church in Anti-Corruption," 5.
84. Sakala, "Corruption Rocks Christians."
85. Sakala, "Corruption Rocks Christians," para. 4.

identify the culprits and the victims, and ultimately determine solutions. Okure is convinced "the survey revealed that corruption was rampant in institutions run by the Diocese of Bafoussam, therefore a Zero Corruption campaign was launched, as the diocese decided that 'doing nothing about corruption was no longer an option.'"[86]

The leadership of the diocese therefore engaged all stakeholders in workshops where they dialogued to ascertain the causes and solutions to the problem of corruption in the diocese. As a result, they crafted a statement of commitment, part of which read:

> After a careful analysis and prayerful reflection on the ills of corruption and how it has negatively impacted us, how it has permeated our educational system, our health care, our social, our political and our family lives, and indeed every fabric of our relations and transactions, we realize that we cannot allow this to continue. This is leading us to doom, and to destruction. . . . We therefore commit ourselves to be agents of change. We commit ourselves to fight corruption in our institutions, using our knowledge and talents, and all the means available to us, so as to restore justice and sanity to our families, to our communities and to our country.[87]

Beyond the statement of commitment, they made resolutions, some of which are captured below, and the members of the diocese were determined to translate them into action:

- "Severe sanctions against all who are found guilty
- Awareness of the consequences of corruption, and a call to resist corruption in all its manifestations and by all means
- Hire and promote workers based on competencies
- Conduct regular audit of institutions
- Offer fair wages and where possible give benefits to workers as part of improving their life conditions. For example, free tuition for one or two children of school staff or free healthcare for a spouse and children of a health center staff
- Publish service fees to empower customers so that they can ask questions when they suspect overcharging or bribes are demanded

---

86. Bahati and Okure, "ACT against Corruption."
87. Bahati and Okure, "ACT against Corruption," 3.

- Create a hotline and a suggestion box for those who wish to lodge a complaint."[88]

Another model emerged in the Church of Pentecost, an influential denomination in Ghana, where, under the leadership of Apostle Eric Nyamekye, a project dubbed Vision 2023 was instituted and themed "Possessing the Nations," with the focus on influencing every sphere of society with the values and principles of the Kingdom.[89] And one dimension of the project was to constitute workers' guilds which comprised professional fraternities committed to the following ideals, among many others:

i. "Members of the various Professional Groups should demonstrate the highest degree of enviable attributes such as honesty, integrity, discipline and humane perspective at all times.

ii. Members should adhere strictly to their professional Code of Ethics and not yield to monetary and material enticements that will dent or soil their image and by extension the image of The Church of Pentecost."

All these notwithstanding, the collective anticorruption efforts of Christian communities in Africa appear to be imperceptible. Balia observes, "African faith communities are growing rapidly, notably Christian churches, but their presence in the ranks of those fighting against corruption must yet be strengthened."[90] The following approaches are therefore suggested as further responses of the church in its antigraft engagement:

The first and most effective contribution the church can make to help minimize corruption in Africa is to educate the populace on the destructive impact of the canker. Anderson and Tayviah are convinced,

> Pentecostal/Charismatic Christianity should focus on awakening and shaping the moral conscience and consciousness and morality of Ghanaians on corrupt practices; instead of fostering unhealthy religious competition, commercialization of religious products and services, search for hegemony, and the display of supernatural power and wealth in Ghana's religious market.[91]

88. Bahati and Okure, "ACT against Corruption," 7.
89. Church of Pentecost, *Vision 2023*.
90. Balia, "African Faith Communities Can Fight Corruption Too."
91. Anderson and Tayviah, "Corruption in the Wake of High Religiosity in Ghana," 118.

For instance, the churches can collaborate and set up a research outfit to collect, collate, and disseminate data on corruption.

Second, the church could advocate for the institution of policies and practices that would curtail corruption. For instance, in Ghana, the church can lobby Parliament to promulgate the law for spot-fines for traffic offenses to eliminate the practice of bribing the police for traffic offenses.

Third, the church can consider offering moral and financial support to anticorruption campaigners and organizations such as Transparency International and investigative journalists. So far, it appears Ghanaian Christian leaders are reticent with their public support for Anas Aremeyaw, whose antigraft investigative journalism has won him international accolades. Probably the Ghanaian churches are hesitant to praise him because the rumor has it that his next target is the church. Little wonder the only public endorsement Anas has received from a Christian leader is the one offered by Prophet Bismarck Amoah, leader of Bohye Prayer and Revival Centre, calling on him to investigate the church.[92] Undoubtedly, resourcing anticorruption agencies financially would significantly serve the interest of the church and the wider society.

Fourth, it is suggested that the church should develop theological content that responds constructively to the problem of graft. According to Balia, corruption and Governance Program head for the Institute for Security Studies (ISS) in Cape Town, "In the case of Christians, we notice in particular the rise of Pentecostal-type churches spreading a prosperity-type gospel that encourages wealth creation among its members. While the coincidence might not be so obvious to some, African churches should be challenged like all institutions in society to examine the moral assumptions of their belief systems or mission statements that may help or hinder the spread of corruption."[93]

Conclusion

Evidently church-state relations in Africa have registered a checkered narrative that varies from constructive and cooperative engagements to unhealthy and sometimes belligerent confrontations. However, since corruption is identified as a factor that significantly hampers economic

---

92. Ghana Web, "Prophet Begs Anas to Investigate Men of God."
93. Balia, "African Faith Communities Can Fight Corruption Too."

progress and undermines the development agenda of any nation, the need for a concerted approach of government and civil society groups to tackle the problem of corruption in Africa cannot be over emphasized. Although the church may not have the mandate to directly engage in the fight against corruption, it can synergize with antigraft agencies, offering support and resourcing such agencies to help minimize, if not exterminate, corruption.

Bibliography

Abdulmalik, Abdulrahman. "Catholic Bishops Blast Jonathan, Governors, over Massive Corruption, Rights Abuses." *Premium Times*, November 2, 2012. https://www.premiumtimesng.com/news/121632-catholic-bishops-blast-jonathan-governors-over-massive-corruption-rights-abuses.html.

Agbiji, Obaji M., and Ignatius Swart. "Religion and Social Transformation in Africa: A Critical and Appreciative Perspective." *Scriptura* 114 (2015) 1–20.

Agyeman-Fisher, Abena. "James Bond of Ghanaian Journalism Debuts 'Ghana in the Eyes of God' Targeting Judges Who Take Bribes." *Face 2 Face Africa*, September 24, 2015. https://face2faceafrica.com/article/ghana-in-the-eyes-of-god.

Akrong, Abraham A. "Religion and Traditional Leadership in Ghana." In *Chieftaincy in Ghana: Culture, Governance, and Development*, edited by I. K. Odotei, and A. K. Awedoba, 193–212. Culture and Development Series 1. Accra: Sub-Saharan, 2006.

Anderson, George, Jr., and Margaret Makafui Tayviah. "Corruption in the Wake of High Religiosity in Ghana: Questioning the Possibility." *E-Journal of Religious and Theological Studies* 5 (2019) 112–20.

Asamoah-Gyadu, J. K. "'God Bless Our Homeland Ghana': Religion and Politics in a Post-Colonial African State." In *Trajectories of Religion in Africa: Essays in Honour of John S. Pobee*, edited by Cephas N. Omenyo and Eric B. Arum, 165–84. Leiden: Brill, 2013.

Assimeng, Max. *Social Structure of Ghana: A Study in Persistence and Change*. Accra: Ghana Publishing Cooperation, 2007.

Auty, R. M. "The Resource Curse in Developing Countries." In *The Companion to Development Studies*, edited by V. Desai and R. B. Potter, 224–29. London: Arnold, 2002.

Awinador-Kanyirige, William. A. "Ghana's National Peace Council." *Global Centre for the Responsibility to Protect Policy Brief*, August 21, 2014. http://s156658.gridserver.com/media/files/awinador-ghana-national-peace-council.pdf.

Ayaga, A. M. "Planning for Church and State Educational Leaders' Partnerships in Ghana: An Examination of Perceptions Impacting Relationships." *Educational Planning* 22 (2015) 37–62

Bahati, Jacques, and Aniedi Okure. "ACT against Corruption: A Project That Mobilized Church Leaders from Christian and Muslim Communities to Fight Corruption and Promote Just Governance in Cameroon." *Africa Faith and Justice Network*, August 1, 2019. https://afjn.org/act-against-corruption-a-project-to-mobilize-church-leaders-from-christian-and-muslim-communities-to-fight-corruption-and-promote-just-governance-in-cameroon/.

Balia, Daryl. "African Faith Communities Can Fight Corruption Too." *Institute for Security Studies*, December 12, 2011. https://issafrica.org/iss-today/african-faith-communities-can-fight-corruption-too.

Bansah, Confidence Worlanyo. "Religious and Moral Education: A Panacea for Nation Building in Post-Colonial Ghana." *Ghana Journal of Religion and Theology* 8 (2018) 97–110.

Biggs, Matthew M. "Ghana Suspends Seven High Court Judges over Corruption Allegations." *Reuter*, October 5, 2015.

Bokpe, Seth J. "Clergy under Fire for Acts Unbecoming of Men of God." *Daily Graphic*, August 15, 2011.

Church of Pentecost. "The Church of Pentecost Membership Hits Over 4.2 Million." May 3, 2020. https://thecophq.org/the-church-of-pentecost-membership-hits-over-4-2-million-2/.

Cochrane, James R. "Corruption and the Role of Religion in Public Life." In *Fighting Corruption: South African Perspectives*, edited by Stanislaus Sangweni and Daryl Balia, 1–17. Pretoria: UNISA, 1999.

Coetzer, Wentzel, and Lutricia E. Snell. "A Practical-Theological Perspective on Corruption: Towards a Solution-Based Approach in Practice." *Acta Theologica* 33 (2013) 29–53.

Dairo, A. O. "Privatization and Commercialization of Christian Messages in Nigeria." In *Creativity and Change in Nigerian Christianity*, edited by David O. Ogungbile and Akintunde E. Akinade, 193–200. Lagos: Malthouse, 2010.

———. "Sacred Corruption in Sacred Places: The Case of Some Selected Neo-Pentecostal Churches in Nigeria." *Arts in Humanities Open Access Journal* 4 (2020) 241–44.

Dummet, M. "How Corrupt Is the Church?" *Blackfriars* 46 (1965) 619–28. https://doi.org/10.1111/j.1741-2005.1965.tb07502.x.

Ennin, Paul Saa-Dade. "The Role of Religious Institutions in Governance in Africa: The Case of the Ghana Catholic Bishops' Conference." MPhil thesis, University of Ghana, 2015.

Ghana Web. "Today in 2018: Prophet Begs Anas to Investigate Men of God." June 15, 2020. https://www.ghanaweb.com/GhanaHomePage/NewsArchive/Today-in-2018-Prophet-begs-Anas-to-investigate-men-of-God-980407#google_vignette.

Ghanian Chronicle. "Contribution of the Methodist Church to Education in Ghana." *Modern Ghana*, November 15, 2020. https://www.modernghana.com/news/304531/contribution-of-the-methodist-church-to-education.html.

———. "Corruption as Mass Murder . . ." January 9, 2014. https://www.modernghana.com/news/512805/corruption-as-mass-murder-.html.

Gifford, Paul. *African Christianity: Its Public Role*. London: Hurst & Company, 1998.

Jere, Qeko. "Public Role of the Church in Anti-Corruption: An Assessment of the CCAP Livingstonia Synod in Malawi from a Kenosis Perspective." *Verbum et Ecclesia* 39 (2018). https://doi.org/10.4102/ve.v39i1.1776.

Keulder, Christiaan. "Africans Think Their Governments Aren't Fighting Corruption Hard Enough." *The Washington Post*, January 29, 2021. https://www.washingtonpost.com/politics/2021/01/29/africans-think-their-governments-arent-fighting-corruption-hard-enough/.

Konings, Piet. "Church-State Relations in Cameroon's Postcolony: The Case of the Roman Catholic Church." *Journal for the Study of Religion* 20 (2007) 45–64.

Kudadjie Joshua, and Robert K. Aboagye-Mensah. *Christian Social Ethics*. Accra: Asempa, 1991.

Kunda, Anthony. "Eight Years after Zambia Became a Christian Nation the Title Is Not Convincing." *Christianity Today*, January 1, 2000. https://www.christianitytoday.com/ct/2000/januaryweb-only/24.0b.html.

Kunhiyop, Samuel J. *African Christian Ethics*. Grand Rapids: Zondervan, 2008.

Leite, Carlos, and Jens Weidmann. "Does Mother Nature Corrupt? Natural Resources, Corruption, and Economic Growth." IMF Working Paper 99/85. https://www.imf.org/external/pubs/ft/wp/1999/wp9985.pdf.

Lindberg, Staffan. "What Accountability Pressures Do MPs in Africa Face and How Do They Respond? Evidence from Ghana." *Journal of Modern African Studies* 48 (2010) 117–42.

Lungu, Gatian F. "The Church, Labour, and the Press in Zambia: The Role of Critical Observers in a One-Party State." *Oxford Journals: African Affairs* 85 (1986) 385–419.

Makumbe, John Mw. "Fighting Corruption in the SADC and Sub-Saharan Africa." Paper presented at the 9th International Corruption Conference, KwaZulu-Natal, 1999.

Mazrui, Ali. "Africa since 1935." In *General History of Africa*, edited by C. Wondji, 8:725–43. London: Heinemann, 1992.

Mbamalu, Socrates. "Sierra Leone: Corruption and the Church in Africa, a Cosy Mess." *This Is Africa*, September 2, 2019. https://thisisafrica.me/politics-and-society/sierra-leone-corruption-and-the-church-in-africa-a-cosy-mess/

McGreal, Chris. "How Secret Camera in Archbishop's 'Love Nest' Silenced Vocal Mugabe Critic." *The Guardian*, July 20, 2007. https://www.theguardian.com/world/2007/jul/21/zimbabwe.chrismcgreal.

Mibiti, John S. *African Religions and Philosophy*. 2nd ed. Oxford: Heineman, 2006.

Myint-U, Athi. "Corruption: Causes, Consequences." *Asia-Pacific Development Journal* 7 (2000) 33–58.

MyNewsGH. "Police, Presidency, Parliament, GES Most Corrupt Institutions in Ghana—UG Survey." January 13, 2019. https://www.mynewsgh.com/police-presidency-parliament-ges-most-corrupt-institutions-in-ghana-ug-survey/.

Ndiyo, Ndem A. *Poverty to Sustainable Development: A Community-Based Approach*. Calabar: University of Calabar Press, 2008.

Norman, Ishmael D. "Separation of Church and State: A Study of Accra City's Use of Public Buildings and Schools for Religious Services." *Advances in Applied Sociology* 3 (2013) 282–88. http://dx.doi.org/10.4236/aasoci.2013.

Nsereko, Daniel D. "Religion, the State, and the Law in Africa." *Journal of Church and State* 28 (1986) 269–87.

Patterson, Collin. "Betraying the Game." BBC production, 2018. https://insighttwi.com/films /betrayingthegame.

Pobee, John .S. *Religion and Politics in Ghana*. Accra: Asempa, 1991.

Presbyterian University–Ghana. "Historical Background." https://www.presbyuniversity.edu.gh/site/about-pucg/.

Quampah, Dela. *Good Pastors, Bad Pastors: Pentecostal Ministerial Ethics in Ghana*. Eugene, OR: Wipf & Stock, 2015.

Quayesi-Amakye, Joseph. "Pentecostals and Contemporary Church-State Relations in Ghana." *Journal of Church and State* 57 (2015) 640–57.

Sakala, Tiyese. "Corruption Rocks Christians." *Lusaka Times*, July 20, 2008. https://www.lusakatimes.com/2008/07/20/corruption-rocks-churches/.

Transparency International. "Citizens Speak about Corruption in Africa." July 11, 2019. https://www.transparency.org/en/news/citizens-speak-out-about-corruption-in-africa.

———. "Corruption Perceptions Index Reveals Widespread Corruption Is Weakening COVID-19 Response, Threatening Global Recovery." January 28, 2021. https://www.transparency.org/en/press/2020-corruption-perceptions-index-reveals-widespread-corruption-is-weakening-covid-19-response-threatening-global-recovery.

———. "CPI 2019: Sub-Saharan Africa." January 23, 2020. https://www.transparency.org/en/news/cpi-2019-sub-saharan-africa.

———. "Where Are Africa's Billions?" July 11, 2019. https://www.transparency.org/en/news/where-are-africas-billions.

United Nations. "Global Cost of Corruption at Least 5 Percent of World Gross Domestic Product, Secretary-General Tells Security Council, Citing World Economic Forum Data." September 10, 2018. https://www.un.org/press/en/2018/sc13493.doc.htm.

Werlin, Herbert H. "The Consequences of Corruption: The Ghanaian Experience" *Political Science Quarterly* 88 (1973) 71–85.

Yirenkyi, Kwasi. "Combating Corruption." *The World Bank*, October 19, 2021. https://www.worldbank.org/en/topic/governance/brief/anti-corruption.

———. "The Role of Christian Churches in National Politics: Reflections from Laity and Clergy in Ghana." *Sociology of Religion* 61 (2000) 325–38.

Zalot, Jozef D. *The Roman Catholic Church and Economic Development in Sub-Saharan Africa*. Lanham, MD: University Press of America, 2002.

CHAPTER 8

A Response to Dela Quampah's "Church-State Relations and the Problem of Corruption in Africa"

Mbanyane Mhango

Introduction

THIS PAPER IS A response to Dela Quampah's chapter on church-state relations and the problem of corruption in Africa. In this response I will identify and discuss salient issues he raises, albeit without necessarily following the structure of Quampah's paper. In addition, I will offer suggestions for strengthening Quampah's case for church-state relations and curbing corruption in Africa. Further, I will provide biblical references and direct quotes wherever I deem appropriate.

Summary

To begin, Quampah asserts that corruption exists in all societies, institutions, and nations, albeit in varying degrees. Similarly, he notes that different types of interventions are employed to curb corruption. Among other things, watchdogs, nongovernmental organizations, periodic reports, legal frameworks, etc., play a role in the fight against corruption. But Quampah's paper focuses on the role of church-state relations in combating corruption. The church's role is partly rooted in its mission to raise citizens with high ethical values that are antithetical to corruption.

Next, Quampah contends that the church contributes to socioeconomic development by establishing schools from kindergarten to university. This way, the church helps in raising an informed populace and in creating employment opportunities. Thus, church-state relations are consequential in fostering socioeconomic development and in fighting against corruption. The case for the church's role in fighting corruption finds strength in the African holistic or nondualist worldview. Africans do not dichotomize public and private, or sacred and secular spheres of life.

Further, Quampah stresses the importance of church-state relations in combating corruption. Religious and political leaders enjoy enormous influence in Africa. For this reason, church-state relations weaken when religious and political leaders engage in corruption. While politicians buy votes from an impoverished populace, prosperity gospel preachers accumulate wealth at the expense of the poor. Thus, the public often accuses such unscrupulous politicians and prosperity gospel preachers of perpetuating corruption. Public trust in religious and political leaders is often low.

By employing suspect hermeneutics, prosperity gospel preachers promise health and wealth to those individuals who sow financial seeds into their ministry. Such clergy undermine the church's credibility in the fight against corruption. Similarly, some politicians often accumulate too much wealth within a relatively short time after they assume public office. This rightly breeds suspicion of corruption and thus undermines public trust in political leaders and religious leaders in Africa.

Moreover, Quampah points out, corruption costs nations several millions of US dollars that could have significantly contributed to socioeconomic growth in Africa. Drawing from reports by watchdogs, investigative journalists, etc., Quampah concludes that corruption pushes people into abject poverty. This is despite the relatively impressive growth of Christianity in Africa.

Quampah provides statistical data that show corruption levels in Africa overshadow the impressive numerical growth of Christians. However, he offers hope in that some churches are reportedly taking steps to tackle corruption. Generally, churches take different approaches to contribute to the fight against corruption in Africa. Whereas some churches operate in isolation, others seek partnership with churches, parachurch organizations, and even nongovernmental organizations.

Quampah recommends a concerted approach between states and civil society groups. Precisely, he argues that synergizing with antigraft agencies could curb corruption and spark socioeconomic growth in Africa. Church-state relations cannot curb corruption without robust institutions. Additionally, the rule of law that privileges democratic values in society plays a role.

Hereafter, I offer a critique of Quampah's paper and make suggestions for the purpose of strengthening the case for seeking church-state relations toward fighting corruption in Africa.

Critique and Recommendations

The poor bear the brunt of corruption in any society. As the church awaits Christ's return, it should endeavor to teach believers to resist corruption. This way, believers reflect the *imago Dei* (the image of God) and carry out the *missio Dei* (the mission of God). Corruption is antithetical to the *imago Dei* and *missio Dei*. Since Christianity is a relationship with Christ in whom dwells the Godhead bodily (Col 2:9), corruption is an affront to God's redemptive mission. The fight against corruption links to ecclesial mission until Christ's reign in the eschatological kingdom.

Seen in this light, partnering with states to fight corruption has theological merit. But the church's role in fighting corruption is not independent of other factors, including the rule of law, democratic values, and nongovernmental institutions. In keeping with this, nations that espouse freedom of expression and encourage public participation in the fight against corruption are in a better place to expose corrupt practices. Democratic systems of government open up space for the church and the public to expose and denounce corruption. However, it is relatively difficult for the church to do so in largely pseudo-democratic regimes in Africa.

In a continent known for military coups and unstable governments, the church can play a crucial role in fostering political stability and socioeconomic development. The poor in society, who depend on state-funded services, largely experience the effects of corruption. As "corruption is the misuse of public office or a position of authority for private material or social gain at the expense of other people,"[1] it is antithetical to political

---

1. Kruger and De Klerk, *Corruption*, 97.

leadership that cares for common good. It is partly in this light that the church's mission and a democratic government's mission resonate.

Because "corruption takes place as an intentional, illegal, and immoral act of behaviour with the purpose of gaining some kind of advantage,"[2] it can engender mistrust, instability, and even hatred among people in a society. Of course, corruption occurs in different ways. Quampah lists some convincing measures toward curbing corrupt behavior. Although there is no universal formula for curbing corruption, Quampah's proposals have potential to restrain corrupt practices.

According to Munyai, measures that can help in fighting corruption, especially in public spaces, are: ending the culture of impunity; protecting whistleblowers; promoting transparency in financial transactions and accountability in state or government administration; encouraging selflessness and ethical standards; and promoting state cooperation in exchange for resources and intelligence in detection, monitoring, investigation, and prosecution of corruption.[3] In particular, promoting selflessness and ethical standards resonates with Christ's teaching. This seems a fitting area for the church to make a significant contribution in the fight against corruption.

Next, limited access to information on corruption renders it difficult to gauge its impact in society. Reported levels of corruption in Africa are often speculative and ought to be taken with a hermeneutic of suspicion. Data that underlies reports of corrupt practices in Africa often relates to macro-level corruption. Quampah shows that corruption in Africa occurs daily at traffic checkpoints, markets, hospitals, government offices, small businesses, etc. It is micro-level corruption that shapes and informs and funds macro-level corruption. By macro-level corruption, I mean large-scale abuse of public funds or office that occurs at corporate or government levels.

Here it is worth citing Jesus, who said, "Whoever is faithful in a very little is faithful also in much; and whoever is dishonest in a very little is dishonest also in much" (Luke 16:10). Jesus offers us an important insight about human nature and behavior. Biblical anthropology reckons that humans wrestle with sinful nature (Rom 3:23; 5:12). Salvation changes people at the heart or soul level (2 Cor 5:17). This change within manifests in one's behavior, in faithfulness or honesty. It is this

---

2. Kruger and De Klerk, *Corruption*, 97.
3. Munyai, *Overcoming the Corruption Conundrum in Africa*, 202.

author's conviction that micro-level corruption is the root of macro-level corruption. Success at curbing micro-level corruption is key to success at curbing macro-level corruption.

Holding accountable those that engage in corruption certainly sends a strong message in a society. But to curb micro-level corruption requires fundamental change at a foundational level. Christian anthropology seems to suggest that those convinced about the sinfulness of micro-level corruption assume that macro-level corruption is also sinful. Put another way, faithfulness or integrity develops in adversity, not in prosperity (Heb 5:8). Corrupt behavior reflects a lack of faithfulness or integrity. The church has a responsibility to train members into Christlikeness.

Interestingly, Western nations, often considered as secular societies, have better rankings on the Corruption Perceptions Index (CPI) than African nations where Christianity is the predominant religion. For example, as an African immigrant to the United States, I am often impressed by the virtue of faithfulness or integrity that people born or raised in the US generally exhibit. It seems that children learn the virtue of faithfulness or integrity early, especially through education systems.

Thus it is not surprising that the micro-level corruption that occurs frequently at traffic checkpoints, businesses, government offices, etc., is not as prevalent in the US as in Africa. An emphasis upon integrity early in children's education helps in raising law-abiding citizens and yields a society with a low level of corruption. The significance of training children in integrity has biblical roots: "Train children in the right way, and when old, they will not stray" (Prov 22:6). Integrity links the fruit of the Spirit (Gal 5:22–23) to anthropology, or pneumatology to biblical anthropology.

Even secular organizations in Western countries seem to value integrity. This partly explains why societies in the largely secular West experience relatively low corruption. To be sure, democratic governments, legal frameworks, financial institutions, etc., contribute to low levels of corruption in the West compared to high levels of corruption in Africa. However, the church's central teaching of Christlikeness, which privileges truthfulness or integrity in life because of Christ the truth incarnate, is the primary foundation for believers to abhor corruption.

Whereas some link high corruption levels to high poverty levels, such a view contradicts Christ's teaching on faithfulness (Luke 16:10). For Christ, faithfulness does not depend upon whether one has little (poverty/adversity) or plenty (abundance/prosperity). In the secular

West, pursuit of truth seems to motivate people toward integrity. The pursuit of truth is a foundation of education[4] that gives rise to a society with low corruption. If the pursuit of truth were central in all church-state relations, it could help curb corruption levels in Africa.

The pursuit of Christlikeness is the goal of believers and the church's central teaching. Notably, the pursuit of Christlikeness relates to the pursuit of faithfulness or truthfulness. This is because Christ is the truth incarnate, truth made flesh, or embodiment of truth (John 1: 14). This transformation into Christlikeness attracts states to partner with the church to fight corruption. In addition, the church's Christlike character gives it the moral authority to mediate in a society.

Quampah reports that the church in Africa has played a role in mediation during political tensions, especially related to presidential elections. Although this is commendable, some church leaders take advantage of political upheavals for personal gain. Precisely, such leaders take sides with a political party that advances their personal interest instead of offering objective counsel, thus promoting rather than curbing corruption in society. The church should have a clear, impartial posture if state-church relations will help curb corruption.

Next, Quampah rightly notes that some churches do not take a stand against politicians engaged in corrupt practices. Such a posture of silence in the face of rampant corruption betrays the church's calling to speak truth to power. Meanwhile, mainline churches, like the Roman Catholic Church, usually take the lead in holding officials that perpetuate corruption accountable. Thus, Africans generally perceive mainline churches as credible in fighting against corruption. Consequently, they often take seriously recommendations of mainline churches compared to smaller churches.

However, this does not suggest that politicians or the public always perceive mainline church leaders as corruption-free. Quampah cites the case of a Roman Catholic bishop in Zimbabwe who called President Robert Mugabe a murderer, even though the bishop was involved in an adulterous affair. This exemplifies the need for a symbiotic relationship between the church and state in fighting against corruption. Thus, the prophetic church that speaks truth to power in matters related to corruption should endeavor to be above reproach (Col 1:22; 1 Tim 3:2; 15).

---

4. Caldecott, *Beauty for Truth's Sake*, 32.

Prophetic Church and Corruption

The prophetic church must boldly declare the sinfulness of corruption. In so doing, it fulfills the call to speak truth to power. If the church is to speak truth to power as Peter did to the Sanhedrin (Acts 5:29),[5] it must live in accord with God's word. The church's audacity to speak truth to power depends on her moral authority. The prophetic church is a gatekeeper of morality in society. The church's influence in society cannot exceed the level of trust the society holds toward her. Laver argues that "the prophetic role of the church and its leaders is intimately related to, and affected by, their own credibility and integrity."[6] To win public trust, the church must not assume her moral credibility and integrity but instead demonstrate these in concrete ways.

Those who speak truth to power should expect to be unpopular when they challenge the corruption of power and prestige.[7] Like Peter and the early church, they should not be concerned about being unpopular but rejoice that they are found worthy to suffer dishonor for Christ's sake (Acts 5:41). As corruption disproportionately affects the poor, the fight against corrupt behavior appeals to Christ's heart. Seen in this light, the church should view corruption through a Christological lens. Since all believers are prophets,[8] they should boldly expose and denounce corruption. Significantly, all believers should adhere to high ethical standards in all their dealings in society. Unfortunately, prosperity gospel preachers make it difficult for the church to combat corruption.

Prosperity Gospel and Corruption

Prosperity gospel, also known as health and wealth, undermines the church's credibility in that the behavior of prosperity gospel preachers weakens the church's moral authority to fight corruption. Since the church has no universal magisterial or central teaching office, it is relatively difficult to halt the threat of prosperity gospel preachers. Precisely, they undermine the church's moral authority to condemn public officials that engage in corruption. Some posit that the prevalence of

---

5. Johnson, *Prophetic Jesus*, 186.
6. Laver, "Christian Faith and the Church," 60.
7. Johnson, *Prophetic Jesus*, 186.
8. Stronstad, *Prophethood of All Believers*.

corruption in society implies a failure of religion to serve as a social control.[9] It is hard to challenge this view.

Religious beliefs influence adherents' behavior. Generally, religions encourage adherents to abide by civil law and to desist from illegal activities that benefit individuals at the expense of the common good. Kramer and Shariff observe, "The emphasis that religions place on honesty is part of a larger association between morality and religion—an association that has, in part, led many to make assumptions about the morality of religious people."[10] Notably, they contend that "thinking about God in the moment increases honest behavior."[11] Thus, it seems reasonable to expect religious people to be less inclined to engage in corrupt behavior. Similarly, one would expect governing officials to value partnership with faith leaders in the fight against corruption.

To begin, there is no universally accepted definition of corruption. Nonetheless, phrases like "abuse of power" or "abuse of public office," "misappropriating public funds," "money laundering," "bribery," "favoritism," "nepotism," etc., are often associated with corruption. Similarly, it is also difficult to pinpoint the exact correlation between corruption and religious affiliation. This is partly because corrupt behavior relates to other factors like social, cultural, economic, and political ideology. Therefore, what constitutes or is regarded as corrupt behavior may differ from society to society. A person's perception or attitude toward corruption is not dependent upon religiosity alone.

Against this backdrop, Treisman notes that countries with high Protestant populations reported lower levels of perceived corruption, while a high proportion of Muslim, Catholic, and Anglican citizens yielded no significant effect.[12] Quampah's paper did not explore the effect of non-Christian religions on corrupt behavior. Notwithstanding this, church traditions espouse different doctrines and practices. Hence, it is difficult to measure an individual's religiosity. Religiosity cannot be measured based on the number of church services one attends. Rather, true religiosity extends beyond places of worship and manifests in how believers interact with others in public.

---

9. Yusuf, *Corruption and Religious Institutions*.
10. Prooijen and Lange, *Cheating, Corruption, and Concealment*, 233.
11. Prooijen and Lange, *Cheating, Corruption, and Concealment*, 233.
12. Allaby, *Corruption and the Church*, 13.

Governing Authorities and Corruption

Paul states that believers ought to be subject to governing authorities as God ordains the latter for the former's sake (Rom 13:1–2). This implies that God has interest in how authorities govern their people. Importantly, God tasks governing authorities to restrain evil behavior and to reward good behavior and expects governing authorities to punish perpetrators of evil without favoritism. Additionally, the Pauline text suggests that governing authorities are natural partners with the church and faith-based institutions in advocating for the common good in all society.

Quampah stresses the importance of this symbiotic relationship in curbing corruption, where governing authorities and the church have distinct but related tasks. Precisely, the task of developing laws belongs to the governing authorities, whereas the church serves as a watchdog to ensure laws are just and applied fairly. Believers engaged in active politics can play a crucial role in helping develop laws that are morally right and biblically grounded.

Despite the claim, "When the righteous rule, people rejoice; when the wicked rule, people mourn" (Prov 29:2), some Christians in public office are accused of engaging in corruption. In fact, other Christians leave office after losing public trust, or with questionable integrity. To be sure, some ascended to presidency of their nation after campaigning to root out corruption. These include but are not limited to Frederick Chiluba of Zambia, Goodluck Jonathan of Nigeria, Pierre Nkurunziza of Burundi, John Magufuli of Tanzania, and Lazarus Chakwera of Malawi, the latter of whom is an ordained minister and former president of Malawi Assemblies of God. Not all the individuals listed above lived up to the promise to lead with integrity and curb corruption. Public office poses a huge temptation even to Christians. As Quampah argues, believers cannot effectively resist corrupt behavior if they don't have an adequate view of the church's role.

Theological Remedy for Corruption

Quampah proposes that the church should develop theological content to respond to the problem of corruption. The church's posture toward governing officials that engage in corrupt behavior relates to believers' understanding of the nature of the church. Precisely, the church is of divine origin and rightly called the body of Christ (Matt 16:18; 1 Cor 12:27). It follows that the church ought to view corruption as sin just as God does (Lev 22:25; 2 Pet 1:4, 2:19). The church should abhor corruption and make her stance clear when dealing with governing officials.

Because the church originates in Christ, her response to corruption should be dictated by the latter's character. It flows from this thinking that a Christ-centered view of the church offers a theological remedy to the problem of corruption. For example, the view of the church as salt and light[13] is a polemic against all forms of corruption. The biblical metaphors of salt and light (Matt 5:13–14) highlight believers' indispensability and utility in dealings with others in society.

Salt and light have self-evident traits that can hardly be misconstrued or manipulated. Salt is used to preserve food or materials from decay whereas light is used to illuminate in darkness. Salt and light remind the church of its telos to fight against corruption or moral decay. "The Church must act as the 'voice of the voiceless' when others remain silent."[14] Through Christ-like words and deeds, believers expose corruption (Matt 5:16). Thus, conceiving the church as salt and light can provide a theological remedy to the problem of corruption in Africa.

Furthermore, the Pauline conception of the church as the body of Christ and the foundation of truth (1 Tim 3:15) is another polemic against corruption. This is partly because corruption thrives wherever and whenever people suppress truth. In keeping with this, Christ identifies himself as the truth (John 14:6). The description of the church as the ground and pillar of truth compels Christ's followers to uphold truthfulness in all their dealings. The church's mandate to fight against corruption is not dependent upon societal or cultural norms. After all, societal or cultural norms may even change over time and may not always resonate with biblical truth. However, the church's fight against corruption continues until the eschaton.

Eschatological View of Corruption

An eschatological view of corruption is helpful for highlighting the value of church-state relations. This eschatological view can augment Quampah's recommendations for curbing the problem of corruption in Africa. Corruption is a mark of the devil's followers while integrity is

---

13. Ilo, et al., *Church as Salt and Light*.
14. Kruger and De Klerk, *Corruption*, 111.

a mark of Christ's followers (John 8:44; 1 Tim. 3:15). The church that awaits Christ's return will endeavor to eschew all forms of corrupt behavior and will expose the same wherever it occurs.

Though the wicked may seem to prosper, God will hold them accountable in the day of judgment (Hos 9:9; Rev 14:5). Instead of asking the Lord why the wicked prosper (Jer 5:28; 12:1), the church should stress that it is better to have a little through righteousness than much through injustice (Prov 16:8). The corrupt may escape punishment in this world, but the judge of all humans will hold them accountable at the end of time (Matt 16:26; Mark 8:36). Thus, Peter is convinced that it is better for believers to suffer for doing good (1 Pet 3:17). Paul adds that this world's sufferings are incomparable to the glory of God's eschatological kingdom (Rom 8:18).

Despite strong church-state relations, the church cannot completely root out the problem of corruption on this side of the eschaton. It is only in God's realized or eschatological kingdom that corruption will not exist. The church lives in the eschatological tension between the already and the not yet. Nonetheless, the church should persist in exposing and denouncing corruption. Quampah rightly posits that the church must use all resources at her disposal to fight corruption. Believers who expose and denounce corruption are sacraments of the eschatological kingdom.[15]

Conclusion

Quampah's paper draws the reader's attention to the problem of corruption in Africa. Further, he demonstrates the need for church-state relations to mitigate the effects of corruption on socioeconomic development. Quampah cites churches that operate schools and mediate in political conflicts especially related to presidential elections. Precisely, he shares examples of churches in Africa that exposed and denounced corrupt practices in their respective nations.

Lastly, Quampah reminds the church to lead by example by exposing corruption in sacred spaces. The clergy should not seek church-state relations because of personal gain. Notably, the church should teach believers to espouse integrity as citizens of God's eschatological kingdom.

---

15. Mhango, *Manifesting the Spirit*.

Bibliography

Allaby, Martin. *Corruption and the Church: Voices from the Global South.* Oxford: Regnum, 2018.

Caldecott, Stratford. *Beauty for Truth's Sake: The Re-Enchantment of Education.* Grand Rapids: Brazos, 2009.

Ilo, Stan Chu, et al., eds. *Church as Salt and Light: Path to an African Ecclesiology of Abundant Life.* Eugene, OR: Pickwick, 2011.

Johnson, Luke Timothy. *Prophetic Jesus, Prophetic Church: The Challenge of Luke-Acts to Contemporary Christians.* Grand Rapids: Eerdmans, 2011.

Kruger, Ferdinand, and Barend Jacobus De Klerk. *Corruption in South Africa's Liberal Democratic Context: Equipping Christian Leaders and Communities for Their Role in Countering Corruption.* Durbanville: AOSIS, 2016.

Laver, Roberto. "The Christian Faith and the Church: Challenges and Opportunities in Promoting a Culture of Public Integrity." In *Deliver Us from Evil: Corruption and the Challenge to the Christian Faith and Church,* 51–64. Minneapolis: Fortress, 2018.

Mhango, Mbanyane. *Manifesting the Spirit: Believers as Sacraments.* Eugene, OR: Resource, 2020.

Munyai, Anzanilufuno. *Overcoming the Corruption Conundrum in Africa: A Socio-Legal Perspective.* Newcastle-upon-Tyne: Cambridge Scholars, 2020.

Prooijen, Jan-Willem van, and Paul A. M. van Lange. *Cheating, Corruption, and Concealment: The Roots of Dishonesty.* Cambridge: Cambridge University Press, 2016.

Stronstad, Roger. *The Prophethood of All Believers: A Study in Luke's Charismatic Theology.* Cleveland, TN: CPT, 2010.

Yusuf, Bilkisu, *Corruption and Religious Institutions: The Score Board, in Corruption, Accountability, and Transparency for Sustainable Development.* Ota: ALF, 2003.

CHAPTER 9

A Pentecostal Response to Home and Urban Mission in Africa

VINCENT ANANE DENTEH

Introduction

IN THE PAST, MISSION work in Africa mostly centred on rural communities, where most of the population lived. But today the trend is changing as a result of urbanization. Urbanization (or rural-urban migration) occurs when the population of a nation tends to drift more heavily to the urban centres and the cities than rural areas. This presentation seeks to discuss the urgency of urban mission today considering the rapid population growth in urban centres. In simple terms, we are looking at ways by which we can fulfill the *missio Dei* in the inner cities of the world. The urgency to focus on urban mission emanates from the fact that there are various kinds of "unreached people groups" in the inner cities or urban centres—more than some rural communities.

In this paper, the biblical antecedents of urban mission, as well as the models and strategies adopted by the early church in the light of urban mission, will be highlighted. God has always been concerned about the salvation of the cities as could be seen in his mission through Jonah to the city of Nineveh and his judgement of the cities of Sodom and Gomorrah. By these two examples, it is felicitous to state that it is not out of place to make urban mission a major tradition of our missionary expedition in this century. The numerous references to the city of Jerusalem, even to the extent that there is a new Jerusalem being prepared by God for believers to spend eternity, affirms this claim.

This paper, therefore, intends to use The Church of Pentecost's Home and Urban Mission model in Ghana as a case study. The megachurch concept of some Pentecostal and Charismatic churches in the inner cities will also be examined to give a broader perspective of urban mission already being practiced by various churches across the globe.

Demographic Realities of Urbanization and Its Effects on Mission

According to Mutavhatsindi, "the word 'urban' refers to that which pertains to or characterizes cities in distinction from rural areas" and it is created over a long period as large numbers of people settle in a particular community.[1] Anderson states that "the world population at the end of the first millennium after the birth of Christ was 275 million, but has today grown into billions."[2] For the first time in human history, more than half of the world's population lives in cities and urban centers. The number is expected to rise to about five billion by the year 2030, particularly in Africa and Asia.[3] Barrett and Johnson estimate that by 2025, the number of urban dwellers will be around 4,611,677,000.[4] According to them, metropolises with populations of over one hundred thousand people will increase from 4,200 in 2002 to 6,500 in 2025, while mega cities with over one million inhabitants will increase from 420 to 650 in the same period.

Sadly, about 1.5 billion in major cities will be urban slum dwellers by the year 2025. However, one striking thing about this trend is that the world's traditionally largest urban conglomerations such as Tokyo, Mumbai, Lagos, and Dhaka are being challenged by emerging cities, mainly from Africa. According to Jenkins, by the middle of the twenty-first century, many African cities will become so densely populated that they will rival the traditionally largest urban centers.[5] This will see the percentage of Africans in urban centers increasing to 63 percent by 2050, against the current proportion of around 40 percent.

1. Mutavhatsindi, "Church Planting in the South African Urban Context," 12.
2. Anderson, *Biographical Dictionary of Christian Missions*, 32.
3. United Nations Population Fund, *Report 2007*.
4. Barrett and Johnson, "Annual Table of World Religions."
5. Jenkins, *Next Christendom*.

The Significance of Urban Mission

1. The high concentration of people in urban centers makes it an imperative task for the church to minister to urban folks.
2. The upsurge of all kinds of ungodly ideologies and worldviews in urban centers make the gospel an urgent need for urban folks.
3. The fallen state of Christianity and values and principles of the kingdom of God in some urban cities across the world makes it a new mission field. For example, in the Western world, huge church buildings and places of worship in urban cities have now become architectural designs with either no one worshiping in those buildings or having just a handful of worshippers that occasionally come to worship there.

The Call for Paradigm Shifts in Mission

Like any other social development, this trend also comes with difficult situations—economically, scientifically, politically, and religiously. According to Samuel and Sugden, "healthcare, housing, education, and employment"[6] are major issues affecting urban settlers. For the gospel to be very relevant to urban dwellers, the church must modify its missional praxis and strategies to address these needs. Despite significant efforts made by mission practitioners over the past twenty years, a universally recognized model has not yet been established, and missiologists continue to find it difficult to create a standardized model for urban mission work because of the complex nature of urban settings.[7] The difficulty some urban mission practitioners have been facing, according to Engen, is their inability to deal with the whole system of the city. At times, those involved in micro-ministry are able to deal with a few individuals in the city and their needs, "but they are often burning out in the process, in part because they are not dealing with the entire system."

Another challenge arises with those aiming at the entire system, making them conduct macro-studies into the characteristics of the city. These people are normally concerned with conducting studies in "sociology, anthropology, economics, politics, and religion in the city," with the aim of finding a standard missiological model or strategy for urban mission,

6. Vinay and Sugden, *Mission as Transformation*, 87.
7. Engen and Tiersma, *Seeking a Theology for Urban Mission*.

but they also face various challenges as that of the micro-ministry system. While these problems continue to confront the standard planning of urban mission, it is in the right place to posit that urban mission has become a very significant mission field that should heed the attention of all Christians. To expand God's kingdom in urban centers, the church must understand thoroughly the dynamics of urban evangelism and discipleship. Mission in the urban setting should therefore be a crucial approach for missionary activities in dealing with this situation because the challenges in Africa and Asia are already enormous.

Urbanization has increased (and continues to increase) the rate of poverty, housing problems, high cost of living, poor sanitation, weather pollution, population explosion, and all kinds of crimes. It has also led to a decrease in the rural population, plunging most rural areas into extremely excruciating poverty. These developments also leave their toll on the church and the work of mission as a whole. There is a possibility that many of those people who come to Christ in rural areas may backslide from their Christian faith when they get to the cities and are confronted suddenly with various kinds of challenges unless they are immediately tracked and introduced to a church.

The Model of Urban Mission in the Early Church

It has been established in this discussion that urban mission is a new mission field today due to urbanization. However, both the concept and practice of urban mission have been in existence since the beginning of Christianity; the Bible is replete with God's plan for people in the cities. According to Engen, the entire ministry of Jesus can be observed from the perspective of his ministry in Jerusalem,[8] where he rode a donkey on his triumphal entry to the city, cried over the city's destruction, and was put on trial by the Jewish authorities. His presence, encounter, and concern for Jerusalem presuppose a model of the urban mission established for the church to follow. Commenting on Jesus' expressions about Jerusalem, Engen writes, "When I hear those words about Jerusalem, I hear the deep pain of an urban missionary"[9] who wanted an urban city to embrace the gospel. In addition to this dimension of Jesus' ministry is that of the apostle Paul.

8. Engen and Tiersma, *Seeking a Theology for Urban Mission*.
9. Engen and Tiersma, *Seeking a Theology for Urban Mission*, 243.

Focus on Paul's Strategy

A critical analysis of Paul's ministry indicates that he embarked on urban mission. Pierson avers, "The early Church followed an urban strategy"[10] and Paul's main focus was to evangelize the cities or urban centers. Paul ministered in cities such as Thessalonica, Corinth, Ephesus, and Rome. For example, during his first missionary journey he ministered in Cyprus, as well as the cities of Salamis, Paphos, and Antioch of Pisidia, while some of the cities in which he ministered during his second missionary trip were Philippi, Athens, Phrygia, and Galatia. He ministered at Antioch, Ephesus, and Corinth during his third missionary trip. There are various reasons associated with Paul's mission strategy. For Boyd, Paul's strategy of establishing churches in urban communities may not have been an intentional approach; rather, his focus on Jewish communities might have produced it. He explains that the Jews in the Diaspora were predominantly into business and liked living in the urban centers.

In contrast to Boyd's statement, Ugo argues that Paul was intentional and strategic about his ministry to urban centers. He used this approach to convert people in the cities and then train and send them to preach in other communities where he could not preach the gospel.[11] He knew that the cities were very strategic to his reaching out to other satellite communities. Another reason for Paul's choice of the cities, as Ugo observes, is the realization that many social problems and evil activities abound in the cities.[12] They were also strategic for church planting and church growth, considering their huge populations. It could also be inferred that churches in the city would have sufficient human and material resources to be self-reliant in their activities without depending on him or external support for growth. Also, "Paul might have realized that many of the cities were not well evangelized, hence focused on breaking new ground."[13]

Paul was so strategic in his missionary career that the list given here cannot exhaust his strategies in mission. His missional strategy and missiological approach were so holistic that they covered every sphere of the religious, social, and political landscape of the Greco-Roman world. Rajendran attests to this claim thus:

---

10. Jenkins, *Next Christendom*, 47.
11. Ashford, *Theology and Practice of Mission*.
12. Ugo, *St. Paul's Church Planting Strategies*, 4.
13. Senior and Stuhlmueller, *Biblical Foundations for Mission*, 184.

> The holistic perspective of Paul's mission strategy has many aspects such as metropolises mission strategy, follow up work, use of local people, contextualization, self-support, hard work, encouraging, edifying and teamwork strategy, all these aspects come under the umbrella of Paul's holistic perspective mission strategy.[14]

Contrary to the argument of some scholars that Paul did not have any missional strategy, our discussion so far indicates that Paul had a good missional strategy and a Christ-centered message as his theology of mission. He neither conducted his mission haphazardly nor ran without a message. It has been observed that Paul's encounter with Jesus on the way to Damascus—his conversion experience—formed the basis of his Christology and the urgency for mission work. Today, some Christians have adopted the preaching of their personal achievements at the expense of focusing their messages on Christ as Paul did. He allowed Christ to take the center stage of his missionary career, resulting in the planting of many churches across Asia and Europe. The Christocentric ministry of Paul, his passion for cross-cultural mission, and his strategy of discipleship among people he felt could spread the gospel rapidly to other regions are vital for mission practitioners today.

The Church of Pentecost Model: Special Ministry for People Groups in Urban Centers

The premise on which this discussion is based has been demonstrated by The Church of Pentecost (CoP) in Ghana. Having seen the need for urban mission, the CoP has established a special ministry known as Home and Urban Missions (HUM). The CoP is of the view that establishing HUM "has become necessary because for a very long time, many churches and mission agencies across the globe have embarked on selective evangelism in which the majority of people groups are neglected"[15] or have not been adequately evangelized. If this is the case, then it is a huge responsibility for the entire Christian community across the globe to identify the various people groups in their urban centers and then develop pragmatic approaches and missional strategies to minister to them.

---

14. Rajendran, "Paul's Mission Strategy," 5.
15. Home and Urban Missions, *Training Manual*, 11–12.

The use of the term "people groups" in this sense refers to "groups of individuals, families and clans who share a common language and ethnic identity" or "an ethnolinguistic group with a common self-identity that is shared by the various members"[16] in a specific geographic context. Some examples could be the Chinese living in Paris or Lagos, the Somalis in Johannesburg, the Albanians in Kiev, the Turks in Hamburg, or the Fulani in Ghana, among others. At times, even in the same nation certain people groups leave their rural communities to settle in urban centers and form a nucleus societyoutside their places of origin.

Reaching Out to the Unreached People Groups as Urban Mission

Among the various people groups in the urban centers are the "unreached people groups." "These groups of people are ethnolinguistic groups that have either a very small number of Christians or have no indigenous Christian community with adequate material and immaterial resources in their own environment without depending on external assistance for their activities."[17] These kinds of people are spread across the nations, and they live in the same communities where our churches are scattered. But to what extent do our churches give them attention? Kwafo asserts, "Every country across the globe, whether developed or under-developed, has expatriates or foreigners, unreached people groups, urban poor and the marginalized."[18] Ghana Evangelism Commission states that "the best way to reach the 'unreached people groups' is the use of their mother tongue in communicating the gospel to them."[19]

It is, therefore, the best missional strategy to get Christian resources such as Bibles, Bible study materials, and audio resources to them in their local languages. Kwafo argues that most churches are so localized or self-centered that they do not pay adequate attention to the various people groups in the urban centers. The Christian church must intentionally, strategically, and consciously seek to plant churches with a special mission that is in consonance with the style of worship of specific people groups in the urban centers. The caveat, however, is that while planting ethnolinguistic churches is a good missional strategy, care must be taken

---

16. International Mission Board, "What Is a People Group?," para. 1.
17. Ghana Evangelism Commission, *Unreached People Groups in Ghana*, 4.
18. Home and Urban Missions, *Training Manual*, 13.
19. Ghana Evangelism Commission, *Unreached People Groups in Ghana*, 4.

to manage those churches very well to avoid them drifting into ethnocentric pressure groups in the mother church. When the missional intent of planting those churches is not properly established and defined, it may give some people an opportunity to form a social activist movement that may exacerbate the already racial and social tensions affecting both the church and society in various places across the globe.

Apart from mission among the various people groups, the identifiable areas of urban mission are numerous and can be a very complex mission field. Missiologists have identified schools, hospitals, prisons, and marketplaces as some of the key "mission fields" within urban centers. Some churches even have mission to politicians (parliamentarians, mayors, etc.), and industrial workers because there are specific challenges relating to professionals in urban centers. Ministry to persons with disabilities, drug addicts, and commercial sex workers are all emerging mission fields that must be explored. The general inference from this section, however, is that urban centers are big mission fields that need to be taken over. As mission fields, the church needs specially trained missionaries who are well equipped and passionate for urban mission. It is not every person or minister of the gospel that can be very effective in this mission field.

Urban Church Planting as Mission

Urban church planting is an urgent assignment for the church today, even though the act of implementing it is very challenging. The concept of urban church planting can be well understood in the context of how various urban and city councils seek to create new districts, municipalities, and "communes" to meet the demand for increasing population and expansion of their cities. City authorities often embark on various approaches by appointing new officials to take charge of the newly created administrative centers. Mission practitioners ought to understand that disciple-making and church planting are very important aspects of mission work. As we propagate the gospel, the Holy Spirit would convict the hearts of people, leading to their conversion to Christianity. As soon as they are converted, missionaries should ensure that these converts are brought together to form a new assembly and disciple them properly to be true followers of Jesus Christ.

Some urban mission practitioners have recommended home cells or house churches as an effective strategy in urban church planting. For them, such groups are where new Christians can be given the needed attention in terms of intentional discipleship, counseling, and addressing their personal challenges. When the home cells are well coordinated in the city, Christians can be well discipled to become a viable Christian community that can also affect their neighborhood with the gospel. Despite the positive aspects of planting house churches in the urban setting, Engen thinks such Christian groups do not generally have "missional intention to be God's agents of the transformation of the city itself."[20] Although Engen immediately recognizes his statement as a generalization, I think it is good to inform urban mission practitioners that such a situation may occur, and they should therefore be conscious of it and factor it into their discipleship programs.

Urban church planters should try to identify the social needs of urban dwellers and find ways and means of addressing those challenges. For example, how would the church handle its members who have just converted from drug addiction or commercial sex work? What about those members with disabilities, and the abject poor people? These are all indications that urban mission must be a well-organized ministry with a deep sense of kingdom-mindedness in the light of the Great Commission. Urban mission is not a "hit-and-run" or "one-time" type of mission work, but one that requires the church to be very meticulous and consistent with its missional strategy to make it very sustainable. When the church has a relevant missional strategy for addressing the needs of urban dwellers, it makes the process of planting churches among them easy.

A Missiological Approach for Urban Mission

As has been stated earlier in this section, urban Missiology is still in its gestation period, and the church needs to continue to "search for a theology of mission" that gives us a new perspective "for our city, informs our activism, guides our networking, and energizes our hope for the transformation of our city."[21] The church needs a missiological approach to urban mission, ensuring that the gospel is preached to non-Christian urban dwellers in a very relevant way, while at the same time tracking

---

20. Engen and Tiersma, *Seeking a Theology for Urban Mission*, 247.
21. Engen and Tiersma, *Seeking a Theology for Urban Mission*, 248.

the movement of migrant Christians from rural areas and elsewhere so that their faith is not consumed by urban challenges. The missiological framework should consider nine key issues:

1. How to evangelize non-Christians in urban communities to win them for Christ and plant churches in urban centers.
2. How to establish small cells in urban centers and use them as disciple-making centers in urban settings.
3. How to track Christian migrants from rural areas or other places to the urban centers.
4. How to restore backsliders in the urban centers to their faith.
5. How to establish churches in migrant communities or refugee camps in the urban centers.
6. How to establish churches that are Bible-based and reflect the true image of Christ without being confused by the multi-religious activities in the urban centers.
7. How to minister to urban slum areas and establish churches in those areas as special places for mission work.
8. How to use social ministry as a missional strategy to sustain the church in urban centers, and also to appeal to prospective converts in Christ.
9. How to break new ground in urban areas without "stealing" another church are members, simply dividing an existing church to form a new one, or rebelling against a mother church to form a new church with the breakaway members. The whole concept of church planting must be biblically oriented just as the apostles evangelized non-Christians and brought them to Christ. The process must begin with non-Christians rather than those who are already "kingdom citizens."[22] Here, the concept of the fresh expressions of the church in mission is vital.

Given the numerous challenges in urban centers, achieving these nine objectives is not an easy task, but with the relevant missiological framework and church planting strategies, the church can make significant strides. The missiological framework should also consider the

---

22. Ashford, *Theology and Practice of Mission*, 203.

numerous social and scientific problems facing urban dwellers and address those problems from a missiological viewpoint.

Urban mission really needs new evangelistic and missional approaches because the social settings of urban dwellers differ in so many ways from life in the countryside. Gilliland's assertion can help us to take action in this regard: "Protestant churches must shed their parochial mindset derived from their small-town origins and begin to think in terms of the city as a whole."[23] Urban dwellers do not necessarily consider their residential neighborhood as the primary locus of their identity as we have in the rural areas. They tend to prefer living in an enclave environment, so reaching out to them with the gospel calls for various approaches that are relevant in twenty-first-century mission—most of which have been discussed in this book.

The Megachurch Concept as a Strategy in Urban Mission

In recent times, the establishment of megachurches has taken centre stage in many ministries, but its advantages and disadvantages need to be examined. In cases where a particular church is very new to a country, the establishment of a megachurch can serve as a grand entry into that society. However, in the context of contemporary urban church planting, the megachurch is gradually posing a difficult situation to the home cells and local assemblies.

There are implications for overemphasizing the establishment of the megachurches; it can affect the disciple-making process of the church and pose a challenge to efforts to track backsliders. While we do not intend to object to the megachurch concept because it has some advantages in certain communities, we recommend that the church should pattern its disciple-making processes on the home cell and Bible study programs, and the establishment of local assemblies in urban centers. "Mission-planted" congregations for special people such as the deaf and dumb as well as the blind should also be established.

The church may also target people in urban subcultures or certain special groups such as Rastafarians, prostitutes, petty traders, artisans, drivers, and drug addicts. For example, in The Church of Pentecost (the church to which I belong), there is a special ministry for persons with disabilities who are being assisted by specially trained ministers. There is

---

23. Gilliland, *World among Us*, 249.

a need to specifically train missionaries or ministers for particular subcultures to enhance the reach of the gospel to such people. The church needs to critically examine areas of special needs in mission and adopt appropriate missional strategies and concepts to address those needs. This can only be achieved if the church is not ignorant of critical contemporary developments in Christian mission that need a response.

The overriding point is that urban mission is crucial for contemporary mission work, more than in the past, and the church today should factor it into its missional approaches. It is also a highly demanding mission enterprise which needs committed ministers and missionaries with adequate knowledge about contemporary issues, as well as those who have adequate skills in church planting. It is time- and energy-consuming mission work, involving huge amounts of money and other resources. Ministers and missionaries being considered for urban mission ought to be people who are seasoned leaders and who understand the conceptual framework of both urbanization and postmodern epistemology as they relate to Christian ministry. In other words, they must understand the culture of urbanization and other phenomena relating to globalization (as the sons of Issachar understood their times in 1 Chr 12:39) before they can achieve much in urban mission. For example, there are three categories of urban dwellers: One is the extremely poor people who cannot afford food, shelter, and clothing. Then there are the middle-class people who are neither very poor nor very rich. And finally there are those who are extremely and fabulously rich.

It must be reiterated that a well-structured urban ministry ought to consider the social and spiritual challenges of these people and confront them with the gospel in a manner that can win them for Christ. However, this mission is very challenging and needs a pragmatic approach by the church as well as its ministers. To enhance our approach and avoid the situation of living in today's city with yesterday's mindset, we ought to conduct empirical research (with multiple methodologies) into this phenomenon in our communities, then come up with the appropriate recommendations that can help the church to know which missional strategy to adopt. The social stratifications and the scientific problems of various cities differ significantly, even in the same nation. Thus, we cannot make many recommendations here, but we can say that the church needs a scientific view of the cultural settings of the urban centers. Therefore, empirical research should be conducted in the various cities of particular nations and the findings brought together for the church to develop a standard missiological framework for its mission in the urban centers.

The urban centers as complex systems with various units need missionaries who have the capacity to integrate all the units into God's redemptive plan. Urban cities are so complex that the church may not adequately understand their social and spiritual developments. This requires the church to conduct research using relevant methodologies that will be able to unearth empirical findings that can inform the *missio Dei* discourse in the church. There are various kinds of research approaches to choose from, including case study, impact studies, evaluative research, longitudinal research, observational research, transformative research, and explanatory research. These research types are just a few examples to guide urban missionaries and mission agencies in their quest to win people in the urban setting for Christ.

Recommendations for the Way Forward of Urban Mission

1. There must be appropriate budgetary allocation for urban mission.
2. The causes of backsliding of rural-urban migrants may need to be investigated.
3. The factors leading to rural-urban migration should be investigated.
4. Address the need for business evangelism. The world is booming in business and ideas, and most of the business community and elites are in the urban centers. Churches that are poised to do effective urban mission work should present a model of Christianity that will appeal to these business leaders.
5. The church's evangelism wing in urban centers should be composed of people who understand the systems of urbanization and fashion their messages to appeal to urban dwellers.
6. Urban mission is so complex that mission practitioners need to conduct missiological research from time to time to identify the trends and developments in urban centers and how the church can missionally position itself to make an impact.

Conclusion

The churches in Africa ought to realize that as their cities become part of the urban conglomerations, so their missional responsibility within the continent increases. Establishing research centers to critically study ways and means for urban mission, as well as other new developments in contemporary mission work, is vital. While we have seen throughout this section the importance of urban mission in this century, it is appropriate to caution ourselves against being passive toward rural missionary activities. Both urban and rural missionary activities are equally important, and the church should develop a viable missional approach in expanding God's kingdom in these settings.

Bibliography

Anderson, Gerald H., ed. *Biographical Dictionary of Christian Missions.* Grand Rapids: Eerdmans, 1999.

Ashford, Bruce R., ed. *Theology and Practice of Mission: God, the Church, and the Nation.* Nashville: B&H, 2012.

Barrett, David B., and Todd M. Johnson. "Annual Table of World Religions, 1900–2025." *International Bulletin of Missionary Research*, January 1, 2002. http://www.wnrf.org/cms/statuswr.shtml.

Engen, Charles V., and Jude Tiersma. *Seeking a Theology for Urban Mission: God so Loves the City.* Eugene, OR: Wipf & Stock, 1994.

Ghana Evangelism Commission. *Unreached People Groups in Ghana.* Accra: Ghana Evangelism Committee, 2020.

Gilliland, Dean S. *The World among Us: Contextualizing Theology for Mission Today.* Eugene, OR: Wipf & Stock, 1989.

Home and Urban Missions. *Training Manual.* Vol. 2. Accra: The Church of Pentecost, 2021.

International Mission Board. "What Is a People Group?" https://www.peoplegroups.org/understand/313.aspx.

Jenkins, Philip. *The Next Christendom: The Coming of Global Christianity.* Rev. ed. Oxford: Oxford University Press, 2007.

Mutavhatsindi, Muthuphei A. *Church Planting in the South African Urban Context—With Special Reference to the Role of the Reformed Church Tshiawelo.* PhD diss., University of Pretoria, 2008. https://manualzz.com/doc/21422234/church-planting-in-the-south-african-urban-the-reformed-c.

Rajendran, Johnson. "Paul's Mission Strategy in the Light of Book of Acts." https://www.academia.edu/10724666/Pauls_Mission_strategies_in_the_light_of_Book_of_Acts.

Senior, Donald, and Carroll Stuhlmueller. *The Biblical Foundations for Mission.* Tottenham: SCM, 1983.

Ugo, Ikechukwu. *St. Paul's Church Planting Strategies as Revealed in Selected Passages in the Book of Acts.* http://ojs.globalmissiology.org/index.php/english/article/view/814/1964.

United Nations Population Fund. *UNFPA Report 2007.* https://www.unfpa.org/sites/default/files/pub-pdf/ar07_eng.pdf.

Vinay, Samuel, and Chris Sugden, eds. *Mission as Transformation: A Theology of the Whole Gospel.* Oxford: Regnum, 1999.

CHAPTER 10

Pentecostalism and the Lordship of Christ in a Religiously Pluralistic Society

Alfred Koduah

It is an undisputed fact that Pentecostalism has always believed in the lordship of Christ. Among Pentecostals, one of the cardinal requirements for a person's salvation is the public acknowledgement and declaration of the lordship of Christ. In other words, before Pentecostals would acknowledge that someone has truly become a born-again Christian and accept that person into membership, that person should make a public declaration of the lordship of Christ Jesus.[1] With their strong belief that "every tongue shall confess that Jesus is Lord" (Phil 2:11), Pentecostals also believe that because Christ Jesus is God, who has authority over all humans and all creation, he is Lord over all. The unequivocal proclamation of the exclusivist message of Pentecostals that Jesus is the only Savior gives further credence to the fact that they believe in the lordship of Christ. In that regard, Pentecostals subscribe to the statement of the American missionary to the Arab world Samuel Marinus Zwemer (1867–1952), "Unless Jesus is Lord of all, He is not Lord at all."[2] For them, the extent to which a person acknowledges and submits to the lordship of Christ determines that person's obedience and surrender to the Lord.

---

1. The declaration is contained in what Pentecostals consider as the "sinner's prayer," which states: "I accept that I am a sinner and that Jesus died for my sins. I, therefore, accept Jesus as my Lord and personal Savior."

2. Zwemer, *Solitary Throne*, 1.

However, the prevailing religiously pluralistic society seems to have launched an attack on the uniqueness of the lordship of Christ by consistently questioning the exclusivist message of Pentecostals that Jesus is the only Savior. This paper examines how the Pentecostal belief in the uniqueness of the lordship of Christ is faring in the prevailing religiously pluralistic society. After considering how religious pluralism has managed to come into prominence, this paper will look at the prevailing religiously pluralistic society as well as the impact religious pluralism is having on Pentecostalism. The discussion will finally explore how Pentecostalism will be able to maintain the proclamation of its message of the uniqueness of the lordship of Christ Jesus in a religiously pluralistic society before the conclusions will be drawn. In this paper, the terms "Christians" and "Pentecostals" are used interchangeably.

The Coming into Prominence of Religious Pluralism

Religious diversity is nothing new. From time immemorial, while the nations worshiped their traditional gods, the Israelites were worshiping Jehovah, God of Israel, the I AM THAT I AM (Exod 3:14).[3] The Egyptians worshiped their perceived "king of the gods and goddesses," Amun-Ra (the hidden one), the Greeks deified Zeus, and the Western Africans engaged in voodoo practices. By the New Testament times, the Romans were very much involved in emperor worship that subscribed to the lordship of Caesar. When the early Christians were preaching that Jesus Christ is Lord, the Romans could not take kindly to that because they thought the gospel had come to challenge their popular notion of "Caesar is lord." The lordship of Christ Jesus, therefore, came into direct conflict with the lordship of Caesar. Some early Christians suffered martyrdom because of their belief in the uniqueness of the lordship of Christ.

During the premodern period in Western civilization, which was characterized by a belief in supernaturalism, the culture was prescientific with prescribed social roles. The people had basically monocultures and religions, with "little exposure to aliens or foreigners" and "minimal or no social change."[4] According to Gene Edward Veith, that society was characterized by a "complex, dynamic and tension-filled era," which "included mythological paganism, classical rationalism as well as biblical

---

3. Groothuis, *Truth Decay*, 33.
4. Groothuis, *Truth Decay*, 33.

revelation."[5] Douglas Groothuis explains that although people in pre-modern societies generally hold onto one religion, it should not be assumed that everybody in the community subscribes to that one faith. There could be a few who hold onto other faiths, but such people were considered marginal groups and were often persecuted.[6]

Religious pluralism was given a greater impetus during the modern era, which was characterized by several philosophies that rejected belief in supernaturalism, and either discouraged people from believing in God (or gods), or simply encouraged them to believe in anything of their choice.

During the postmodern era, much emphasis has been placed on rejection of absolute truth, metanarratives, and claims of universality. There has also been a systematic promotion of individually or community-constructed truth, permissiveness, moral relativism, omni-choices, and omni-tolerance, as well as disregard for established rules and authority. In addition to bringing to the fore issues concerning the marginalized and minorities, the postmodern era has also promoted pluralism of all kinds, including religious pluralism. This has resulted in a situation referred to as "religion-quake," where two new religions are started every day in this world. These new religions generally reject the unique lordship of Christ Jesus because they teach their adherents to return to pre-Christian primal religions by synchronizing spiritualities and beliefs from various sources into a do-it-yourself religion.[7]

Through migration, better communication technology, and globalization, people now have greater access to different religious traditions and cultures, making religious plurality an everyday reality.[8] Clark H. Pinnock observes that religious pluralism has become urgent in this generation because it has cultural and ecclesiastical implications. He explains that the closer interaction between people from different faiths and cultures in today's globalized world has made religious pluralism a major issue.[9] The contemporary, religiously pluralistic environment is encouraging people to ask questions about the key doctrines of the Christian faith, especially those concerning the uniqueness of Jesus

5. Veith, *Post-Christian*, 29.
6. Groothuis, *Truth Decay*, 33.
7. Pocock et al., *Changing Face of World Missions*, 79, 89.
8. Johnson, "Three-Pronged Defense."
9. Pinnock, "Inclusivist View," 96–97.

Christ and salvation.[10] Thus, although religious pluralism has been in existence from time immemorial, it has now come into prominence and impacting lives in an unprecedented manner because of the prevailing postmodern environment.

The impact of pluralism is being felt in virtually every facet of human endeavor. Politics, religion, the media, the economy, science, and technology have all been affected by pluralism. Today, there is multiparty democracy in several countries, acceptance of multireligious beliefs, multimedia outlets and a multifaceted approach to economics, science, and technology.

The prominent evangelical scholar D. A. Carson identifies three types of pluralism. The first is empirical pluralism, which highlights the increasing diversity in human culture. Second, cherished pluralism approves and celebrates variety and diversity as something good. The third is philosophical/hermeneutical pluralism, which rejects any notion, claim, or suggestion that one ideology or religion is superior to another.[11] Religious pluralism, which is of major concern to this paper, falls under philosophical/hermeneutical pluralism.

The Prevailing Religiously Pluralistic Society

Contemporary society appears to have embraced religious pluralism, which advocates that because one religion is as good as any other, all religions must be given equal recognition and acceptance. No one religion must consider itself as the only way. According to the teaching of the New Age movement, all religions are the same since Jesus, Buddha, Krishna, Muhammad, and founders of other religions "all taught the same thing (how to be at-one with God)."[12] The New Age movement further claims that Jesus is not the only begotten Son of God, and that if human beings are all "gods" or part of God, then Jesus' death on the cross accomplished nothing, and so there is no need for Jesus. Rather, men and women need direction to realize their unlimited potential by connecting with the supernatural soul of the universe. As far as the New Age movement is concerned, "The path to God is broad enough to take

---

10. Johnson, "Three-Pronged Defense," 2.
11. Carson, *Gagging of God*, 13, 18–19.
12. Schwarz, *Christian Faith*, 198–99.

in all men."[13] Accordingly, since New Agers believe that salvation could be found in any or all faiths, Christianity or any other religion should not claim monopoly over salvation.[14]

Bruce J. Nicholls states that because "it is axiomatic that no one religion can claim uniqueness and finality, no one religious founder can claim to be the only savior of the world."[15] Islam even reduces Jesus to the level of a mere human being and accuses Christianity of elevating a human being to the place of God and worshiping him.[16]

The renowned philosopher and proponent of religious pluralism John Hicks (1922–2012), takes the matter a little further. He sees a contradiction between 1 Timothy 2:6, which describes God's desire to save all people, and John 14:6, which teaches that Jesus is the only way to salvation. According to Hicks, if only one religion is salvific, then it is doubtful that God is truly interested in the salvation of all people. For him, therefore, "the only way to overcome this contradiction is to believe that all religions are salvific."[17]

Dennis L. Okholm and Timothy R. Phillips point out that in matters of salvation, no one religion should claim uniqueness or superiority, or even think that it has closer access to the ultimate reality than the rest.[18] Groothuis quotes Steve Turner as saying, "We believe that all religions are basically the same. They all believe in love and goodness and differ only in matters of creation, sin, heaven, hell, God and salvation."[19] This statement raises some questions because the stated areas of difference constitute the heart of any religion. After all, if religious groups differ in fundamental theological areas of creation, sin, salvation, the afterlife, and God himself, then there is no way they could be "basically the same" as Turner wants people to believe.

The Indian-born, Canadian American Christian apologist Ravi Zacharias (1946–2020) refutes the arguments that all religions are the same by saying:

---

13. Schwarz, *Christian Faith*, 199.
14. Wright, "Case against Pluralism," 33.
15. Nicholls, *Unique Christ in Our Pluralist World*, 9.
16. Smith, *World's Religions*, 236. See also Beaver, *Eerdmans' Handbook to the World Religions*, 316.
17. Quoted from Jones et al., *Blackwell Companion to Modern Theology*, 804.
18. Okholm and Philips, *Four Views on Salvation in a Pluralistic World*, 17.
19. Zacharias, *Jesus among Other Gods*, 4–5.

> All religions are not the same. All religions do not point to God. All religions do not say that all religions are the same. At the heart of every religion is an uncompromising commitment to a particular way of defining who God is or is not and accordingly, of defining life's purpose. . . . Anyone who claims that all religions are the same betrays not only an ignorance of all religions but also a caricatured view of even the best-known ones. Every religion is at its core exclusive.[20]

The debate on the relationship between the world's major religions has been concentrated around three terminologies that deal with the various opinions on the matter. The first, exclusivism, has from time immemorial been the central position of the church, including Pentecostals.[21] Explaining exclusivism, Johnson asserts:

> Key to this position is the understanding of God's general and special revelations. God is manifested through creation (general revelation), but man has responded by freely going against this revelation and, thus, stands guilty before a holy God. However, God has demonstrated a reconciliatory mercy through His word and deed fulfilled completely in Jesus Christ. The historical person of Jesus, then, is the unique, final, decisive, and normative self-revelation of God to man (special revelation). Exclusivists believe that Jesus Christ is the sole criterion by which all religions, including Christianity, should be understood, and evaluated.[22]

Chris Wright explains that there are two types of exclusivists: Christians, including Pentecostals, who "argue that no human being can be saved apart from explicit knowledge of faith in Jesus Christ," and those who believe that even though salvation can be found only through Christ, the gracious God will save people "who have never heard of Christ yet turn to God in some kind of repentance and trust."[23]

The second major terminology in the discussion of religious pluralism is inclusivism. This serves as a sort of "middle way" between exclusivism and pluralism, as it seeks to avoid claiming monopoly over the gospel of redemption. Although inclusivists accept that salvation is possible outside the Christian faith and can be available to those who have no church

---

20. Pocock et al., *Changing Face of World Missions*, 99.
21. Lakeland, *Postmodernity*, 76. See also Wright, "Case against Pluralism," 31.
22. Johnson, "Three-Pronged Defense," 3.
23. Wright, "Case against Pluralism," 31.

membership, they still believe that Christ is the agent of that salvation. As far as inclusivists are concerned, Christian salvation is not limited to any specific cultural setting. Also, when people from a different religious culture respond to the available general revelation, they need no special knowledge of Christ's work before obtaining salvation.[24]

While some inclusivists are concerned about people who, through no fault of their own, have not had access to the gospel, others argue that the purpose of Christian mission is not conversion per se, but "to help people discover and unveil the Christ already within their religious tradition."[25] This argument, however, appears to be at variance to the biblical concept of evangelism, which aims at making converts (Matt 28:18–20; Acts 2:38–41; 14:15; Rom 10:13–15).

There are two types of inclusivists: those who think that although there could be some degree of divine revelation among adherents of other faiths, it is not possible for anyone to be saved through any of those religions, and those who see "the saving work of Christ, present in hidden and anonymous ways in those faiths."[26] There are, however, some overlaps within these two types of inclusivists.

The third important terminology in the religious pluralism debate is pluralism, which argues that to "promote justice in an intolerant world," no religion should "claim an absolutist stance."[27] Hicks argues that even though all the world's religions are attempting to relate to the unknowable ultimate reality, their various cultural and historical contexts make them naturally apply different methods. That is why their conceptions of the real and the salvation(s) they are seeking differ.[28]

For pluralists, Christ is not better than any other religious figure or concept. Rather than confessing that Jesus Christ is the one Lord over all, some pluralists accept that "the one Lord who has manifested himself in other names is also known as Jesus."[29] Pluralism considers "all the faiths as different responses to the one Ultimate Divine Reality," so "even apparent contradictions between different faiths could be seen as merely the result of human limitations."[30] Hicks and Knitter, therefore, admonish

24. Johnson, "Three-Pronged Defense," 1.
25. Johnson, "Three-Pronged Defense," 3–4.
26. Wright, "Case against Pluralism," 31.
27. Hicks and Knitter, quoted in Johnson, "Three-Pronged Defense," 5.
28. Hicks, quoted in Johnson, "Three-Pronged Defense," 5.
29. Johnson, "Three-Pronged Defense," 5.
30. Wright, "Case against Pluralism," 32.

Christians to discard any claim of Christian uniqueness and accept that the Christian faith is one among many options.[31]

Commenting on the three main terminologies under religious pluralism, Wright maintains that one objective common to exclusivist and inclusivist scholars is that they aim at preserving "the centrality and normativeness of Christ."[32] However, of late, some other scholars are advocating that people embrace a "theocentric theology of religions" which hopes to see "God at the centre of the religious universe," and not "Christ or Christianity."[33]

Tying the three terminologies together, Wright cites Hicks as proposing that the church has moved from "exclusive ecclesiocentrism" (the church at the center of all salvation) to "inclusive Christocentrism" (Christ is normative, but he has revealed himself to people in other religions, some of whom he may save).[34] Accordingly, the church must now adopt "pluralist theocentrism," which projects "neither Christ nor the church at the centre, but only God."[35] The reason is that while Jesus himself "preached the kingdom of God (theocentric proclamation)," the church started preaching Jesus (Christocentrism) when it was "faced with the apparent failure or delay of that kingdom."[36] However, Wright correctly argues that it is "impossible within the framework of the New Testament to be theocentric without being Christocentric."[37]

Wright again declares that "the pluralist view cannot be reconciled with authentic Christianity, because to relativize Jesus Christ is to deny him."[38] He subsequently states that "the uniqueness of Jesus is not something Christianity invented," and since it was God who exalted Christ and gave him a supreme name, the final proof rests with God.[39] Additionally, since the uniqueness of Christ and God have been emphasized in pluralistic societies of old,[40] even the small early church in the pluralistic Graeco-Roman world, there is no reason why Christians today should

---

31. Hicks, and Knitter, quoted in Johnson, "Three-Pronged Defense," 5.
32. Wright, "Case against Pluralism," 32.
33. Wright, "Case against Pluralism," 32.
34. Wright, "Case against Pluralism," 33.
35. Wright, "Case against Pluralism," 33.
36. Wright, "Case against Pluralism," 34.
37. Wright, "Case against Pluralism," 34.
38. Wright, "Case against Pluralism," 35.
39. Wright, "Case against Pluralism," 44.
40. Wright, "Case against Pluralism," 42–44.

attempt to sacrifice it on the altar of modern-day pluralism.[41] Debunking the pluralistic view, Calvin E. Shenk opines:

> Christ did not come just to make a contribution to the religious storehouse of knowledge. The revelation, which he brought, is the ultimate standard. Since in Christ alone is salvation and truth, many religious paths do not adequately reflect the way of God and do not lead to truth and life. Jesus is not, therefore, just the greatest lord among other lords. There is no other lord besides him.[42]

Comparing religious pluralistic beliefs in premodern and postmodern periods, Peter Berger is quoted by Groothuis as saying that during the premodern times, anybody who chose a belief outside the culturally accepted one was considered a heretic. In the postmodern world, however, because people are expected to select their religious preference from an array of options, it is acceptable to be a "heretic."[43]

The issue of reasonability structures in cultures cannot be overlooked in the discussion of religious pluralism. In every society, some beliefs are viewed as reasonable and others unreasonable. Being a Christian in a predominantly Christian society makes it easy to practice the Christian faith. Conversely, practicing the Christian faith in another culture that is dominated by another major religion can be challenging. Presenting and defending the exclusivist "Jesus only" message of Christianity in such a society would obviously call for convincing apologetics. Pocock and his coauthors suggest that to bring the Christian message to the postmodern culture would require a comparison of the existing plausibility structures to the Christian worldview.[44] He laments that instead of doing this, some contemporary missionaries spend time trying to find a way to communicate the Christian faith in terms of commonality.[45]

It is in the context of the numerous arguments being developed in favor of religious pluralism that Pentecostalism has consistently maintained the uniqueness of the lordship of Christ. For Pentecostals, the uniqueness of the lordship of Christ is a *sine quo non* to their very existence. They vehemently reject the notion that all religions are salvific.

---

41. Tan, "Challenge of the 'Pluralistic' Theologians," 70.
42. Shenk, *Who Do You Say I Am?*, 35.
43. Groothuis, *Truth Decay*, 53.
44. Pocock et al., *Changing Face of World Missions*, 102.
45. Pocock et al., *Changing Face of World Missions*, 102.

They also reject the belief that all founders of major religions qualify to be referred to as lords. For them, even if these founders claim some form of lordship, they will ultimately bow before the King of kings and Lord of lords, who is Christ Jesus. Pentecostals continually affirm this belief through their numerous songs and sermons that Christ Jesus is the Lord of lords and the King of kings (1 Tim 6:15; Rev 1:5; 17:14; 19:16). One such song is:

> *He is Lord, he is Lord,*
> *He is risen from the dead, he is Lord,*
> *Every knee shall bow, every tongue confess,*
> *That Jesus Christ is Lord.*

Continually singing such songs implies that Pentecostals are declaring Jesus as the King of kings and Lord of lords who has the power to exercise absolute dominion over all creation, including kings and lords. As an unchallengeable king and lord, he alone would eventually exercise rulership in all the earth. The questions, however, are: Can Pentecostalism withstand the onslaught of religious pluralism? Can Pentecostals continue to tenaciously hold onto their claim of the uniqueness of the lordship of Christ Jesus in this fast-changing, permissive, and religiously pluralistic society?

The Impact of Religious Pluralism on Pentecostalism

Religious pluralism has had (and continues to have), a profound impact on Pentecostalism. First, even though Pentecostalism was initially perceived by the mainline Christian denominations as a sect,[46] respect for religious pluralism and the fast growth of Pentecostalism have brought forward issues relating to Pentecostals to the extent that they are now one of the most recognized and respected traditions within Christianity.

---

46. The other Christian denominations initially looked down upon Pentecostals until the South African-born Pentecostal minister David Johannes Du Plessis (1905–87), popularly known as "Mr. Pentecost," became the first Pentecostal to have been invited to the third session of the Vatican II (1963–65), and all the six assemblies of the World Council of Churches between 1948–83. The title "Mr. Pentecost" was given to him by the International Missionary Council in 1952 when the council recognized Du Plessis as a "rational Pentecostal." See Burgess and McGee, *Dictionary of Pentecostals and Charismatic Movements*, 252–53.

Second, religious pluralism has compelled Pentecostals to embrace ecumenism. In their quest for distinctiveness and doctrinal purity, Pentecostals were initially skeptical of ecumenism. According to the Pentecostal scholar Cecil M. Robeck Jr., before the 1940s, Pentecostal founders condemned ecumenism and prevented their ministers from fellowshipping with ecumenical bodies such as the World Council of Churches.[47] In the process, Pentecostals "contributed to the fragmentation and pluralization" of global Christianity.[48] They have now abandoned that position to embrace ecumenism.

Third, religious pluralism has compelled Pentecostals to respect other religious faiths. In the past, some Pentecostal preachers in Ghana mounted evangelistic platforms to condemn other religious faiths such as Islam. However, in line with respect for religious pluralism, this is no longer the case as Pentecostals have now tried to avoid public offense to those faiths. Today, many Pentecostal leaders are enjoying various degrees of fellowship with Islamic leaders in their communities in the interest of peaceful interreligious coexistence.

Maintaining the Proclamation of the Pentecostal Message of the Uniqueness of the Lordship of Christ in a Religiously Pluralistic Society

Undoubtedly, maintaining the proclamation of the uniqueness of the lordship of Christ Jesus in a religiously pluralistic society is not an easy task. It is, therefore, imperative for Pentecostals to develop a proper response to religious pluralism. According to Pocock et al., Christians have generally responded to religious pluralism in two ways: outreach and ambivalence. The outreach response makes Christians consider people from other faiths as "unreached people" who need to be introduced to the gospel. The ambivalent response, which appears to be gaining popularity in the world today, has made Christians think that it is safer to allow for a peaceful coexistence with people from other faiths since, in this globalized world, everyone has a right to a religion of their choice.[49]

In this regard, it appears Pentecostals uphold both the outreach and ambivalent positions. On the one hand, they consider people from other

---

47. Robeck, "Pentecostal and Ecumenism in a Pluralistic World," 340–44.
48. Robeck, "Pentecostal and Ecumenism in a Pluralistic World," 351–55.
49. Pocock et al., *Changing Face of World Missions*, 56.

faiths as unreached who need to be evangelized, while on the other hand, they wish to coexist with people from other faiths. The only challenge is that the popularity of the ambivalent response is leading some Christians to lose interest in evangelism and missionary work in this generation. It is also leading to compromises in biblical values.

In the view of Bruce L. Shelley, churches have responded to religious pluralism in three ways: (a) accommodating the views of other religious faiths, (b) refusing to accommodate the views of other religions, and (c) adopting an intermediate position where, to varying degrees, they accommodate and resist at the same time. From his perspective, many churches today have adopted the intermediate position.[50] To varying degrees, Pentecostals appear to hold the intermediary position. Harold Coward, however, thinks that to open a dialogue with other religions, the churches have only altered their ecclesiology, but not their Christology. For him, "until the issue of the uniqueness of Jesus is examined and reinterpreted in relation to the claims to truth by other religions, the changed ecclesiology will lack a firm foundation."[51]

Coward is right when he asks, "Can Christianity accept other religious traditions as valid ways to salvation without giving up its fundamental conviction about the absoluteness and uniqueness of Jesus Christ?"[52] This question lies at the heart of the development of any response to religious pluralism. Coward notes that even though religious pluralism has always been around, it poses a "special challenge" to world religions today.[53] The reason is that the world today has become a global village where people with different religious persuasions are able to interact better and faster with one another than before. It is, therefore, imperative for churches to develop a response to religious pluralism. To effectively develop a response to religious pluralism would require Pentecostals to adequately defend the uniqueness of Christ as the truth, as presented in the Bible (John 14:6).

To maintain the uniqueness of Christ Jesus in a religiously pluralistic society, Pentecostals should remain resolute in their convictions about the faith. Pentecostals should carefully draw a line between what is expressly biblical and what is church tradition. This will help them to recognize what constitutes the church's "negotiable" and

50. Shelley, *Church History in Plain Language*, 490.
51. Coward, *Pluralism*, 15.
52. Coward, *Pluralism*, 14.
53. Coward, *Pluralism*, 94.

"non-negotiable" beliefs and traditions. This will also help to determine which of the negotiables worked yesterday but are no longer relevant today. In other words, Pentecostals must clearly define their biblical absolutes or basic tenets, which will constitute their non-negotiables. In addition to Christianity's basic tenets, which include the uniqueness of the lordship of Christ Jesus, other non-negotiable areas that may have to be maintained at all costs include an emphasis on prayer, holiness and discipline, total reliance on the Holy Spirit, and absolute respect as well as reverence for the Word of God.

In addition to these are several written and unwritten church traditions. Good as some of them may appear, Pentecostals cannot honestly and sincerely say that they are all absolutely biblical. Those that cannot be classified as the expressed word of God should be categorized as negotiables. These include seating arrangements in church and church administrative structure, which may change with time and circumstances.[54] If this is not done, with time, people may think that church traditions are as sacred as Scripture and guard them as jealously as biblical doctrines. That situation will lead to the accommodation of doctrinal errors, which abound in contemporary times.

Pentecostals should also demonstrate the power of God through miracles, signs, and wonders, even in today's religiously pluralistic society. The early apostles did not compromise within their equally religiously pluralistic societies. They preached the "Jesus only" message, which resulted in massive church growth. Contemporary Pentecostals should, therefore, not sacrifice biblical and doctrinal absolutes on the altar of religious pluralism.

To enable Christians to maintain the proclamation of the unique lordship of Christ Jesus in a religiously pluralistic society, Groothuis, in his authoritative book *Truth Decay: Defending Christianity against the Challenges of Postmodernism*, offers eight points of the biblical view of truth. First, Christians should reject the notion that "truth" is relative and socially constructed and continue to hold on tenaciously to the "real truth" that has been revealed by God.[55]

Second, because God is the source of all truth, Christians, including Pentecostals, must uphold the fact that there is an objective truth, which can be revealed to all genuine seekers. That revealed truth should not be

---

54. Koduah, "Church of Pentecost in a Postmodern Society," 127–28.
55. Groothuis, *Truth Decay*, 65–82.

subjected to any human experiences or interpretations. Christians should, therefore, not soften their position on the absoluteness of God's truth as revealed in the Bible because doing so would constitute unfaithfulness to the truth of God. Groothuis admits that proving the absoluteness of truth involves long "intellectual claims and counterclaims," but that should not stop Christians from believing in the absoluteness of truth as presented in the Bible. Therefore, he encourages Christians to continue to engage in apologetic discussions on the absoluteness of God's truth.[56]

Norman Anderson agrees with Groothuis on this point. He indicates that Christians must continue to use proclamation, dialogue, argumentation, and friendship approaches to declare the uniqueness of Christ. He explains that Paul used dialogue (Acts 28:23–28), argumentation (Acts 17:16–31), and friendship (1 Cor 9:19–23) approaches to proclaim the uniqueness of Christ to his pluralistic audience (Rom 10:9; 1 Cor 8:6; 12:3; Phil 2:11).[57]

Third, because God is immutable, his truth is not relative or revisable, and should, therefore, not be subject to any human procedures.[58] Fourth, because truth is universal, the message of the gospel and God's moral requirements should not be changed or limited by any cultural situations. Even though Providence allows for diversity, matters relating to God's truth should not be localized because it is universal in scope and application.[59] Johnston buttresses this point by asserting that Christians, including Pentecostals, should not make any compromises concerning God's truth because "he who marries the spirit of the age soon becomes a widow."[60]

Fifth, because God's truth is anchored in his eternal being, it goes beyond all trivialities and, therefore, needs no modifications.[61] Sixth, God's "truth is exclusive, and specific," because "what is true excludes all that opposes it."[62] Accordingly, "if there is but one God, all other claimants are impostors."[63] By implication, because all truth belongs to God, not all truth

---

56. Groothuis, *Truth Decay*, 69–71.
57. Anderson, *Christianity and World Religions*, 176–94.
58. Groothuis, *Truth Decay*, 67, 69.
59. Groothuis, *Truth Decay*, 72–73.
60. Johnston, *Preaching to a Postmodern World*, 10.
61. Groothuis, *Truth Decay*, 74.
62. Groothuis, *Truth Decay*, 75.
63. Groothuis, *Truth Decay*, 75.

can be logically and factually fit together.⁶⁴ Carson takes this matter further by stating that even though other religions may express faith in several deities, and recognize many "lords," "baptisms," and "hopes," Christians should continue to express the exclusive biblical truth of "one Lord, one faith, one baptism, one God and one hope" (Eph 4:4–5).⁶⁵

The seventh point is that because there is only one truth, just as there is only one God who created a *uni-verse* and not a *multi-verse*, all truths come together to express "God's harmonious objective reality."⁶⁶ The eighth point is that Christians, including Pentecostals, must continue to affirm that biblical truth is an end, and not a means to any other end.⁶⁷ The American missiologist David J. Hesselgrave (1924–2018) agreed with Groothuis when he stated that the Christian faith is absolutely unique because there is no faith like it. There is also no other God, Christ, Calvary, empty tomb, redemption, salvation, or heaven.⁶⁸

By all standards, the above suggestions by Groothuis and other scholars are quite revealing and good. It is important to emphasize that there is no need for Pentecostals to modify their belief in the lordship of Christ in a religiously pluralistic society. The reasons are fourfold. First, the belief in the lordship of Christ has the ability to positively change and transform lives. Despite all the technological advancement, there is no medical doctor who can spiritually transform the life of anyone for the better. However, through the acceptance of the lordship of Christ Jesus, the lives of millions of evil-minded people have been changed into responsible citizens.

Second, it is a proven fact that the acceptance of the lordship of Christ can change and transform communities and cultures for the better. For example, before Christianity was established in many cultures, several inhumane practices were carried out, including panyarring, ritual murder, infanticide, scarification, honor killing, early child marriage, forced marriage, widowhood rites, female genital mutilation, breast pressing/ironing, burning of perceived witches, and tribal marks cutting. However, when people in such cultures accept the lordship of Christ, some of these harmful practices are abandoned. Even though some of

---

64. Groothuis, *Truth Decay*, 76.
65. Carson, *Gagging of God*, 497.
66. Groothuis, *Truth Decay*, 79.
67. Groothuis, *Truth Decay*, 80.
68. Pocock et al., *Changing Face of World Missions*, 99.

these practices are still upheld in some cultures, Christianity has helped to reduce their influence on the people.

Third, the acceptance of the lordship of Christ enables people to control their sexuality. In this sex-crazed world in which unrestrained sexual activities are not only encouraged but glorified, it is only the gospel that is able to help people exercise self-control. No wonder the Scottish theologian William Barclay (1907–78) pointed out that even though Christianity came to meet a sex-crazed world, it has succeeded in bringing about chastity.[69]

Fourth, the acknowledgment of the lordship of Christ enables Christians to confront powers of darkness and evil forces. Taking inspiration from the biblical declaration that "at the name of Jesus every knee should bow . . . and every tongue confess that Jesus Christ is Lord" (Phil 2:10–11), many Christians, especially the Pentecostals, are able to demonstrate God's power over evil forces. This proves the uniqueness of the lordship of Christ over all other lords.

The English Anglican cleric and theologian John Stott (1921–2011) cautioned that although Pentecostals must not impose their religion on people of other faiths, they should also not be indifferent to the activities of other religious faiths. Rather, they should show respect to those who subscribe to other religious traditions and use persuasion to convince them about the absoluteness of God's truth as presented in the Bible.[70]

It is obvious from the foregoing points that, to maintain the proclamation of the uniqueness of the lordship of Christ Jesus in the religiously pluralistic society, Pentecostals must adopt a non-compromising position. The reason is that while other religions leave little or no room for dissenting views and religious diversity, they want Christianity to adopt an inclusivist position when it comes to issues of faith. For example, in various totalitarian countries where Christians are persecuted without mercy, the militantly Islamic nations have little or no freedom for "religious pluralism or public debate on religious matters."[71]

Pentecostals must, therefore, maintain the presentation of their exclusivist "Jesus only" gospel message based on Jesus' declaration: "I am the way, the truth, and the life. No one comes to the Father except through me" (John 14:6). Pentecostals should remain resolute because any departure from the exclusivist gospel message would render their

---

69. Barclay, *Letter to the Galatians*, 51.
70. Stott, *New Issues Facing Christians Today*, 53–62.
71. Groothuis, *Truth Decay*, 193–94.

evangelistic mission enterprise a futile activity. After all, what is the point of going around evangelizing if all religions were salvific?

Conclusion

This paper has examined how the Pentecostal belief in the lordship of Christ is faring in the prevailing religiously pluralistic society. It has been observed that although religious pluralism has been in existence since time immemorial, it has come into prominence within contemporary society because of the prevailing emphasis on the rejection of absolute truth, metanarratives, and claims of universality, as well as the promotion of moral relativism, omni-choices, omni-tolerance, and permissiveness.

This discussion has noted that religious pluralism has helped to bring to the fore the activities of Pentecostalism, which was initially perceived by the mainline Christian churches as a sect. In addition to compelling Pentecostals who originally did not want to associate with any ecumenical group to change their stance, religious pluralism has also literally forced them to move away from preaching against other religious faiths.

Concerning how Pentecostals could continue to propagate the message of the unique lordship of Christ Jesus in a religiously pluralistic society, the paper observed that they should never compromise their stance. Pentecostals must carefully differentiate between biblical teaching and church tradition to enable them to determine what constitutes the church's "negotiable" and "non-negotiable" beliefs and traditions. While they may compromise on the negotiable beliefs and traditions whenever it becomes necessary, they should tenaciously hold on to the non-negotiable ones.

Pentecostals should also demonstrate the power of God through miracles, signs, and wonders, even in the religiously pluralistic society. They must learn lessons from the early apostles who did not make any compromises but preached the uniqueness of the lordship of Christ Jesus in their equally religiously pluralistic societies.

Additionally, Pentecostals must remain resolute in matters of the Christian faith because the immutable God, who is the source of all truth, has revealed his one universal, unchangeable, exclusive, objective, and real truth to all genuine seekers. That truth, which is anchored in God's being, is an end and not a means to an end. As such, that truth must never be revised. Furthermore, Pentecostals must continue to proclaim the uniqueness of the lordship of Christ because it has the power to positively transform lives and communities. It has the ability to control human sexuality in this sex-crazed world, as well as confront evil spirits. Pentecostals must, therefore, continue to proclaim the unique lordship of Christ in the religiously pluralistic society. They should never sacrifice the core values of the Christian faith on the altar of religious pluralism.

Bibliography

Anderson, Norman. *Christianity and World Religions: The Challenge of Pluralism.* Downers Grove, IL: InterVarsity, 1984.
Barclay, William. *The Letter to the Galatians.* Edinburgh: Saint Andrew, 1954.
Beaver, R. Pierce. *Eerdmans' Handbook to the World Religions.* Grand Rapids: Eerdmans, 1982.
Burgess, Stanley M., and Gary B. McGee, eds. *Dictionary of Pentecostals and Charismatic Movements.* Grand Rapids: Zondervan, 1988.
Carson, D. A. *The Gagging of God: Christianity Confronts Pluralism.* Downers Grove, IL: InterVarsity, 1996.
Coward, Harold. *Pluralism: Challenge to World Religions.* Maryknoll, NY: Orbis, 1985.
Groothuis, Douglas. *Truth Decay: Defending Christianity against the Challenges of Postmodernism.* Downers Grove, IL: InterVarsity, 2000.
Johnson, Brad. "A Three-Pronged Defense of Salvific Exclusivism in a World of Religions." http://www.leaderu.com/theology/salvific.html.
Johnston, Graham. *Preaching to a Postmodern World.* Downers Grove, IL: InterVarsity, 2001.
Jones, Gareth, ed. *The Blackwell Companion to Modern Theology.* Oxford: Blackwell, 2007.
Koduah, Alfred. "The Church of Pentecost in a Postmodern Society." In *James McKeown Memorial Lectures: 50 Years of the Church of Pentecost*, edited by Opoku Onyinah, 105–32. Accra: Church of Pentecost, 2004.
Lakeland, Paul. *Postmodernity: Christian Identity in a Fragmented Age.* Minneapolis: Fortress, 1997.
Nicholls, Bruce J. *The Unique Christ in Our Pluralist World.* Carlisle: Paternoster, 1994.
Okholm, Dennis L., and Timothy R. Philips, eds. *Four Views on Salvation in a Pluralistic World.* Grand Rapids: Zondervan, 1995.
Pinnock, Clark H. "An Inclusivist View." In *Four Views on Salvation in a Pluralistic World*, edited by Dennis L. Okholm and Timothy R. Philips, 93–123. Grand Rapids: Zondervan, 1996.
Pocock, Michael, et al. *The Changing Face of World Missions: Engaging Contemporary Issues and Trends.* Grand Rapids: Baker Academic, 2005.
Robeck, Cecil M. "Pentecostal and Ecumenism in a Pluralistic World." In *The Globalization of Pentecostalism: A Religion Made to Travel*, edited by Murray W. Dempster et al., 338–62. Carlisle: Regnum, 1999.
Schwarz, John. *A Handbook of the Christian Faith.* Minneapolis: Bethany House, 1998.
Shelley, Bruce L. *Church History in Plain Language.* 3rd ed. Nashville: Nelson, 2008.

Shenk, Calvin E. *Who Do You Say I Am?* Scottdale, PA: Herald, 1997.
Smith, Huston. *The World's Religions.* San Francisco: HarperSanFrancisco, 1999.
Stott, John. *New Issues Facing Christians Today.* London: HarperCollins, 1999.
Tan, Kim-Sai. "Challenge of the 'Pluralistic' Theologians." In *The Unique Christ in Our Pluralist World*, edited by Bruce J. Nicholls, 67–76. Grand Rapids: Baker, 1994.
Veith, Gene Edward. *Post-Christian: Guide to Contemporary Culture.* Wheaton, IL: Crossway, 1994.
Wright, Chris. "The Case against Pluralism." In *The Unique Christ in Our Pluralist World*, edited by Bruce J. Nicholls, 31–44. Grand Rapids: Baker, 1994.
Zacharias, Ravi. *Jesus among Other Gods.* Nashville: Nelson, 2000.
Zwemer, Samuel Marinus. *The Solitary Throne.* London: Pickering & Inglis, 1937.

CHAPTER 11

Re-thinking Church in the Light of COVID-19

Patrick Tetteh Kudadjie

Introduction

COVID-19 WAS INITIALLY THOUGHT to be a public health emergency of international concern by the World Health Organization (WHO) on January 30, 2020.[1] However, the WHO later declared it as a pandemic due to its rapid rate of spread.[2] COVID-19 is believed to be the worst modern pandemic, after the Spanish flu.[3] It has undoubtedly disrupted the world, affecting virtually every aspect of life—political, economic, religious, psychological, and social. The church has not been insulated from this disruption, with COVID-19 posing significant challenges to the way churches operate and interact with their congregations. It was also observed that in the face of the challenges posed by the COVID-19 menace, the church was resilient, creating opportunities that enabled it to survive the pandemic. This paper focuses on how Pentecostal-Charismatic churches can respond by mitigating the challenges and taking advantage of the opportunities for a sustained future. Putting it in another way, the paper aims to suggest to Pentecostal-Charismatic churches lessons they can draw from their experiences with the COVID-19 pandemic as they

1. Durkin et al., "Touch in Times of COVID-19," 1–2.
2. Lekoa and Ntuli, "Attack on the Cross," 1.
3. Lekoa and Ntuli, "Attack on the Cross," 1.

build a robust and glorious church. Let us, first consider an overview of the COVID-19 situation in Ghana.

An Overview of the COVID-19 Situation in Ghana

The COVID-19 pandemic spread throughout many countries of the world including Ghana. Prior to the presence of the virus in Ghana, the president, His Excellency Nana Addo Dankwa Akuffo, oriented the entire country about preparations made to reduce its impact. This he did through periodic updates on TV stations in the country. As part of the preparations, readiness assessment research was conducted by the National Surveillance Department of the Ghana Health Service to indicate how ready the country was for the pandemic. As part of the preparatory strategy, various training and orientation programs were organized for stakeholders, especially, those at the various borders and ports. Ghana's first experience of the virus was reported on March 12, 2020, by the then minister of health, Agyeman Manu. Within a space of two weeks after the first case, it had spread to other parts of the country, mainly in Accra and Kumasi.

With the presence of COVID-19 in Ghana, like all other countries the Ghana government came up with several regulations to curtail the spread of the virus. The first step the government took was the closure of all universities, senior high schools, and basic schools both public and private. As the situation worsened, a ban on social gatherings was imposed. This included a ban on all religious activities, funerals, conferences, political rallies, sporting events, and workshops. However, private burial with a maximum of twenty-five people was permitted at the time. There was also a mandatory quarantine of all travelers that arrived in the country forty-eight hours prior to the closure of the country's borders. The government further introduced a partial lockdown in the Greater Accra Metropolitan area, including Kasoa, and the Greater Kumasi Metropolitan area of the country. These places were considered the epicenters of the virus in Ghana. Another innovation by the government to clamp down on the spread of the disease was contact tracing. This involved a process of identifying, assessing, and managing people who were exposed to the virus in order the prevent further transmission. Like all other nations, Ghana was not spared the devastating effects of COVID-19. At the time of this writing, Ghana recorded a total of 171,653 COVID-19 cases with 1,462 deaths since the epidemic began.[4]

Economically, COVID-19 had distressing effects on every sector of life. Many businesses were affected, leading to a high unemployment rate. For instance, the income of over 770,000 workers was reduced, the working hours of about 700,000 workers were slashed, and 42,000 workers lost their jobs.[5] One sector that was heavily affected was transport. The fortunes of many commercial drivers were reduced as they were told to limit the number of passengers to allow for social distancing. Nevertheless, the period opened economic fortunes for others. People made gains through the sale of personal protective equipment (PPE), nose masks, hand sanitizer and many other related items. The period was a business boom for ICT experts as many businesses made transactions digitally.

Additionally, COVID-19 affected the social lives of Ghanaians. The ban on social gatherings cut down on social interactions. Some cultural values were challenged. The usual practice of shaking hands with people, which is an integral part of communal life, was halted. Family members could not embrace each other for fear of being infected with the virus. People could not pay their last respects to their dead relatives due to COVID-19 regulations. The Ghana government did its best to respond to some of the economic hardships that COVID-19 brought on its citizens. The government set up the Coronavirus Alleviation Programme (CAP). It also supported small and medium enterprises (SMEs) with loans that have a one-year moratorium and two-year repayment period.[6] As part of the COVID-19 relief to the citizens, the president in his fifth address to the nation avers:

> Ministries of Gender, Children's Protection, and Local Government and Rural Development, and the National Disaster Management Organizations and MMDCEs and faith-based organizations are to provide food for up to 400,000 individuals and homes in Accra and Kumasi. Ghana Water Company Ltd and Electricity Company of Ghana were to ensure a stable supply of water and electricity during the period, the government was also to absorb the water and electricity bills for the months of April–June.[7]

---

4. WHO Coronavirus Dashboard: http://covid19.who.int.
5. World Bank, "COVID-19."
6. Adams, "President Launches COVID-19 Alleviation Programme."
7. Akuffo-Addo, "5th Address to the Nation."

In this section, we presented some preparations that were made by the Ghana government as well as the regulations put in place to check the spread of the virus. We also discussed some devastating effects that the virus brought on Ghanaians. Finally, some interventions by the government to reduce the adverse impacts were highlighted. The next section discusses the effects of the virus on the church.

Effects of COVID-19 on the Church

One group of society that was heavily affected by the COVID-19 pandemic was religious bodies. A number of research studies conducted around the world indicated that the pandemic "severely disrupted the religious life of millions of people around the world."[8] Writing from the context of England, Leslie Francis and Andrew Village disclosed, "In the Church of England there was no access to churches during the first lockdown from March to July 2020 and access was restricted to those churches that opted to provide socially distanced worship during the lockdown from January to July 2021."[9] The situation was not different in Ghana. The ban on social gatherings including religious activities affected the church in diverse ways. It became a challenge because churches in Ghana at the time were used to physical meetings in large auditoriums. Moreover, almost every activity of the church involves contact with people. The restrictions on religious activities, therefore, meant that normal church activities could no longer be done. The situation brought some discomfort to churches.

First, many churches faced financial difficulties. This is because the source of finances of the church in Ghana is largely from members' tithes and offerings, which, are taken during church services. Many churches in Ghana do not have systems that encourage electronic payments of offerings. Even at churches where they are available, the majority of their adherents are not acquainted with them. Due to these challenges, many churches could not meet their expenditures. Some had to put projects and other related issues on hold. Moreover, due to the lockdown and economic hardship that people faced, church members expected their leaders to assist them with food items and other necessities of life. All these put some form of pressure on churches. Research carried out by

---

8. See Cavaliere, "Religious Institutions in Japan," 31; Osei-Tutu et al., "Ban of Religious Gatherings," 340; Village and Francis, "Effect of Spiritual Wellbeing," 2900.

9. Village and Francis, "Effect of Spiritual Wellbeing," 2900.

Annabella Osei-Tutu et al. indicated that some church leaders admitted that the ban on religious restrictions had some adverse financial difficulties for them and their churches. Part of their findings read:

> Some of the religious leaders we interviewed indicated that some of their members had difficulty meeting basic needs. One participant stated, "Someone can call me, 'Pastor even what my children and I will eat I do not have, so we beg you to get something small for me.'" Other religious leaders noted that some of their congregants who did informal sector work faced a decline in their work as customers were not patronizing their goods. They also said that the pandemic had put financial stress on congregants who were involved in farming.[10]

Financially, the well-being of some church leaders and their congregants was affected. One other challenge for the church was how to reach its members during the period of the lockdown and restriction on religious activities. In fact, there was a loss of fellowship and a sense of community. Apart from meeting in church auditoriums, many churches, especially, Pentecostal-Charismatic churches do not have other means of meeting their congregants. This became a real challenge for them. There was the need to meet the spiritual needs of their members. Many Ghanaian Pentecostal-Charismatics usually take their spiritual insights from the pulpit rather than studying the Bible for themselves.[11] A study revealed that during the COVID-19 period, there was "a decline in religious practices such as prayer and listening to the word of God among congregants."[12]

Furthermore, during the period of religious restrictions, some religious rituals could not be held. For example, key rituals such as water baptism, communion, blessing of marriages, and burial services were not held in some churches. Despite these challenges, some real opportunities were presented to the church. One such is the use of technology. Churches that embraced technological innovations were able to survive the period of COVID-19. Through this medium, it was possible for many churches to reach their congregants. Some Pentecostal-Charismatic churches organized virtual church services through television, Facebook, and WhatsApp. The period saw the proliferation of online activities in

---

10. Osei-Tutu et al., "Ban of Religious Gatherings," 340.
11. Kudadjie, "Holy Spirit in Moral Character Formation," 195.
12. Osei-Tutu et al., "Ban of Religious Gatherings," 340.

the church's life. Time consciousness is another positive gift that COVID-19 brought to the church. Church service during the COVID-19 period was brief. Prior to COVID-19, most Pentecostal services could last for about three to three and a half hours. However, during the period of COVID-19, church services were done within two hours. In the post-COVID era, some churches have maintained this brevity because it works for them. Other equally important opportunities that COVID-19 brought to the church include the importance of small group meetings, the need for effective pastoral care ministry, the relevance of fellowship and community, the need for state-church partnership, social intervention as a key ministry of the church, and health consciousness, just to mention a few. In the section that follows, we will reflect on the ways Pentecostal-Charismatic churches can harness the challenges and opportunities of COVID-19 for effective ecclesiology.

Harnessing the Challenges and Opportunities of COVID-19 for Effective Pentecostal-Charismatic Ecclesiology

As has been highlighted in the previous section, COVID-19 presented both challenges and opportunities to the church. The question that remains is, how can Pentecostal-Charismatics control the challenges and take advantage of the opportunities to enhance their form of Christianity? It must be pointed out that COVID-19 is not the first pandemic to have hit the church. History is replete with examples of pandemics that affected the world and the church in the past. Mention can be made of the Spanish flu, the Asian flu of 1957 (H2N2) and the Hong Kong flu pandemic of 1968. It is believed that these pandemics "had a similar effect on the global scale like COVID-19."[13]

One lesson that could be gleaned from these pandemics was that the church embraced the challenges and came out stronger. Pentecostal-Charismatic churches should understand that society is dynamic and would from time to time go through changes. They should, therefore, adjust themselves and take advantage of the changing situations to enhance themselves. Our goal is to point out some key areas for consideration for an effective Christian ministry in the post-COVID-19 era. These include embracing technological innovations, the need for flexibility and adaptability, understanding the fragility of life, sustaining

---

13. Arthur, "African Pentecostal Church Life," 5.

social intervention systems, encouraging family and personal devotions, acknowledging suffering as part of the Christian call, strengthening pastoral care ministry, strengthening state-church relations, building a health-conscious church, the need for effective time management, and encouraging small group meetings.

Embrace Technological Innovations

One lesson that COVID-19 taught the church is the relevance of technological innovations in the church's life. Religion and technology had been bedfellows for some time now. However, it was during the COVID-19 era that the relationship because obvious. Technology became a savior to the church. Many churches and Christian leaders took to their social media platforms such as Facebook, Google Meet, Microsoft Teams, WhatApp, Cisco, WebEx, etc., to provide for the devotional needs of their followers. Some churches organized their services on TV and radio broadcasts. For example, The Church of Pentecost held its 44th and 45th General Council Meetings virtually in 2020 and 2021, respectively, for the first time.

Although some Christian leaders employed technology to meet the needs of their members, it was inevitable that some struggled with the technology. Aside from employing technology for devotional purposes, it was used as a fundraising tool. Pentecostal-Charismatic churches should invest heavily in technology. They should continue its usage and train their leaders on the use of technology. They should have a department that will oversee their technological needs. They should blend physical meetings with online ones, especially for church business meetings. They should employ the use of technology for mission work as it can help to reach people faster. In this case, training in digital missions at all levels of the church is ideal. Pentecostal churches should also encourage their members to pay their tithes and offerings through digital means.

The Need for Flexibility and Adaptability

Pentecostal-Charismatic churches should also learn from the COVID-19 experience that change is inevitable. They should be ready to change some of their practices when there is a need. For example, The Church of Pentecost (CoP) was not used to organizing funeral services in church auditoriums. However, COVID-19 caused leadership to revisit such a position. When the ban on social gatherings was imposed with a restriction on funeral services, the leadership of the church saw it expedient to allow funeral services to take place in church buildings. In the post-COVID era, the church is still encouraging it.

Pentecostal churches should critically reflect on their practices and see which ones could go through modifications in light of COVID-19. For instance, during the COVID-19 restrictions in Ghana, many Pentecostal-Charismatic churches could not perform water baptism. This is because they ascribe to baptism by immersion, which requires that the whole body is completely immersed in water. However, it was detected that COVID-19 could spread through this medium. The question that one may raise is, if COVID-19 had persisted, does it mean that there would be no baptism? The humble suggestion is that Pentecostal-Charismatic churches should think through their rituals and practices and allow for modification where necessary.

Emphasize the Fragility of Life

COVID-19 has taught the world that human life is fragile and could be lost at any time. This notion is firmly established in Scriptures. James reminds us of the fragility of life when he writes:

> Now listen, you who say, "Today or tomorrow we will go to this or that city, spend a year there, carry on business and make money." Why, you do not even know what will happen tomorrow. What is your life? You are a mist that appears for a little while and then vanishes. (Jas 4:13–14)

We are reminded that we do not have control over life, and also emphasizes the fact that tomorrow is never guaranteed, in the sense that everything in this world could be taken away in an instant. Pentecostal-Charismatic churches should teach this reality of life so that their adherents will not be overwhelmed when the unexpected happens.

Acknowledging Suffering as Part of the Christian Call

Another lesson that can be drawn from the COVID-19 experience is the need to accept that suffering is part of the Christian life. Not many Pentecostal-Charismatics readily accept the above notion. Some Christians question the reality of God during crises like COVID-19. During the

COVID-19 era, some people asked about "God's care and love amid situations where they could not mourn the loss of loved ones."[14] COVID-19 restrictions and regulations along with the daily death toll left many people to question the rule of God or sovereignty over the pandemic.[15] That is, people questioned God's characteristics such as love, mercy, kindness, and empathy. Pentecostal churches should teach about the sovereignty of God. Their adherents should be made to understand that God's character does not change despite the crises that humanity faces.

Sustaining Social Intervention Systems

The indispensable role of social intervention came up during the COVID-19 era. Church members expected their churches to support them in the moment. Some even threatened to leave their churches because they did not remember them when it mattered. However, a number of churches did well to assist their members during that era. The CoP made various donations to the government and to individuals. Donations to the central government were made by the headquarters of the church.[16] The administrative areas, districts and local assemblies also made donations either to their members who were in need or to their respective communities.[17]

Pentecostal-Charismatic churches should take this aspect of the ministry seriously. They should make budgetary allocations for it. Social intervention is not only an expectation, but also biblical. This is made clear in the book of Matthew: "For I was hungry and you gave nothing to eat, I was thirsty and you gave me nothing to drink, I needed clothes and you did not clothe me, I was sick and in prison and you did not look after me" (Matt 25: 42–43).

Encourage Family and Personal Devotions

COVID-19 has re-echoed the importance of family and personal devotion. When it became impossible for people to congregate for church service, family and personal devotions were the surest means of building

---

14. Resane, "Where Is God When It Hurts?," 1.
15. Resane, "Where Is God When It Hurts?," 7.
16. MyJoyOnline, "Pentecost Church Donates 10 Vans"
17. Nyamekye, "Church of Pentecost."

one's spirituality. People who did not have the habit of having personal or family devotions are at risk of losing their spirituality. Such people would become prayerless and would not have the Word of God in them. It is very important for individuals and families to build a consistent devotional life. Pentecostal-Charismatic churches should continue to encourage and teach their adherents in this area.

Strengthen Pastoral Care Ministry

During the COVID-19 era, it was observed that pastoral care ministry became an unavoidable tool in keeping church members. Churches with strong pastoral care ministries were able to flow with their followers. In the post-COVID era, Pentecostal churches should strengthen this aspect of their ministries. It is the best way to minister and maintain church members. It is a means of demonstrating care and love to the flock.

Encouraging Small Group Meetings

Another key lesson learned from COVID-19 is the role of small group meetings in the church's life. It was observed that churches with excellent small-group meetings were not affected much as compared to those without them. Small group meetings favored COVID-19 regulations. The home cell system in the CoP was what helped the church to survive during the period because church services were organized at that level. Pentecostal-Charismatic churches should not relent in this area. They should encourage it and make it a central part of their system.

Strengthen State-Church Relations

The need to strengthen state-church relations was seen during the COVID-19 era. But for the church, it would have been difficult to control the virus in Ghana. The cooperation between the state and the church made things easier. The churches helped in keeping their adherents abreast with the developments leading to a new normal. Also, when it was becoming difficult for people to accept the Coronavirus vaccine, a number of church leaders came out publicly to give evidence that they had taken it. This helped the congregants to follow suit. During the period of the lockdown, several churches donated relief items to support community members. The CoP, for instance, released its ultra-modern Convention Centre to be used as an isolation center. This brought some relief to the government and Ghanaians. This helped to create a positive public image of the church. Pentecostal-Charismatic churches should maintain a strong relationship with the state for development. Through it, the church can influence some decisions of the government.

Building a Health-Conscious Church

Additionally, COVID-19 has taught humanity the need to be conscious about our health. The COVID-19 experience has taught us to take personal hygiene seriously through regular washing of hands and the use of hand sanitizer. Prior to COVID-19, not many people were used to these practices including the church. However, during the COVID-19 era, the church needed to educate its congregants about the importance of maintaining personal hygiene and being conscious of underlying health challenges. Pentecostal-Charismatic churches should make health education paramount in their ministry.

Need for Effective Time Management

Finally, the need for effective time management is a blessing that COVID-19 brought to the church in general and Pentecostal-Charismatics in particular. Prior to COVID-19, these churches were spending long hours for church services. However, COVID-19 church services were brief but effective, sometimes taking a maximum of two hours. In the post-COVID era, this new trend works for many churches in Ghana. Church members now prefer short services to longer ones. Pentecostal-Charismatic churches should, therefore, structure their programs to avoid prolonged services.

Conclusion

This paper has reviewed the effect of COVID-19 and has indicated that it has brought both challenges and opportunities. We argued that Pentecostal-Charismatic churches can work on the challenges and take advantage of the opportunities to enhance their ministries. The paper identified and shed light on eleven areas for their attention. It will be of great benefit to the church and its congregants if they did attend to these 11 areas.

Bibliography

Adams, Claude Nyarko. "President Launches Gh 600 Million COVID-19 Alleviation Programme Today." *All Africa*, May 19, 2020. http://allafrica.com/stories/202005190844.html.

Akuffo-Addo, Nana. "Akuffo-Addo's 5th Address to the Nation on Measures Taken to Combat Coronavirus." https://www.ghanaweb.com/GhanaHomePage/television/news/Akuffo-Addo-s-5th-address-tothe-nation-on-measures-taken-to-combat-Coronavirus-96286.

Arthur, Justice Anquandah. "African Pentecostal Church Life in the Post-COVID-19 Era: Analysis and Proposal." *Majam* 6 (2022) 1–15.

Cavaliere, Paola. "Religious Institutions in Japan Responding to COVID-19-Induced and Uncertainty." *Journal of Religion in Japan* 10 (2021) 31–63.

Durkin, Joanne, et al. "Touch in Times of COVID-19: Touch Hunger Hurts." *Journal of Clinical Nursing* 30 (2020) 331–65.

Kudadjie, Patrick Tetteh. "The Holy Spirit in Moral Character Formation: Perceptions within Ghanaian Pentecostal-Charismatic Christianity." PhD diss., Akrofi-Christaller Institute of Theology, Mission and Culture, 2022.

Lekoa, Mammusa Rosinah, and Sibuso Louis Ntuli. "An Attack on the Cross: Spiritual Leaders' Accounts of Fear and Resilience during COVID-19 Pandemic." *Pharos Journal of Theology* 102 (2021) 1–12.

MyJoyOnline. "Pentecost Church Donates 10 Vans to Support NCCE's Public Education Coronavirus." March 24, 2020. https://www.myjoyonline.com/pentecost-church-donates-10-vans-to-support-ncces-public-education-on-coronavirus/.

Nyamekye, Eric. "The Church of Pentecost, Chairman's Circular Letter to All Assemblies, Ghana," May 4, 2020.

Osei-Tutu, Annabella, et al. "Ban of Religious Gatherings during the COVID-19 Pandemic: Impact on Church Leaders' Well-Being in Ghana." *Pastoral Psychology* 70 (2021) 335–47.

Resane, Kelebogile T. "Where Is God When It Hurts? Theodicy from the Pain of COVID-19." *In die Skriflig* 57 (2023) 1–7.

Village, Andrew, and Leslie J. Francis. "The Effect of Spiritual Wellbeing on Self-Perceived Health Changes among Members of the Church of England during the COVID-19 Pandemic in England." *Journal of Religion and Health* 62 (2023) 2899–915.

World Bank. "COVID-19 Forced Businesses in Ghana to Reduce Wages for Over 770,000 Workers and Caused about 42,000 Layoffs—Research Reveals." August 3, 2020. https://www.worldbank.org/en/news/press-release/2020/08/03/covid-19-forced-businesses-in-ghana-to-reduce-wages-for-over-770000-workers-and-caused-about-42000-layoffs-research-reveals.

CHAPTER 12

Church Governance and National Transformation: A Case of The Church of Pentecost, Ghana

JOHNNY LARTEY PEPRAH

Introduction

THIS PAPER ATTEMPTS TO examine the role played by governance of The Church of Pentecost (CoP), in Ghana's national development and transformation. The paper traces the origin of Ghanaian Pentecostalism to Peter Newman Anim, who started a very small rural fellowship of Christians in Asamankese, Ghana, in the 1921.[1] The Pentecostal movement grew into three major branches: Anim's Christ Apostolic Church International (CACI), The Apostolic Church of Ghana (ACG), and The Church of Pentecost. The CoP has grown and spread into a global-impact movement of 4.2 million members in 152 nations worldwide as of December 2022.[2]

The fundamental factor responsible for the phenomenal growth of the CoP is identified as "the God factor." This pneumatic movement has been driven by a system of government under the guidance of a very disciplined and militant leadership full of integrity. The CoP governmental ethos is peculiar in that the executive, legislative, and judiciary branches

---

1. Larbi, *Pentecostalism*, 98.
2. Nyamekye, "State of the Church Address," 3–9.

function in unity and diversity. The CoP has achieved such spectacular results through its system of government that they warrant theological and scientific investigation. The CoP's governance has contributed significantly to Ghana's national transformation, especially through its five-year vision dubbed Vision 2023 under the theme, "Possessing the Nations: Equipping the Church to Transform Every Sphere of Society with Values and Principles of the Kingdom of God."

The CoP, since its establishment in 1953, has contributed to national development and transformation in the following spheres: (i) Moral and Spiritual Guidance, (ii) Social Welfare and Community Development, (iii) Advocacy and Social Justice, (iv) Leadership and Empowerment, and (v) Moral Accountability and Anti-Corruption Efforts. The impact of the CoP on Ghana's national transformation has been influenced by numerous factors, including the commitment and wise actions of CoP leadership, the level of engagement of the CoP's ministers, officers and members at all levels, the cooperation of the communities in which the CoP functions, and the broad social and political contexts.

While the CoP has been very influential in Ghana's positive national transformation, collaboration and synergy with other stakeholders including the government, civil society organizations, and other faith groups, have been crucial for comprehensive and sustainable national transformation. This chapter concludes with lessons that other institutions, movements, and national governments can learn from the CoP's governance systems.

Background

The church has from its inception been a transformative force in society. The Jewish leaders complained that Jesus Christ was turning all the people away from the traditional religious systems (John 12:19). Paul and his companions were persecuted because they were "people who turn the world upside down" (Acts 17:6). Church history and theological research has records of the transforming power of the church on society. Onyinah and Tsekpoe have posited that Ghana has experienced five generations of Christianity, with each making its impact on the society.[3] Scholars of Pentecostalism in Ghana like Tsekpoe, Asamoah-Gyadu, and Onyinah agree that Pentecostalism owes a lot to the Traditional Western Mission

3. Onyinah and Tsekpoe, "Pentecostal-Charismatic Ecumenism in Ghana," 237–46.

Churches (TWMCs) who "had contributed significantly to the building of schools, hospitals, and the translation of the Bible and other literature into various vernacular languages."[4] The first of the five generations of Christianity was the Western Traditional Mission Churches with their ethnocentric replication model of mission that reflected the exploitative colonization agenda of their governments. This was followed by the African Independent churches with their indigenous traditional and spiritual paradigms of worship. The third generation of Christianity is the classical Pentecostal movement with its contextualization of the gospel to suit its host environment. The CoP belongs to this contextualization model of missions. The fourth generation of Christianity emerged in the 1970s as the Charismatic renewal movement with its American models of worship. This attracted the youth significantly and continues to transform the sociocultural dynamics of the nations. The fifth generation of Christianity in Ghana is the one-man prophetic church model, where one charismatic figure arises as a spokesperson of God with miraculous signs and wonders accompanying his or her ministry.

The CoP has contextualized all these five generations of Christianity under its umbrella to provide a forum where all people of all backgrounds can conveniently fellowship and be satisfied. This is the unique strength of the CoP's contextualization model. It is in this light and through the "God factor" under the well-structured governmental system that the CoP envisages to "possess the nations and transform every sphere of society with values and principles of the kingdom of God." Vision 2023 had outlined the strategies and tactics necessary to achieve the agenda. What lessons lie in the CoP's success story for governments and others?

Biblical Principles of Good Governance (Acts 6:1–7)

The Bible described a church governance issue in Acts 6:1–7 as follows:

> Now in these days when the disciples were increasing in number, a complaint by the Hellenists arose against the Hebrews because their widows were being neglected in the daily distribution. And the twelve summoned the full number of the disciples and said, "It is not right that we should give up preaching the word of God to serve tables. Therefore, brothers, pick out from among you seven men of good repute, full of the

---

4. Tsekpoe, "Navigating the Shades," 27–46.

Spirit and of wisdom, whom we will appoint to this duty. But we will devote ourselves to prayer and to the ministry of the word." And what they said pleased the whole gathering, and they chose Stephen, a man full of faith and of the Holy Spirit, and Philip, and Prochorus, and Nicanor, and Timon, and Parmenas, and Nicolaus, a proselyte of Antioch. These they set before the apostles, and they prayed and laid their hands on them. And the word of God continued to increase, and the number of the disciples multiplied greatly in Jerusalem, and a great many of the priests became obedient to the faith.

Brian Schuette posited that "there are five key principles for church governance that stand out from this passage."[5] The key principles are (i) the necessity of godly leadership, (ii) the characteristics of godly leadership, (iii) the benefits of broad participation, (iv) the synergy between godly leadership and broad participation, and (v) the impact of a healthy church in action. These principles are explained below:

The Necessity of Godly Leadership

The passage in Acts 6:1–7 describes a conflict between Hellenists and Hebrews in the Jerusalem church. This conflict shows that wherever two or more people gather, conflict is inevitable. Jesus reiterated the fact that offenses will definitely come between people. The church must, therefore, be structured to deal with conflict in ways that glorify God and protect the body of Christ. Leadership at all levels of the church organization must address conflict peacefully. This is possible when leaders are given organizational authority commensurate with their spiritual responsibilities. Administratively, there must be constitutions, rules, regulations, bylaws, policies, and statutes that clearly specify the roles of the clergy, lay ordained officers, and members of the church for peaceful coexistence and operations.

The Characteristics of Godly Leadership

Godly leaders are needed to decisively anticipate and address conflicts with humility and love. This allows everyone to focus on the mission of evangelism and transformational discipleship. Godly leaders

---

5. Schuette, "5 Principles of Good Church Governance."

demonstrate the character of Christ by bearing the fruit of the Spirit for the benefit of the entire congregation and community. Godly leaders equip the saints for works of ministry by preaching, teaching, and portraying Christ for the edification of the church.

The Benefits of Broad Participation

Godly leadership promotes broad participation of clergy and laity in decision-making and policy implementation at all levels. Godly leadership acknowledges the importance of all clergy and laity in doing ministry as members of the body of Christ. Leadership that encourages broad participation facilitates church growth and development in peace. At all times they encourage leadership input and membership participation.

The Synergy between Godly Leadership and Broad Participation

Godly leadership produces synergy that creates a whole that is greater than the sum of its parts. This means that godly leadership unites people into a team to achieve more than they could have achieved if they worked separately. The body of Christ achieves far more for the kingdom of heaven, when working as a united team motivated by the love of God through godly leaders.

The Impact of a Healthy Church in Action

The synergy produced by godly leadership participating with faithful members has significant impact beyond the local church. The synergy produced by godly leadership impacts the church, the community, and nations, and creates waves that flow into eternity.

Models of Church Governance

There is no single generally accepted church governance structure prescribed in the Bible, though the Bible contains divine principles of leadership and governance. All church governance models aim to be shaped by biblical principles but they each sit on a continuum in terms of which principles they accept and their practical theological application of those principles. Thus, there are as many church governance structures as there are doctrinal differences and cultures. Three key questions are most relevant to understand any church structure: (i) where is power distributed—with the local congregation or a centralized structure, or somewhere in between? (ii) Who makes and reviews decisions—a single minister, a small group of pastors, or a large group of church members? (iii) What happens when something goes wrong? Who steps in when there is a crisis, conflict, or change in leadership? Answers to these questions determine the governance model of a church, whether centralized or congregational.

According to Andrew Judd there are five major models along the church governance continuum: Catholic (papal control), megachurch (senior pastor control), Anglican (bishop and synod control), Presbyterian (regional ministers and elders control), and Baptist (congregational control).[6] There are other minor models and mixed models along the continuum. The most centralized model is the Catholic structure where the church reports to the pope. This structure implies that one single personality, with the assistance of a small group of clergy (*episcopoi*), control the church decisions and activities. The megachurch model has a senior pastor, assisted by selected clergy, controlling the decisions and activities of the church. This is very common among North American Charismatic ministries. With the Anglican model, control is exercised by a bishop and a synod. The synod is a local or provincial assembly of bishops and other church officials meeting to resolve questions of discipline or administration. The Presbyterian model involves a more democratic position which combines clergy and laity from the congregation to form a governing body. The Baptist congregational model involves a governing body made up of members at various levels and departments of the church, forming a governing body.

The Carver Model or the Universal Principle of Governance

According to Jamé Bolds, "If God through Christ has reconciled all things to himself, then it seems that a Christian theory of governance must by definition be a universal theory applicable to any given governance structure."[7] Bolds posited that, on the basis of Colossians 1:15–20, there

---

6. Judd, "Five Models of Church Governance," 1–3.
7. Bolds, "Universal Principles of Governance," 1–5.

must be a universal model of governance of all organizations, adaptable for faith-based nonprofits and, to a lesser degree, for local church governance structures once due consideration is given to the authoritative inputs of Scripture, ecclesiology, and tradition.

Governance Structure of The Church of Pentecost

The governance structure in the CoP is significantly the Presbyterian model, but also has a mixture of other models. It is more congregational at the local level, and Presbyterian at the district and area levels. At the global level, the Anglican and Catholic models blend to project the chairman like the Catholic pope and Anglican archbishop. This structure has evolved over many eras of leadership in the evolution of the CoP. The evolution from congregational model to a Catholic/ Presbyterian model is described below.

According to Opoku Onyinah,

> The CoP has a centralised structure of governance "that is similar to the Apostolic Church in the UK. . . . At the top of the church's structure is the General Council which consists of all confirmed ministers of the church, area executive committee members, chairmen of boards and committees and ministries directors. Below the General Council is the 15-man Executive Council that sees to the administration of the church. The area (and national) presbyteries, chaired by apostles and prophets, come below the Executive Council. Under the area presbyteries, are the district presbyteries. The district presbyteries are headed by pastors. At the bottom of the administrative structure of the church are the local presbyteries, headed by presiding elders. . . . The structure may have its weaknesses, as with all structures. However, on the whole, it seems to fit in with the Ghanaian culture, especially that of the Akan with its various military organs (Busia 1951, 1–22; Nukunya 1992, 67–74). Thus, it makes the members feel secure in its formality, accountability and disciplinary measures.[8]

---

8. Onyinah, "Distinguished Church Leader Essay," 186–87.

The Apostolic Church Era (1937–53)

Peter Anim, who is recognized as the father of Pentecostalism in Ghana, started his church in 1921 with a congregational governance model. This was when the movement was called Faith Tabernacle Church (1923–30) and Apostolic Faith Church (1930–35). After affiliating the movement to the Apostolic Church, UK in 1935, the governance structure changed to a more Presbyterian model.[9] In 1935 Anim, against the objection of some assemblies, invited George Perfect of the Apostolic Church, UK to visit the church in Asamankese. Anim later made a request to George Perfect for a resident missionary to help the church in Africa. The Apostolic Church sent James McKeown to the Gold Coast as a missionary in March 1937. The African church did not have any elaborate governance structure. Anim, together with his elders and ministers, formed a presbytery that took all executive, legislative, and judicial decisions.

In 1939, the presbytery decided to terminate their relationship with the Apostolic Church, UK, due to doctrinal differences on faith healing. Anim renamed his church Christ Apostolic Church (CAC), which later became Christ Apostolic Church International (CACI).[10] By 1950, CAC had established an episcopal governance structure with a centralized General Executive Council as the main ruling body in charge of all activities and decisions of the church.[11] The Apostolic Church, UK, had an episcopal governance model with a hierarchical administrative structure headquartered in Bradford, where final executive, legislative, and judicial decisions were taken by the Executive Council. The Apostolic Church, UK resolved in 1953 that the Latter Rain abused the privileges granted them in condemning both in public and in private the recognized Church Government in the Apostolic Church. McKeown objected to the Executive Council decision to enshrine in the constitution that white apostles were superior to black apostles and refused to endorse the decision, because he considered it un-Christian, not biblical, discriminatory, and biased. He was dismissed in 1953.[12]

---

9. Larbi, *Pentecostalism*, 98–105.
10. Larbi, *Pentecostalism*, 108.
11. Larbi, *Pentecostalism*, 109.
12. Larbi, *Pentecostalism*, 213–14.

James McKeown's Era (1953–82)

After his dismissal by the Apostolic Church, UK in 1953, McKeown returned to the Gold Coast to lead his faction of the Apostolic Church. He established an administrative structure like that of the Apostolic Church, UK. McKeown's Executive Council was to oversee an administrative hierarchy of regional/area heads, district ministers, and presiding elders. These were assisted by Executive Committees for policy implementation. The legislature was structured likewise, with the General Council, regional/area, district and local presbyteries. Larbi has posited that "the discipline of the church has made the 'structure' effective. . . . The kind of hierarchical structure that is found in the CoP is also found, for example, in CAC and the Apostolic Church, Ghana." McKeown's CoP is noted for discipline for effective governance structure.[13]

F. S. Safo's Era (1982–87)

Fred Safo introduced administrative reforms to strengthen the existing structure by directing that all area heads open offices, engage the services of area deacons for financial management, and staff the offices with competent administrators. This policy facilitated the smooth administration of the church at all levels and accelerated growth and development in all spheres. Safo was a very strong disciplinarian and diplomatic leader who kept the spiritual and disciplinary standards of the church very high. He created more areas and districts out of existing ones for efficiency, maximum growth, and development.[14]

M. K. Yeboah's Era (1988–98)

Yeboah's leadership and governance was so peaceful and impactful that he made the CoP to experience spectacular national and international growth. During Yeboah's tenure of office as the chairman of the church, the CoP grew from 302,421 members in 1988 to 869,889 members in 1998. The church spread rapidly into neighboring nations such as Togo, La Cote D'Ivoire, Liberia, Burkina Fasso, and Benin. The office of the International Missions Director (IMD) was created in 1991 to promote

13. Larbi, *Pentecostalism*, 109, 180.
14. Noble-Atsu, "Phenomenal Growth of The Church of Pentecost," 76.

the Great Commission agenda of global evangelization and transformation. Ghanaians in Europe and America started CoP fellowships and sent requests to the IMD's office for recognition and supply of missionaries to give them spiritual leadership. Monthly offerings were raised in all local assemblies to support the mission enterprise. Yeboah's excellent leadership and governance in the CoP led to his appointment to the Council of State, where he contributed significantly to national development and transformation.[15]

M. K. Ntumy's Era (1998–2008)

The public image of the CoP was raised very significantly under the leadership of M. K. Ntumy. Relations between the CoP and the state and traditional leadership were improved, and tensions between the church and traditional systems were calmed to foster peaceful cooperation for community development. Within ten years Ntumy's leadership as chairman of the CoP from 1998 to 2008, the church's membership doubled from 869,889 to 1,788,114.[16] He was noted for developing diplomatic relations between the CoP and the state, promoting development, and improving the media presence of the CoP. Ntumy established the Pentecost University College to promote liberal and theological education within and outside the CoP. The CoP increased its media presence by preaching more frequently and powerfully on radio, television, and other international mass media platforms. Ntumy's diplomacy, leadership, and governance made so much impact on Ghana's development and transformation that the president of the Republic of Ghana awarded the young CoP chairman the prestigious medals. Noble-Atsu wrote that:

> Chairman Ntumy received, at a glamorous ceremony, one of Ghana's highest national awards in recognition of his leadership excellence, contribution to national peace and development, and as a distinguished clergyman. President John Agyekum Kuffuor, acting on behalf of the whole nation, decorated Apostle Ntumy with, The Order of the Volta, Companion. There is no doubt that the image of The Church of Pentecost was boosted thereby. He was also appointed by the President to

---

15. Noble-Atsu, "Phenomenal Growth of The Church of Pentecost," 77.
16. Noble-Atsu, "Phenomenal Growth of The Church of Pentecost," 58.

serve the nation as a member of the Ghana AIDS Commission, a body chaired by the President himself.[17]

Ntumy's tenure lifted the image, national significance, and international impact of the church. Ntumy did not alter the governance structure of the CoP. He only added more glory and power to the system. He handed over the chairmanship to Opoku Onyinah in 2008.

Opoku Onyinah's Era (2008–18)

Opoku Onyinah inherited a governance structure that he worked with for his ten years of leadership of the CoP. He introduced the Regional Coordinating Committee (RCC) to facilitate executive decision-making, implementation, and supervision at the regional and national levels. The RCC addressed judicial and legislative issues at the regional levels also. To arrive at more informed leadership decisions at the global level, Onyinah expanded the Executive Council membership from nine to fifteen apostles and prophets. He added the eleventh tenet, Christian Marriage and Family Life, to the ten tenets. Through the very strong governance structures of the CoP, Opoku was able to extend the influence of the CoP into other spheres like chieftaincy, chaplaincy, national peace, and development. As an academic and theologian, he championed theological education in the CoP and expanded the scope of theological education for ministers and officers in the CoP and beyond. He was appointed member of the Ghana National Peace Council by the President of Ghana. He played several roles of national significance. Noble-Atsu stated, "When the church's university was established in 2003, he was appointed its first rector. . . . [H]is flagship legacies in the church would include the construction of an ultra-modern Pentecost Convention Centre at Gomoa-Fettheh." Opoku Onyinah was recognized internationally for serving on many boards and committees across many Christian organizations globally.[18] Onyinah handed over the leadership and government to Eric Nymaekye peacefully and smoothly in 2018.

---

17. Noble-Atsu, "Phenomenal Growth of The Church of Pentecost," 79.
18. Noble-Atsu, "Phenomenal Growth of The Church of Pentecost," 78–79.

Eric Nyamekye's Vision 2023 (2018–)

Eric Nyamekye was elected chairman of the CoP in May 2018. He presented a five-year vision which spans from 2018–23, dubbed *Vision 2023*. The agenda for this vision is to transform every sphere of society with values and principles of the kingdom of God. One of his strategies to achieve the goal is to restructure the church systems in order to achieve maximum impact in the nations. The restructuring efforts introduced intervention ministries to promote more effective and efficient implementation of activities. Some of the intervention ministries are the Ministry to Persons with Disabilities (MPWD), Home and Urban Missions (HUM), Schools Outreach Ministry (SOM), ministry to chieftaincy institution, and chaplaincy ministry. The intervention ministries of Vision 2023 did not change the executive, legislative, or judiciary structures of the CoP, but rather increased the implementation organs of the church to achieve maximum impact in the national transformation agenda.

The CoP Local Assembly Government Structure

The CoP local assembly is a community-based group of believers who meet occasionally to pray, worship, sing songs of praises to God, preach the gospel, study the Bible, give offerings to support the church, discuss issues, solve problems, and perform any other activity for the welfare and edification of the church. The local assembly is led by a presiding elder and assisted by supporting elders to form the executive organ of local government. There is a legislature called the local presbytery made up of all ordained officers (i.e., elders, deacons, and deaconesses). The local executive and presbytery join to form the local judiciary. A case may be referred to a disciplinary committee for investigations and recommendations. The final judicial decisions at the local level are taken by the local presbytery. Plaintiffs or defendants who feel unsatisfied with the local presbytery's judicial decisions may appeal to higher authorities for redress.

The CoP District Government Structure

A group of local assemblies in a designated geographical space is referred to as a district. The district is headed by a full-time minister (apostle, prophet, evangelist, pastor, overseer or probationary overseer). The district minister is the chairman of the district executive committee, which comprises the district secretary, district finance committee chairman, four other elders, the district women's ministry leader and the assistant women's ministry leader. These office holders are elected by the district presbytery to serve for two-year terms of office. The district legislature is the district presbytery made up of all ordained officers (elders, deacons, and deaconesses) within the district. The judiciary at the district level is made up of the executive committee, acting in consultation with the presbytery. A committee may be constituted to investigate cases and make recommendations to the executive committee and presbytery for consideration and decision. Complainants, plaintiffs, defendants, or any person who considers the decisions of the judiciary unsatisfactory may appeal to the area or national executive committee for redress.

The CoP Area Government Structure

A group of districts in a designated geographical space is called an administrative area. The area is administered by an area head, who functions as the chief executive officer, chief justice, and speaker of the legislature. The area head is the chairman of the executive committee, made up of an area secretary, two ministers in the area, the area deacon, and two other elders in the area, all elected to serve a two-year term and may be reviewed for further terms. The area women's ministry leader and her assistant are co-opted members of the area executive committee. The area head is the chairman of the area presbytery, which is made up of the area head and his wife, all ministers in the area and their wives, leaders of various ministries (evangelism, youth, women's, children's, and men's ministry), and eleven ordained officers from each district. The area judiciary is the executive committee acting in consultation with the area presbytery. A victim of "injustice" may appeal to the national executive committee or executive council for redress.

The CoP Regional Coordinating Committee[19]

The regional coordinating committee (RCC) is a body of apostles, prophets, evangelists, area heads, and directors in an administrative region. The RCC is headed by a coordinator who is a member of the executive

19. Church of Pentecost, *Ministerial Handbook*, 152–54.

council. Where there are more than one executive council members in a region, the executive council shall appoint one of them as coordinator subject to yearly reviews. Where there is no executive council member in a region, the executive council shall appoint one of the area heads in that region as coordinator. The appointment is subject to annual review and a coordinator may serve for further terms. The committee shall appoint one of the area heads as secretary. The RCC may co-opt any person(s) to its meetings. The functions of the RCC include the reception and discussion of annual and half-year reports from the areas within the region. The RCC is to present a composite regional report to the general council through the chairman's office, with a copy to the general secretary's office. The RCC shall make recommendations on intraregional transfers of ministers to the Executive Council for consideration. The RCC shall discuss recommendations for upgrading to overseership and callings to the pastorate from the areas and present a report to the Executive Council for consideration. The RCC shall investigate matters that may be referred to it by the Executive Council or an area head in the region and make appropriate recommendations. The RCC shall receive, discuss, and act on all memos coming out from the region and report on the memos to the Executive Council. The RCC shall coordinate activities of head office ministers such as PENSA traveling secretaries within the region. The RCC is to endeavor, at all costs, to build consensus on all matters.

The National/International/Global Government Structure

The Executive Council is a body of fifteen apostles and prophets elected to lead the church for five years per term. The council is headed by a chairman and assisted by a general secretary. There is an international mission's director responsible for the administration of international and internal missions. The decision of the Executive Council, ratified by the General Council, is final. Executive Council decisions are communicated in the annual "White Paper" and subsequent circulars. The foundation of apostolic authority and structure inherited from the Apostolic Church, UK has been developed into a global system of hierarchical administration with levels of authority at the continental block, and the national, regional, area, district, and local assembly levels. The degree of discipline is military in style and the theology is Christological theocracy. According to Michael Ntumy, governance in the CoP is practically a "theomocracy," which is a fusion of theocracy (rule of God) and democracy (rule of the people).[20] There are delegated authorities at all levels, but final authority is constitutionally vested in the chief executive officer (the chairman), who functions with the assistance of the Executive Council with the approval of the General Council.[21]

CoP's Vision 2023: "Possessing the Nations"

Nyamekye stated that he intended to build on what has been achieved by previous leadership, with the intention to produce a refreshed church that equips and releases its members into ministry as agents of transformation wherever they go. The overall goal of Vision 2023 was to "possess the nations by transforming every worldview, thought and behaviour with values, principles and lifestyles of the Kingdom of God and thereby turning many people to Christ." Nyamekye added, "The transformation agenda of Vision 2023 demands the efficient and effective implementation of well-designed interventions in order to fulfil the requirements of the Great Commission." Nyamekye identified seven strategic objectives of the "possessing the nations" agenda to include the following:

1. To teach our members to understand the dual purpose of the church (i.e., the church is called out of the world to belong to God and sent back to the world to witness and to serve).

2. To equip our members with the knowledge of God's Word for ministry.

3. To create the awareness that whatever a person does in any aspect of life is an opportunity and a setting for ministry.

4. To deploy our members to transform their societies and take the nations for Christ.

5. To further strengthen existing institutions and structures of our church and realign their activities to drive Vision 2023.

6. To undertake structural adjustments to get the church system freed from crowded programs to release members to witness and to serve beyond the church.

---

20. Annor-Antwi, *Myth or Mystery*, 351–61.
21. Church of Pentecost, *Constitution*, 7–12.

7. To strengthen existing institutions and structures to continually assess the effectiveness of interventions aimed at achieving the objectives of Vision 2023 (accountability).

The above may be summarized as "teaching, equipping, ministry awareness creation, social transformation, strengthening existing institutions, structural adjustments, and continual assessment and accountability." When all these are pursued with the discipline characteristic of the CoP, national development and transformation are assured.

CoP's Three-Pronged Strategic Approach and Twenty-Five Commitments

The global transformation agenda is designed to be achieved through a three-pronged approach that involved (i) equipping the local church, (ii) realigning structures for transformation, and (iii) promoting community development projects for transformation.[22] The Vision 2023 document identified twenty-five commitments as the spheres to influence to achieve the "possessing the nations" agenda in the short, medium, and long term. The commitments are summarized as follows:

> We are committed to make the local church an equipping centre for all members, where intentional discipleship programmes will be implemented to realigning the activities of the various ministries of the church for national and international transformation. The church will re-organise its counselling services and make the home a transformative arena. Evangelism, church planting and discipleship will be intensified at all levels of the church. Moreover, the nation's existing governance structures (the Executive, Judiciary and Legislature) will be engaged through the Ministry to politicians. Strategic partnerships will be developed with government for the development of the nation. The church will raise leaders for the nation's governance structures, and provide chaplaincy services to institutions including the palace and persons with disabilities. The media ministry will be restructured for impact. We will increase our presence in the nations through our mission fronts. The Pentecost University College will continue to be assisted to become a university of choice in Ghana, where excellent graduates will be produced. The Pentecost Theological Seminary (PTS) will be

22. Nyamekye, *Vision 2023*, 1–5.

assisted to strengthen ministerial formation, refresher courses, higher theological education and missionary training for the church. The Pentecost Convention Centre (PCC) will continue to provide Christian-centered hospitality services with excellence. The Regional Coordinating Committees shall continue to be empowered and given more room to effectively carry out their constitutionally assigned mandate. The church will harness the resourceful human capital of the PIWCs and enhance the activities of the Pension Board. Fraternal relationships with other Christian churches and para-church organisations across the globe will be enhanced, while accelerating the provision of a conducive worship environment for all our local assemblies, as well as ensuring that all our building projects meet the value for money requirement. The administration and finance functions of the church will be improved. The Executive Council shall be committed to serving the church wholeheartedly and with integrity in the fear of the Lord, as mandated. Again, efforts shall be made to make the General Council more functional. We shall adopt both biblical and best practices to improve our finances in order to mobilise the needed financial resources for the expected outputs of Vision 2023.[23]

The Role of Governance in Ghana's National Transformation

The CoP Governance structure and practices have made very significant impact on the development of Ghana. Some of the spheres of impact include national morality, spiritual guidance, social welfare, community development, advocacy, social justice, leadership development, youth empowerment, gender enhancement, anticorruption efforts, peacebuilding, conflict resolution, counseling, infrastructure, education, and health services, among others.

Observations and Recommendations

The governance structures, systems, and operations of the CoP have facilitated the phenomenal growth development and impact of the church on Ghana's development and transformation. The Church of Pentecost, like many other religious institutions, plays a crucial role in providing

---

23. Nyamekye, *Vision 2023*, 6.

moral and spiritual guidance to its members and the wider society. Through its teachings, sermons, and religious practices, the church promotes values such as integrity, honesty, compassion, and respect for human dignity. These values can have a positive impact on individuals and communities, fostering a sense of personal responsibility, social cohesion, and ethical behavior. By instilling these values in its members, the church contributes to the moral fabric of the nation, which is essential for sustainable national transformation.

The Church of Pentecost in Ghana is known for its commitment to social welfare and community development initiatives. The church operates numerous schools, hospitals, orphanages, and other social welfare institutions that provide essential services to the communities they serve. These institutions contribute to education, healthcare, and social support, which are critical components of national development. By actively engaging in social welfare and community development, the church helps address societal needs and uplifts the living standards of individuals, contributing to the overall transformation of the nation. Another role of church governance in national transformation is advocacy and social justice. The Church of Pentecost, like many other churches, often takes a stand on important social and political issues, advocating for justice, equality, and the well-being of the marginalized and vulnerable. Through its pastoral messages, public statements, and engagement with policymakers, the church can influence public discourse, raise awareness about societal challenges, and push for policy changes that promote social justice and equitable development. Such advocacy efforts can contribute to positive transformations in areas such as human rights, gender equality, poverty alleviation, and social inclusion. The Church of Pentecost places strong emphasis on leadership development and empowerment. The church provides training, mentorship, and pastoral care to its leaders and members, equipping them with the necessary skills and values to become effective leaders in their communities. This emphasis on leadership and empowerment can have a ripple effect on national transformation by nurturing a generation of leaders who are committed to ethical governance, community development, and nation-building. The church's leadership development programs, entrepreneurship initiatives, and emphasis on education can contribute to the development of human capital and foster a culture of innovation and productivity within the society. Church governance can also contribute to national transformation by promoting moral accountability and combating corruption. The Church of Pentecost, along with other religious organizations, can play a role in raising awareness about the detrimental effects of corruption and encouraging its members and society at large to uphold ethical standards in public and private life. By promoting transparency, integrity, and accountability, the church can contribute to a culture of good governance and responsible citizenship, which are essential for national transformation.

It is important to note that the impact of church governance on national transformation is contingent on various factors, including the commitment and actions of church leaders, the level of community engagement, and the broader social and political context. While religious institutions can play a positive role in national development, its collaboration and synergy with other stakeholders, including the government, civil society organizations, and other faith-based groups, are crucial for comprehensive and sustainable national transformation.

Conclusion

This paper attempted to examine the role played by governance of the CoP in Ghana's national development and transformation. The paper traced the origin of Ghanaian Pentecostalism to Peter Anim, the father of Ghanaian Pentecostalism and founder of Christ Apostolic Church International. The CoP, an offshoot of the Apostolic Church, UK has grown and spread into a global-impact movement of 4.2 million members in 152 nations worldwide as of December 2022. The "God factor" is responsible for the phenomenal growth and impact of the CoP. Moreover, the system of government, the disciplined members, militant leadership, and high standard of integrity have combined to make a glorious impact. The CoP, since its establishment in 1953, has contributed to national development and transformation in the following spheres: (i) moral and spiritual guidance, (ii) social welfare and community development, (iii) advocacy and social justice (iv) leadership and empowerment, and (v) moral accountability and anticorruption efforts. The impact of the CoP on Ghana's national transformation has been influenced by numerous factors, including the commitment and wise actions of CoP leadership; the level of engagement of CoP ministers, officers, and members at all levels; the cooperation of the communities in which the CoP functions; and the broad social and political contexts. The CoP has been very influential in Ghana's positive national transformation, in collaboration with other stakeholders including government, civil society organizations, and other faith groups. This was necessary to achieve the desired synergy crucial for comprehensive and sustainable national transformation. The author recommends that government institutions, groups, and churches learn the secrets of the CoPs success story and thus adopt and adapt the key principles for their survival, growth, development, and positive transformation.

Bibliography

Annor-Antwi, G. *Myth or Mystery: A 'Bio-Autobiography' of Apostle Professor Opoku Onyinah*. London: Inved, 2016.

Bolds, Jamé. "Universal Principles of Governance for Biblically Normed Institutions." https://www.acton.org/node/6424.

Busia, K. A. *The Position of the Chief in Modern Asante*. Oxford: Oxford University Press, 1951.

Judd, Andrew. "The Five Models of Church Governance (and How They Cope under Pressure)." March 31, 2022. https://www.ridley.edu.au/resource/the-five-models-of-church-governance-and-how-they-cope-under-pressure/.

Larbi, E. K. *Pentecostalism: The Eddies of Ghanaian Christianity*. Accra: CPCS, 2001.

———. "Sustaining the Growth." In *James McKeown Memorial Lectures: 50 Years of the Church of Pentecost*, edited by Opoku Onyinah, 137–58. Accra: Pentecost, 2004.

Nyamekye, Eric. "The State of the Church Address Delivered at the 46th Session of the General Council Meetings of the Church of Pentecost at PCC, Accra Ghana." May 2023.

———. *Vision 2023 of The Church of Pentecost*. Accra: Pentecost, 2019.

Noble-Atsu, D. K. "The Phenomenal Growth of The Church of Pentecost." In *God's Faithfulness to The Church of Pentecost*, edited by Opoku Onyinah and Michael Ntumy, 54–96. Mumbai: Quarterfold Printabilities, 2019.

Nukunya, G. K. *Tradition and Change in Ghana*. Accra: Ghana Universities Press, 1992.

Onyinah, Opoku. "Distinguished Church Leader Essay: The Church of Pentecost and Its Role in Ghanaian Society." In *African Initiated Christianity and the Decolonisation of Development: Sustainable Development in Pentecostal and Independent Churches*, edited by Philipp Öhlmann et al., 183–94. Abingdon: Routledge, 2020.

———. "The State of the Church Address Delivered at the 43rd Session of the General Council Meetings of the Church of Pentecost at PCC, Accra Ghana." May 2018.

Onyinah, Opoku, and Christian Tsekpoe. "Pentecostal-Charismatic Ecumenism in Ghana: A Response to The Church: Towards a Common Vision." In *Towards a Global Vision of the Church*. Vol. 1, *Explorations on Global Christianity and Ecclesiology*, edited by Cecil M. Robeck Jr. et al., 237–46. Geneva: WCC, 2022.

Schuette, Brian. "5 Principles of Good Church Governance." *Schuette Law Group*, June 29, 2021. https://www.slg.legal/5-principles-of-good-church-governance/.

The Church of Pentecost. *Constitution*. Accra: Pentecost, 2016.

———. *Ministerial Handbook*. Accra: Pentecost, 2016.

———. *Vision 2023*. Accra: Pentecost, 2019.

Tsekpoe, Christian. "Navigating the Shades and Nexus of Ghanaian Pentecostalism(s): A Search for an Appropriate Metaphor." *Ghana Journal of Religion and Theology* 10 (2020) 27–46.

Author Index

Aboagye-Mensah, Robert, 72, 83, 102, 103, 119
Agbiji, Obaji M., 77, 98, 102, 111, 112, 117
Agyeman-Fisher, Abena, 102, 108, 117
Anderson, Allan, 5, 15, 64, 65, 69
Anderson, Georg, 110, 115
Anderson, Norman, 160, 164
Anim, Emmanuel, v, vii, 11, 49, 51, 54, 55, 58, 60, 63
Apaah, Felicity, 67, 69
Asamoah-Gyadu, Johnson, 4, 15, 75, 83, 87, 99, 117, 179
Ashford, Bruce R., 137, 142, 146

Barclay, William, 162, 164
Barrett, David, 51, 134, 146
Benyah, Francis, 4-6, 15, 65, 70
Biggs, Matthew M., 107, 118
Bird, Matt, 93, 95
Bolds, Jamé, 183, 187
Bright, Bill, 87, 94
Bruce, Nicholls J, 151, 164, 165
Burges, Richard., 4, 15, 65, 68, 70
Burgess, Stanley M., 156, 164

Calvin, Shenk E., 155, 165
Cameron, Helen, 38, 48
Cochrane, James R., 105, 118
Coetzer Wentzel, 98, 99, 105, 118
Coward, Harold 158, 164
Cox, Harvey, 51, 61

Cross, Terry L., xxiii, 41, 46, 47, 48
Cunningham, Loren, 87, 94

Dairo, A O, 110, 118
Debrunner, Hans, 9, 15, 27, 32, 34, 46, 48
Denteh, Vincent Anane, vi, vii, 13, 133
Donkor, Lord, iii–v, vii, viii, xxiv, 10, 29, 34, 36, 69, 70
Dulles, Avery Cardinal, 19, 25, 26, 31
Dummet, M., 110, 118

Engen, Charles V., 134–36, 141, 146
Ennin, Paul Saa-Dede, 98, 101, 102, 104, 106, 118

Fee, Gordon, xviii
Freeman, Dena, 52, 54, 55, 61

Gaiya, Musa A. B., 66, 70
Gifford, Paul, 55, 58, 61, 101, 103, 104, 118
Gilliland, Dean S., 143, 146
Goodall, Norman, 15, 86, 95
Green, Michael, 86, 95
Groothuis, Douglas, 148, 149, 151, 155, 159, 160, 161, 162, 164

Hesselgrave, David, 34, 161
Hilborn, David, 93, 95
Hodges, Melvin, xxiii
Höschele, Stefan F., 72, 83

Jenkins, Philip, 51, 61, 134, 137, 146
Jere, Qeko, 112, 113
Johnson, Todd M., 87, 88, 95, 134, 146
Johnston, Graham, 160, 164
Judd, Andrew, 183, 197

Kärkkäinen, Veli-Matti, 4, 15, 20, 34
Keulder, Christian, 107, 118
Klinken, Adrain van, 67, 68, 70
Koduah, Alfred, vi, viii, 14, 147, 159, 164
Konings, Piet, 102–4, 112, 118
Kudadjie, Joshua 72, 83, 84, 95, 102, 103, 119
Kudadjie, Patrick, vi, viii, 14, 166, 170, 177
Kunda, Anthony, 110, 111, 119
Kunhiyop, Samuel, 97, 105, 119

Leite, Carlos, 106, 119
Leonard, Christine, 28, 32, 34, 55, 61
Lindberg, Staffan, 101, 106, 119

Makumbe, John, 105, 119
Mazrui, Ali, 103, 119
Mbiti, John S., 74, 83, 98
McAlpine, Thomas H, 3, 16
McGreal, Chris, 111, 119
McKeown, James, iii, iv, xv, xiv, xx, xxi, 1, 9, 10, 17, 19–49, 55, 61, 64, 93, 94, 164, 185, 186, 187
Menzies, William, 37, 39, 49
Mhango, Mbanyane, vi, ix, 13, 31, 109, 110, 121, 131, 132
Millar, Gary, 45, 49
Mutavhatsindi, Muthuphei A., 134, 146

Ndiyo, Ndem, 105, 119
Niebuhr, Richard, 18, 19, 33, 35, 38, 47
Norton, Allison, v, ix, 11, 63, 67, 69
Nsereko, Daniel, 98, 99, 119

Ohlmann, Philp, 5, 16, 61, 197
Okure, Aniedi, 114, 115, 117

Onyinah, Opoku, v, ix, 9, 10, 17, 21, 32, 35, 36–49, 57, 164, 179, 184, 188, 197
Osei-Tutu, Annabella, 169, 170, 177
Otabil, Mensa, 6, 58, 60, 61

Peprah, Johnny Lartey, vi, x, 14, 178
Petersen, Douglas, 3, 65, 70
Pinnock, Clark H., 149, 164
Pocock, Michael, 149, 152, 155, 157, 161, 164

Quampah, Dela, vi, x, 12, 13, 96, 98, 119, 121–31

Rajendran, Johnson, 137, 138, 146
Robeck, Cecil M., iii, xxiii, 95, 157, 164, 197

Schuette, Brain, 181, 197
Shelley, Bruce, 158, 164
Snell, Lutricia E., 98, 99, 105, 118
Stott, John, 47, 49, 54, 62, 162, 165
Sugden, Chris, 135, 146
Swart, Ignatius, 77, 83, 94, 98, 102, 112, 117

Tayviah, Margaret Makafui, 110, 115
Thomas, John Christopher, xxiii, 20, 35
Tsekpoe, Christian, v, vi, x–xxiv, 1, 2, 9, 12, 16, 23, 26, 35, 55, 62, 85, 90, 93, 95, 179, 180, 197

Ugo, Ikechukwu, 137, 146

Veith, Gene Edward, 148, 149, 165
Viney, Samuel, 135, 146

Weidmann, Jens, 106, 119
Wright, Chris, 151–54, 165
Wright, Christopher J. H., 76, 84

Zacharias, Ravi, 151, 165
Zalot, Jozef D., 106, 120
Zwemer, Samuel Marinus, 147, 165

Subject Index

accountable / accountability, 10, 15, 96, 97, 98, 101, 103, 106, 112, 119, 124, 125, 126, 131, 132, 179, 184, 193, 195, 196
Action Chapel International, 5, 6
Africa/ African, i, iii, iv, vii, viii, ix–xi, xiii, xiv, xvi, xix, xxviii, 1–16, 18, 20, 22, 24, 26, 28, 30, 32, 34–36, 38, 40, 42, 44, 46, 47, 48, 50–52, 54–56, 58, 60–70, 72, 74, 76–78, 80, 82–84, 86–88, 90, 92, 94–126, 128, 130–46, 148, 150, 152, 154, 156, 158, 160, 162, 164, 168, 170–72, 174, 176, 177, 180, 182, 184–86, 188, 190, 192, 194, 196, 197
African Christianity, viii, xiii, xiv, 2, 50, 55, 60, 61, 88, 101, 103, 104, 118
African diaspora, xvi, xix, 1, 9
African Pentecostal-Charismatic, i, iii, iv, xi, xiii, xix, 1–4, 6, 8, 10, 12, 14, 16, 18, 20, 22, 24, 26, 28, 30, 32, 34, 35, 38, 40, 42, 44, 46, 48, 52, 54, 56, 58, 60, 62, 64, 66, 68, 70, 72, 74, 76, 78, 80, 82, 84, 86, 88, 90, 92, 94, 98, 100, 102, 104, 106, 108, 110, 112, 114, 116, 118, 120, 122, 124, 126, 128, 130, 132, 134, 136, 138, 140, 142, 144, 146, 148, 150, 152, 154, 156, 158, 160, 162, 164, 168, 170, 172, 174, 176, 180, 182, 184, 186, 188, 190, 192, 194, 196
antigraft, 13, 96, 97, 108, 115, 116, 117, 123
antigraft agencies, 13, 108, 117, 123
apostles, x, 2, 10, 20, 24, 25, 36, 37, 39, 40, 42–44, 52, 142, 159, 163, 181, 184, 185, 188, 190, 191
prophets, x, 10, 20, 24, 25, 36, 37, 39, 40, 42, 43, 44, 71, 79, 109, 127, 184, 188, 190, 191

baptism in the Holy Spirit, 21, 22, 39

Christian(s) / Christian(ity), iii–xii, xiv, xv, xvi, xx, xxiv, xxvi, 1, 2, 5–8, 10, 12, 14, 16, 18, 19, 21–23, 26, 28, 29, 34–36, 39, 43–45, 47, 49, 52, 53, 56, 60–62, 70–85, 87–91, 94–97, 100, 101, 103–5, 108–13, 115–20, 125, 127, 128, 132, 134, 136, 138, 139, 141, 142, 144, 146, 147, 149, 150–56, 161, 163–65, 171–73, 183, 185, 188, 194, 197
Christlike/ Christlikeness: 8, 13, 12, 19, 73, 75, 78, 82, 88, 94, 125, 126, 130
church governance, vi, xvi, 14, 24, 39, 40, 178, 179, 180–85, 187, 189, 191, 193, 195–97

church-state relations, vi, xvi, 12, 96, 97, 99, 101–5, 107, 109, 111–13, 115–19, 121–23, 130, 131

Classical Pentecostal, xxiii, xxv, 39, 55, 73, 79, 180

contemporary, viii, xiii, xiv, xv, xxvii, 8, 12–14, 20, 62, 72, 78, 87, 93, 94, 96, 98, 102, 105, 119, 132, 143, 144, 146, 149, 150, 155, 159, 163–65

contextual(izing) / contextualisation/ contextualised, xi, 11, 47, 60, 138, 146, 180

CoP, vii, viii, x, xv, xvi, xix, xx, 1, 6–12, 15, 36–38, 40–43, 47, 48, 57, 58, 60, 61, 66, 70, 73, 89, 90–92, 118, 138, 160, 172, 173, 175, 176, 178–80, 184, 186–89, 191–93, 197

corruption, xiv, xv, xvi, xviii, 2, 6–8, 12, 13, 15, 73, 88, 96, 97, 99, 101–3, 105–11, 113–18, 122–32, 196

Covid-19, ix, xvi, 11, 14, 56, 59, 64, 66, 166–69, 171–75

development, x, xxiii, 5, 12, 15–17, 55, 57, 63, 65, 66, 88, 91, 97, 99–102, 107, 108, 117, 122, 123, 136, 144, 145, 176, 179, 187, 193–97

diakonia: 11, 50, 52, 53, 55, 59, 60, 61–63, 69

dialogue: xiii, xv, xix, 1, 64, 101, 158, 160

direct mentoring: 10, 12, 26, 92, 93, 95

disciple(s) / discipled / discipleship: ix, xvii, xviii, xxv, xxvii, 8, 9, 12, 13, 19, 20, 26, 43, 71, 73, 75, 77, 78, 85, 86, 89, 90, 92, 93, 95, 136, 138, 140, 141, 180, 181, 193

disciple-making, xvii, 140, 142, 143

ecclesiology/ ecclesiological, xiii, xvi, xxiii, xxiv, xxviii, 4, 6,8, 10,12, 14, 17–26, 31, 33, 36, 37, 39, 44, 46, 48, 52, 72, 86, 88, 89, 158, 171, 184

ecumenical: ix, xxiv, xxviii, 60, 72, 82, 84, 111, 157, 163

education(al), ix, xi, 4–6, 11, 15, 21, 25, 33, 55, 56, 59, 64, 66, 84, 87, 90, 93, 94, 95, 96, 97, 99–101, 107, 114, 117, 118, 125, 126, 132, 135, 176, 177, 187, 188, 194, 195

eschatological, 10, 20, 27, 36, 44

evangelism/ evangelized: xxiv–xxvi, 3, 4, 6, 9, 15, 27, 32, 34, 44, 46, 47, 53, 54, 68, 79, 86, 87, 95, 136, 137, 138, 139, 142, 145, 146, 153, 158, 181, 190, 193

existential encounter: 10, 20, 28, 44, 45

Ghana/ Ghanaian(s), vii, viii, ix, 1, 7, 11–13, 15, 20, 27, 30, 40, 57, 59, 63–65, 73, 87, 90–92, 94, 99, 101, 104, 107, 108, 134, 157, 167–69, 178, 188, 195

global/ globalisation/ globalized/ globally, vii, x, ix, xiii, xix, xxiv, xxv, 2, 3, 20, 51, 63, 64, 87, 88, 105, 108, 120, 157, 171, 178, 184, 187

Gospel, viii, xiv, xviii, 3, 4, 6, 11, 41, 47, 50, 51, 53, 58, 60, 63, 71, 76, 83, 86, 135, 141, 143, 144, 148, 153, 157, 162, 180

government/ governance, vii, xv, xvi, xix, xxvi, 2, 4, 6, 10–17, 20, 24, 25, 32, 33, 39, 40, 47, 51, 56, 58–60, 64–66, 69, 72, 77, 79–81, 87, 90–92, 96, 97, 99–108, 111–13, 116, 117, 124, 160, 176, 178–81, 183–85, 188, 189, 191, 193, 195–97

Great Commission, xvii, 31, 43, 85, 141, 187, 192

holistic mission, 3, 6, 8, 9, 15, 16, 46, 70, 86, 95

Holy Spirit: xx, xxvii, 2–4, 10, 19, 21–23, 28–32, 37, 39–45, 47, 48, 51, 74, 75, 82, 85, 109, 140, 159, 170, 177, 181

SUBJECT INDEX 203

Home and Urban Mission (HUM), vi, xi, xvi, 13, 133, 134, 135, 137, 138, 139, 141, 143, 145, 146, 189

indigenous, x, xxiii, 9, 11, 26, 55, 68, 100, 139, 180
intentional/ intentionality, 3, 12, 76–78, 82, 88, 89, 97, 124, 137, 141, 193
International Central Gospel Church, 5, 6, 11, 50, 55, 58, 60, 63

James McKeown, xv, 1, 9, 21, 22, 32, 33, 34, 35, 37, 39, 41, 43, 45–47, 49, 55, 61, 64, 93, 94, 164, 185
James McKeown Memorial Lectures, iii, iv, xv, xx, xxi, 10, 35, 49, 94, 164, 197
Jerusalem, xviii, 81, 133, 134, 136, 181
Jesus/ Jesus Christ, xiv, xvii, xx, xxvi, 8, 20, 23, 27, 28, 32, 37, 43, 44, 71, 76, 78, 80, 85, 92, 102, 124, 136, 138, 147–56, 158, 159, 161–63, 179, 181

Kingdom of God, xiii, xv, xvii–xix, xxvi, 19, 46, 65, 89, 92, 135, 154, 179, 180, 189, 192

leaders/ leadership, viii, ix, xvi, xxvi, 4, 10–12, 15, 17, 20, 23, 24, 26, 27, 33, 36, 38–40, 42–44, 54, 60, 63, 67, 76, 78, 81–83, 88, 90–93, 98, 100–102, 111, 112, 114–16, 122, 124, 126–28, 144, 145, 157, 170, 172, 173, 175, 178, 179, 181–83, 187, 188, 192, 196
light shining in darkness, 10, 20, 32, 37, 46
Lordship of Christ, vi, xvi, 14, 147, 148, 149, 151, 153, 155, 156, 157, 159, 161–65

megachurches, ix, 14, 68, 143
mission, vii, viii, x, xi, xvi, xx, xxiv, xxv, 3, 6, 9, 11, 13, 14, 19, 20, 26, 40, 42, 43, 46–48, 50, 52–55, 63, 64, 66–68, 72, 75, 76, 83, 85–87, 90, 93, 100, 104, 117, 122–24, 134–46, 153, 163, 172, 179–81, 187, 193
mission praxis, xx, 11, 13, 23, 26, 50, 63, 66, 67

New Testament, xvii, 71, 85, 109, 148, 154

Old Testament, vii, xviii, 71, 109

pandemic, xi, 11, 14, 56, 59, 60, 63–67, 166, 167, 169–71, 174
Pentecost University, viii, xx, 1, 56, 187, 193
Pentecostal ecclesiology, xvi, xxiii, 10, 17, 20, 37, 52
Pentecostal mission, viii, xvi, 3, 9, 11, 52
Pentecostal theologians, xxiii, xxiv, xxviii, 79
Pentecostal/ Pentecostalism, vii–x, xiii, xvi, xviii, xxiii, xxiv, xxv, xxviii, 2–5, 9–12, 17, 19, 21, 36, 37, 39, 41, 47, 48, 50–53, 55, 57, 60, 63–69, 71, 73, 76, 77, 79, 104, 110, 134, 148, 157, 163, 171–75, 178, 180
Pentecostal-Charismatic, vii, viii, ix, x, xiii, xvi, xviii, xxiii, xxiv, xxv, xxviii, 2–5, 9–12, 17, 19, 21, 36, 37, 39, 41, 47, 48, 50–53, 55, 57, 60, 63–69, 71, 73, 76, 77, 79, 104, 110, 134, 148, 157, 163, 171–75, 178, 180
pneumatological sensitivity, 10, 20, 21, 36, 39
pneumatology/ pneumatological, xx, 10, 125
politics/ political/ politicians, xix, xxiv, xxv, 4, 5, 7, 11, 13, 51, 54, 63–67, 72, 77, 79, 83, 90, 91, 93, 94, 96, 98, 99, 101–7, 110–12, 114, 122, 126, 128, 129, 135, 137, 140, 150, 166, 167, 179, 193, 195, 196
Possessing the Nations, xv, xix, 31, 65, 68, 69, 115, 179, 192, 193

SUBJECT INDEX

power/ empowerment/ empowered, x, xix, xviii, xx, xxiv, xxvii, 2–4, 10, 11, 13, 15, 30, 22, 28, 30, 31, 37, 51, 56, 63, 65, 67,69, 75, 76, 79, 83, 93, 96–98, 103, 108, 126–28, 156, 162, 164, 179, 183, 187, 188, 194–96

practical, ix, x, xi, xix, 1, 2, 25, 26, 28, 42, 44, 86, 99, 182

principles, xiii, xv, xvi, xvii, xviii, 8, 12, 20, 23, 26, 31, 32, 34, 53, 71–76, 78, 82, 87–100, 115, 135, 171, 179, 181, 182, 189, 192, 197

public sphere, xiv, xv, xvi, xix, xx, xxiv, 1, 2, 4, 5, 7–12, 15, 64, 65, 69, 72–74, 78, 82, 85–89, 92, 94, 99

reflection, xix, xxiv, xxv, 73, 86, 94, 114
religious pluralism, 14, 148–59, 163, 164
religiously pluralistic society, xvi, 14, 148, 150, 156–59, 161–64
Re-Visioning, xiii, xv, xix, 1, 50, 63

salt and light, xvii, 6–8, 12, 33, 34, 80, 82, 86, 91, 109, 110, 130
scientific, xix, 1, 109, 143, 144, 149, 179
social action, xiv, 3, 4, 6, 8, 9, 52, 53, 66, 68, 92
social concern, 3, 4, 54, 68
social transformation, xvi, 2, 5, 8, 11, 15, 50, 52–54, 63, 64, 67–69, 86, 112, 193
society, vii–xxvii, 7, 8, 11, 12, 14, 15, 18, 33, 47, 50, 51–54, 57, 64, 69, 72, 73, 76, 77, 79, 80, 81, 85–89, 94, 96, 97, 103, 107, 108, 110, 112, 113, 117, 123–25, 127–30, 139, 140, 143, 148, 156, 157, 161–64, 169, 179, 180, 189, 195–97

Spirit/ Spiritual, ix, xx, xxvi, xxvii, 2–4, 7, 10, 15, 19, 21–24, 28, 29, 32, 33, 37, 39–45, 47, 48, 50–52, 64–66, 68, 74, 78, 85, 88, 98, 109, 125, 140, 145, 159, 160, 164, 170, 175, 179–82, 187, 194–96

The Church of Pentecost, vii, viii, ix–xi, xv, xix, 1, 6, 17, 19, 21–26, 31, 33, 34, 36, 50, 51, 55–57, 59, 60, 63–65, 67, 69, 73, 89, 90, 93, 100, 115, 134, 138, 172, 178, 184, 194–96

transformation/ transformational, x, xiii, xv, xvii, xix, 2–5, 8, 11, 13, 15, 42, 48, 50, 51, 53–55, 57, 63–69, 73, 75, 76, 86, 104, 112, 126, 141, 178, 179, 181, 187, 189, 192–97

United States, xvi, 20, 53, 68,69, 125
urbanization, xxvii, 13, 133, 134, 136, 144, 145

Vision 2023, xv, xix, 7, 8, 15, 65, 73, 77, 83, 89, 94, 115, 179, 180, 189, 192, 193, 194, 197

World Council of Churches, xxiv, 15, 62, 72, 75, 84, 95, 156, 157

Scripture Index

OLD TESTAMENT

Genesis

1	xviii
11	xviii
22:18	xiv

Exodus

3:14	145

Leviticus

22:25	130

Deuteronomy

6:4	xiii

2 Samuel

6:20	52

Nehemiah

2	76
2:4–10, 8:9	81

Esther

2:8–18	78, 92

Psalm

51:17	28

Proverbs

16:8	131
22:6	125
28:13	28
29:1	28
29	90
29:2	129

Jeremiah

5:28	131
12:1	131
17:19	41
29:7	81

Daniel

1:3–21	78, 92
2:16–19	82
6:1–3	76
6:5–10	82
9:1–23	82
10:1–12	82

Hosea

9:9	131

Amos

8:3–5	109

Malachi

3:1	28

NEW TESTAMENT

Matthew

5:13–16	8, 80, 85, 94, 109, 130
5:16	130
6:1–4	xxv
11:28–30	xxv
13:33	89
14:13–21	xxv
16:18	19, 129
22:16–22	80
25:42–43	174
28:18–20	xvii, 153
28:19	85
28:20	43, 72

Mark

8:36	131
12:29	xiii

Luke

10:27	87
16:10	124

John

1:14	126
8:44	131
12:19	179
14:6	130, 151, 158, 162
17:1–26	xvii
20:21	8

Acts

1:1–3	xiv, xviii
2:2	87
2:38–41	153
5:41	127
5:29	127
6:1–7	xxv, 180, 181
6	11
8:18	109
14:15	153
17:6	179
17:16–31	160
28:23–28	160

Romans

3:23	124
5:2	124
8:18	131
10:9	160
10:13–15	8, 153
12:2	74
13:1–2	129
13:1–7	xxv, 80

1 Corinthians

8:16	160
9:19–23	160
12:3	160
12:13	22
12:27	129

Galatians

3:26–29	xiv
4:19	45
5:22–23	125

Ephesians

3:10	xv
4:11–12	37
4:11–13	43
4:4–5	161

Philippians

2:10–11	162
2:11	147, 160
2:12–13	75

Colossians

1:15–20	183
1:22	126
2:9	123

1 Timothy

2:1–4	81
2:6	151
3:2	126
3:15	126, 130, 131
4:12	87
6:15	156

Titus

2:13–14	xv

Hebrews

5:8	126

1 Peter

2:13–17	xxv
3:17	131

2 Peter

1:4	109, 130
2:19	130

Revelation

1:5	156
7:9	xviii
14:5	131
17:4	156
18:2–3	xviii
19:16	156
21:1–4	xviii

www.ingramcontent.com/pod-product-compliance
Lightning Source LLC
Chambersburg PA
CBHW070250230426
43664CB00014B/2470